TARGETING THE AIMS IN WRITING

(2006)

BRIAN FREEL, DR. FRANK J. PINTOZZI, AND MARIA STRUDER

AMERICAN BOOK COMPANY
P O BOX 2638
WOODSTOCK, GEORGIA 30188-1383
Toll Free: 1 (888) 264-5877   Phone: 770-928-2834   Fax: 770-928-7483
Web site: www.americanbookcompany.com

ACKNOWLEDGMENTS

The authors would like to acknowledge the editorial assistance of Marsha Torrens in the preparation of this book.

This product/publication includes images from CorelDRAW 11 which are protected by the copyright laws of the United States, Canada, and elsewhere. Used under license.

All the characters, places, and events portrayed in this book are fictitious, and any resemblance to real people, places, or events is purely coincidental.

Contents

PREFACE   v
Test-Taking Tips   vi
Frequently Asked Questions   vii

DIAGNOSTIC WRITING TEST   1

WRITING EVALUATION CHART   4

CHAPTER 1
Writing Paragraphs   5
Paragraph Structure   5
Writing a Topic Sentence   8
Improving a Topic Sentence   9
Supporting Details   12
Developing Supporting Details   14
Organizing Paragraphs   16
    Time Order   16
    Spatial Order   16
    Order of Importance   17
    Contrasting Ideas   18
Writing a Concluding Sentence   20
Chapter 1 Review   22
Additional Activities   25

CHAPTER 2
Voice   26
Author's Purpose   26
Audience   29
Language   32
Tone   35
Chapter 2 Review   41
Additional Activities   44

CHAPTER 3
Creating Ideas and Content   45
Basic Structure of an Essay   45
The Writing Process   46
Read the Writing Prompt Carefully   47
Generating Ideas   48
Focusing Ideas   50
Thesis or Main Idea   51
Making a Plan   53
Chapter 3 Review   55
Additional Activities   58

CHAPTER 4
Organizing and Drafting the Essay   59
Improving Word Choice   59
Writing Introductions   64
Writing Conclusions   68
Using Transitional Words   70
Order of Importance   71
Developing Coherence   76
Writing the Draft   79
Chapter 4 Review   81
Additional Activities   82

CHAPTER 5
Revising the Essay for Sentence
    Fluency   83
How to Revise   83
Adding Clarifying Information   85
Deleting Unrelated Sentences   86
Eliminating Unnecessary Words   88
Correcting Shifts in Tense or Person   90
Checking for Parallel Sentence
    Structure   93
Developing Sentence Variety   95
Chapter 5 Review   98
Additional Activities   100

CHAPTER 6
Proofreading the Essay for
    Conventions   102
Proofreading Notation   102
Capitalization   103
Internal Punctuation   104
Grammar and Usage   109
Spelling   120
Sentence Formation   123
Chapter 6 Review   128
Additional Activities   131

CHAPTER 7
Persuasive Writing   **132**
Purpose and Audience   132
Using Persuasive Language   133
Building an Argument   135
Ethical Arguments   145
Appealing to Emotions   147
Chapter 7 Review   149
Additional Activities   152

CHAPTER 8
Expository Writing   **153**
Basic Expository Essay   153
A Process Essay   157
A Cause-Effect Essay   163
A Comparison-Contrast Essay   168
Writing a Comparison-Contrast Essay   171
Chapter 8 Review   175

CHAPTER 9
Narrative Writing   **180**
Key Steps for Writing a Narrative   181
Step I Analyzing the Topic   184
Step II Organize Your Narrative   186
Step III The Rough Draft   188
Step IV Edit and Proofread
Step V Write Final Copy   189
Chapter 9 Review   190

CHAPTER 10
Scoring the AIMS Essay   **198**
Scoring Overview   198
Holistic Grading   200
Scoring Scale   201
Ideas/Content   202
Organization   204
Voice   206
Word Choice   208
Sentence Fluency   210
Writing Conventions   212
Chapter 10 Review   214

Practice Writing Test 1   **221**
Practice Writing Test 2   **223**

APPENDIX A   **225**
Additional Writing Prompts
Persuasive Prompts   225
Expository Prompts   227
Process Prompts   228
Mixed Expository Prompts   230
Narrative Prompts   232

APPENDIX B   **234**
Writing Resources

APPENDIX C   **239**
Student Essays Progress Chart

Preface

About the Book

Targeting the AIMS in Writing will help Arizona students develop or review writing strategies and writing applications (essays) for the AIMS Writing Test. This book will also assist students who are preparing or reviewing editing (proofreading) tasks. In addition, *Targeting the AIMS in Writing* teaches the concepts and skills emphasized in high school English classes. Each chapter contains concise lessons and frequent practice exercises.

Students can begin this book by taking the *Diagnostic Writing Test* to determine their strengths and areas in which they need to improve their writing. Each chapter ends with a comprehensive chapter review.

In Appendix C, students and teachers can use the Essays *Progress Chart* to record student grades on each essay. The *Diagnostic Test* also includes a *Writing Evaluation Chart* which can be used to evaluate both the *Diagnostic Writing Test* and the *Practice Writing Tests* at the end of this book. Appendix A contains many additional writing prompts for further practice. A separate key includes answers to tests and exercises as well as interactive writing games and activities.

The authors welcome comments and suggestions about this book. Please contact them at:

American Book Company
PO Box 2638
Woodstock, GA 30188-1383

Toll Free: 1 (888) 264-5877
Phone: (770) 928-2834
Fax: (770) 928-7483

Web site: www.americanbookcompany.com

About the Authors

Brian Freel has a Bachelor of Arts degree from Amherst College in Amherst, MA, and a Master of Arts degree from St. Mary's University in Baltimore, MD. He's a writer specializing in language arts and history and has taught students at middle school, high school, and adult levels.

Dr. Frank J. Pintozzi is an adjunct Professor of Education at Kennesaw State University, Kennesaw, Georgia. For over 29 years, he has taught writing and reading at the high school and college levels. He has authored numerous textbooks on writing, grammar, reading, and social studies.

Maria L. Struder received a B. A. degree in English from Kennesaw State University (Kennesaw, GA), graduating Magna Cum Laude with course work in the Bagwell College of Education at Kennesaw. She has taught writing skills at the college level. She is now a writer and editor, specializing in English Language Arts. Currently, Maria is enrolled in the Master's program in Professional Writing at Kennesaw State University.

These writers have produced best-selling books on passing end-of-course and exit exams in Alabama, California, Florida, Georgia, Indiana, Louisiana, Minnesota, Mississippi, Nevada, New Jersey, Ohio, South Carolina, Texas, and Tennessee.

TEST-TAKING TIPS

1. **Complete the chapters and practice tests in this book.** This text will help you review as thoroughly and specifically as possible key writing concepts you will need to learn for high school and the AIMS Writing Test.

2. **Be prepared.** Get a good night's sleep the day before an exam. Eat a well-balanced meal, one that contains plenty of proteins and carbohydrates, prior to your exam.

3. **Arrive early.** Allow yourself at least 15–20 minutes to find your room and get settled. Then you can relax before the exam, so you won't feel rushed.

4. **Think success.** Keep your thoughts positive. Turn negative thoughts into positive ones. If you have put in good study and preparation time, you will reap the benefits of that.

5. **Practice relaxation techniques.** Some students become overly worried about exams. Before or during the test, they may perspire heavily, experience an upset stomach, or have shortness of breath. If you feel any of these symptoms, talk to a close friend or see a counselor. They will suggest ways to deal with test anxiety. **Here are some quick ways to relieve test anxiety:**

   • Imagine yourself in your most favorite place. Let yourself sit there and relax.
   • Do a body scan. Tense and relax each part of your body starting with your toes and ending with your forehead.
   • Use the 3-12-6 method of relaxation when you feel stress. Inhale slowly for 3 seconds. Hold your breath for 12 seconds, and then exhale slowly for 6 seconds.

6. **Read directions carefully.** If you don't understand them, ask the proctor for further explanation before the exam starts.

7. **Write Legibly.** Write your response clearly so that those who will grade your writing can give you the best score for your effort.

8. **Proofread your work.** After you have written your essay, check over your response, making corrections in grammar, punctuation, capitalization, and spelling as neatly as possible.

FREQUENTLY ASKED QUESTIONS

1. **What is AIMS?**
   AIMS is Arizona's Instrument to Measure Standards. This test is designed to measure all Arizona students' progress in learning the Arizona Academic Standards in grades 3, 5, 8, and high school.

2. **Why is AIMS important?**
   Beginning with the class of 2006, high school students must "Meet" the content standards in Reading, Mathematics and Writing in order to receive a diploma.

3. **What if I fail the AIMS test?**
   High School students who do not meet or exceed the standard must retake the tests until the standards in that subject area are met. Each student will have five opportunities to take the AIMS. If any high school student has failed one or more attempts at passing any portion of the AIMS test, he or she is entitled to nine hours of free personalized tutoring sessions.

4. **Do my parents have a right to see my test scores?**
   Yes. Each school district must provide parents or guardians of students copies of their test scores.

5. **Are these tests required by law?**
   Yes. Federal law mandates that every child in a public/charter school in Grade 10 participate in the state's AIMS test. Local school district governing boards may determine specific graduation requirements for special education students.

6. **Will the AIMS test result appear on my official transcript from high school?**
   Yes. Your transcript will record the performance level achieved, the content level assessed, and the date the score was attained. If you take the tests more than once, only your highest score in each content area will be recorded on your transcript.

7. **When are the AIMS tests given?**
   The Writing Test is given in October, with alternate dates in November. The Writing Test is also given in February, with a March make-up date.

NOTES

Targeting the AIMS In Writing Diagnostic Test

Imagine that you were participating in the AIMS Writing Test today. How would you do? In what areas would you perform best? The diagnostic test that follows can help you answer these questions. It can show you where your strengths and weaknesses lie. With this awareness of your strengths and weaknesses, you will be able to plan your studies accordingly. This test is based on the Arizona AIMS content standards that focus on writing.

For assessment purposes, this diagnostic test will consist on one essay preceded by one writing prompt. Make sure you understand what the prompt is saying and respond correctly.

How to Use Your Time

To use your time wisely, you may want to follow the suggestions below.

Planning/Prewriting

Read each writing prompt carefully, make brainstorming lists of your ideas, and organize those ideas into a clustering diagram or outline.

Drafting

After organizing your ideas, write them in complete sentences and develop them into well-formed paragraphs.

Revising

Now is the time to read over each draft and make improvements. You want to make sure all of your ideas are developed in a logical order and supported by relevant reasons and examples. You also want to eliminate unrelated ideas and unnecessary words. This is a good time to improve your word choice as well. Make sure all of your corrections are neat and legible.

Proofreading

Take advantage of the last few minutes of the testing time to review your essay one more time. This time look for errors in capitalization, punctuation, and grammar. These small corrections can make a big difference.

Review your paper using the **Checklist for Your Writing** listed at the end of your prompts.

At the end of your essay, you or your teacher should complete the **Writing Evaluation Chart**. It will help you identify your areas of strength and areas for improvement in writing essays. You can also use the **scoring guidelines** in **Chapter 10** to help you evaluate your essays.

DIAGNOSTIC WRITING TEST

To demonstrate mastery of your abilities for this diagnostic writing exam, you will be asked to produce an essay that demonstrates your writing capability. The competencies are identified below.

In particular, each piece of writing will

1. develop a clear, focused main idea or ideas related to the prompt.

2. demonstrate completeness.

3. include supporting details appropriate to the audience, purpose, and topic.

4. follow purposeful organization.

5. make connections among ideas, paragraphs, and sentences.

6. use a variety of words appropriate to the audience, purpose, and topic.

7. use a variety of sentence structures and/or phrases appropriate to the audience, purpose, and topic.

8. exhibit standard conventions competently (mechanics, usage, grammar, and spelling).

9. be legible.

GENERAL DESCRIPTION

You will be given one prompt, which reflects one of these writing modes: narrative, expository, or persuasive. Successful responses to the prompt focus on the topic, reflect a discernible organizational structure, use appropriate language conventions, and contain pertinent supporting material such as ideas, examples, and/or commentary.

To permit an evaluation of your writing, you are encouraged to write several paragraphs. The test is timed, giving you two to three hours to complete your essay.

Below is one **writing prompt** that gives you instructions about writing an essay. Read the prompt carefully so you understand the topic and the purpose of your essay. Then, use the **Writer's Checklist** below to make sure you write an effective and interesting essay.

Use your own paper for your planning, drafting, and final copy. Your instructor will tell you when to begin and when to stop writing. Do your best, and remember, this is just your first attempt. As you study the chapters in this book, you will have more time for improvement.

Writing Prompt

In the past, schools hired their own staff to provide students nutritious, cafeteria-prepared lunches at a low price. Today, private food service companies are claiming that they can provide better school lunches at lower prices. Your local school board is considering a proposal which would allow several food service companies to set up operation in the school cafeteria. Some parents are concerned that students will eat nothing but "fast food." Decide what you think about private companies providing school lunches.

WRITER'S CHECKLIST

❑ Does my paper have a specific audience and a specific purpose?

❑ Does my paper contain a strong controlling idea?

❑ Does my paper stay on topic?

❑ Does my paper include specific and relevant details, reasons, and examples?

❑ Does my paper have an effective beginning, middle, and end?

❑ Does my paper progress in a logical order, and do my ideas flow smoothly?

❑ Does my paper contain words that make it interesting?

❑ Does my paper contain sentences that are clear and varied in structure?

❑ Does my paper include effective use of paragraphing?

❑ Does my paper include correct grammar/usage, punctuation, capitalization, and spelling?

Writing Evaluation Chart
Diagnostic and Practice Writing Tests

The chapters in this book will provide you with many opportunities to practice writing essays. In addition, you will find many writing prompts in **Appendix A** for writing practice. Keep all of your essays in one folder. As you practice writing essays, you can use the **Writing Evaluation Chart** below to help you assess your progress.

For each essay, work with your teacher or tutor to assign a grade in each category listed. If you have an excellent grasp of the skill, write **E** for **Excellent**. If you use the skill well enough to pass, write **P** for **Passing**. If you need to practice a skill more in order to master it, write **NP** for **Needs Practice**. The number listed next to each skill indicates the chapter which discusses that skill. Read and review the chapters you need to improve each concept and skill. Your teacher may also use the six point scale from Chapter 10, **Scoring the AIMS Essay**.

Writing Progress Chart

Writing Skills	Chapter Number	Student Name:					
		Essay 1	Essay 2	Essay 3	Essay 4	Essay 5	Essay 6
Writing Paragraphs	1						
Voice	2						
Creating Ideas, Content	3						
Organizing and Drafting the Essay	4						
Revising the Essay for Sentence Fluency	5						
Proofreading the Essay for Conventions	6						
Persuasive Writing	7						
Expository Writing	8						
Narrative Writing	9						
Scoring the AIMS Essay	10						

Writing Paragraphs

The goal of this book is to help you produce essays that are clearly focused, well-supported, and effectively written. Each chapter in this book will help you with different aspects of this task. You will begin by writing well-organized paragraphs because these are the building blocks of an effective essay. In this chapter, you will learn about the following aspects of writing paragraphs:

- **Paragraph Structure**
- **Writing a Topic Sentence**
- **Improving a Topic Sentence**
- **Supporting Details**

- **Developing Supporting Details**
- **Organizing Paragraphs**
- **Writing a Concluding Sentence**

PARAGRAPH STRUCTURE

A **paragraph** is a series of related sentences that make a single point about one subject.

Choose one subject: A paragraph is too brief to discuss more than one subject.

Make a single point: To "make a point" is to tell readers something that you want them to know. Usually, you will state your point in the **topic sentence** of your paragraph. The topic sentence often begins a paragraph, though it may also be at the end or in the middle.

Relate other sentences to the topic sentence: Though you *state* your point in the topic sentence, you must *make* your point by providing **supporting details**. Other sentences in the paragraph provide readers with information and evidence to explain your topic sentence. If the topic sentence does not end the paragraph, a **concluding sentence** can bring the paragraph to a close, and if appropriate, lead into the next paragraph.

An easy way to understand the structure of a paragraph is to compare it to a table. The topic sentence is like the table top. Just as the table top's purpose is to provide a flat surface for writing or eating, the topic sentence's purpose is to give the reader a broad view of the topic. Of course, without legs, the table top will not stand. In a similar way, the topic sentence must be supported by details, examples, and explanations.

Finally, a table that rocks on an uneven floor makes people wonder if objects they place on it will fall off. Similarly, a paragraph that does not provide a clear conclusion may leave the reader wondering if the writer has left out some important ideas.

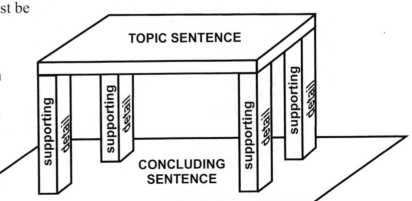

Writing a well-organized paragraph may seem difficult, but do you realize that you talk in paragraphs every day? Here is an example of a paragraph spoken by a cheerleading coach at the season's first practice.

Gather around here and listen up! **If you really want to be cheerleaders, you have to be ready to stretch yourselves to the limit!** *Be sure you really want to do this, people! You will need to be at practice every day after school. There will be no time for any other extracurricular activities! All of you must be ready to give of yourselves and endure pain as you never have before! You will also need to rely on each other. Some of you will be learning how to trust someone else for the first time in your lives. Above all, this job will bring out your character and show you what you're made of. Now, if you still feel up to the task, I want to see you here tomorrow evening at five o'clock, ready to work hard.*

Though spoken, the coach's instruction is like a well-written paragraph. It states the main idea in a topic sentence (indicated in bold) and then supports that idea by describing how the cheerleaders will need to "stretch themselves." The coach concludes by challenging the cheerleaders to action. The speech has overall **coherence** in that all the ideas and sentences relate to one another.

STRUCTURE OF A PARAGRAPH

Topic Sentence (Introduction)
↓
Supporting Details (examples, reasons, testimony, observations)
↓
Concluding Sentence (Summary)

Practice 1: Paragraph Structure

All of the sentences in each series make a paragraph, but they may not be in order. For each sentence, write T if the sentence is the topic sentence, S if the sentence supports the topic sentence, and C if the sentence concludes or summarizes the paragraph.

1. A. Constantly surrounded by beeping faxes, ringing cell phones, and flashing computer screens, many business people are sitting down at the end of the day to enjoy some quiet time with knitting needles and a big ball of yarn.
    B. Men and women with fast-paced, high-powered careers are turning to knitting as a way to unwind.
    C. So, as you speed through modern society, remember, knitting isn't just for Grandma anymore!
    D. Besides the peace and quiet, these knitting professionals say they find it refreshing to focus on the process of creating something, instead of looking only at deadlines and finished products.

    Sentence A _____   Sentence C _____
    Sentence B _____   Sentence D _____

2. A. As she climbed the stairs, her nose was filled with the musty smell of old things.
   B. She walked to the door of her old refuge: the attic.
   C. Times at home had always been happy, but now Sheila needed a break.
   D. The memories of good times made the present situation seem bearable.
   E. Sheila dusted off an old picture frame and found a picture of her mother, smiling.

   Sentence A _____   Sentence C _____   Sentence E _____
   Sentence B _____   Sentence D _____

3. A. With the sale of each bike, he offered a monthly maintenance program.
   B. These regular check-ups kept the bikes in good working condition and brought customers back to the store where they could see new products he was selling.
   C. The success of Alek's young business shows the importance of keeping the customer happy.
   D. His work in other bicycle shops had shown him that a successful business is based on quality products and good service.
   E. With several years' experience under his belt, Alek Siegers established a successful bicycle shop in Aspen, Colorado.

   Sentence A _____   Sentence C _____   Sentence E _____
   Sentence B _____   Sentence D _____

4. A. While Brad, Katya, and Willy were strolling down Eighth Street, they heard a disturbing noise.
   B. They looked up and saw an elderly woman calling out from a second floor window, "Help me, please."
   C. The look on the woman's face propelled the three teens up the stairs to her door.
   D. The woman could not speak but brought them to the kitchen where her husband lay on the floor.
   E. Immediately, Katya called 911, while Brad checked the man's pulse, and Willy tried to reassure the woman.
   F. Within minutes, police officers arrived and commended the teens for their quick thinking.

   Sentence A _____   Sentence C _____   Sentence E _____
   Sentence B _____   Sentence D _____   Sentence F _____

5. A. Training involves many hours of lifting weights and running sprints.
   B. Without this preparation, performance will drop and injuries are more of a risk.
   C. Like the other athletes you see at the Olympics, javelin throwers deserve respect.
   D. The javelin is not a very heavy object, but throwing it long distances requires great arm and leg strength.
   E. Javelin throwing may look easy on TV, but in reality, it is a very demanding sport.

   Sentence A _____   Sentence C _____   Sentence E _____
   Sentence B _____   Sentence D _____

WRITING A TOPIC SENTENCE

The previous section shows that a paragraph is organized around a single idea that is stated in the **topic sentence**. The topic sentence tells the reader two important pieces of information:

1) the subject of the paragraph,
2) what the author wants the reader to know about that subject.

As a writer, you can use these statements to help you develop a topic sentence. Begin by answering the following two questions:

What is the subject of the paragraph?
What do I want the reader to know about that subject?

Then, use the answers to these questions to form a topic sentence. For example,

Subject:	fuel-efficient cars
Want reader to know:	help the environment
Sentence:	Buying a fuel-efficient car is one way you can help the environment.

This simple method of forming a topic sentence can help you stay focused in your writing. The topic sentence is like your compass while you write. It tells you what direction you want to go. Then, if you feel yourself getting lost in your writing, you can return to your topic sentence to get your bearings. For each sentence in a paragraph, ask the two questions above. If the sentence doesn't relate in some way to the subject and what you want the reader to know about the subject, it doesn't belong in the paragraph.

The topic sentence states the subject of the paragraph and what the author wants the reader to know about that subject.

Practice 2: Writing a Topic Sentence

For each of the following, write a topic sentence based on the subject and what you want the reader to know.

1. Subject: baseball cards
   Want reader to know: it's an interesting hobby

Topic Sentence: _____

_____

2.   Subject: computers in classrooms
     Want reader to know: provide learning opportunities

Topic Sentence: _____

_____

3.   Subject: refugees in the United States
     Want reader to know: struggle without knowledge of English

Topic Sentence: _____

_____

4.   Subject: exercise
     Want reader to know: important for good health

Topic Sentence: _____

_____

5.   Subject: school uniforms
     Want reader to know: decrease learning distractions

Topic Sentence: _____

_____

IMPROVING A TOPIC SENTENCE

The previous exercise may make writing a topic sentence seem easy, but writing a *good* topic sentence is a little more challenging. It is like deciding the best way to begin a conversation. Some people are very good at starting a conversation and keeping it going. They have a talent for inviting others into dialogue by picking a good topic and introducing it in an interesting way. When you write, you are starting a conversation with the reader. The topic sentence provides the basis for this conversation. A good topic sentence should present a **single idea** that is **broad enough** to **invite discussion**.

1.   **Single Idea.** Because a paragraph is focused on one idea, the topic sentence also should be limited to a single idea. The sentence should have only one subject and one verb.

     A. Incorrect: *Baseball players and lawyers get paid too much for the work they do.*

          This sentence has two subjects: baseball players and lawyers. The support needed for this sentence requires more than one paragraph. Choose one subject for one paragraph.

     Correct: *Professional baseball players get paid too much for the work they do.*
     Correct: *Lawyers get paid too much for the work they do.*

B. Incorrect: *The Internet provides computer users with a vast resource of information and creates worldwide marketing opportunities for businesses.*

The Internet is a single subject, but the sentence describes two services provided by the Internet. Either service provides the basis for a good paragraph.

> **Correct:** *The Internet provides computer users with a vast resource of information.*
>
> **Correct:** *The Internet creates worldwide marketing opportunities for businesses.*

C. Incorrect: *Young children bring parents great joy as well as tremendous responsibility.*

This sentence introduces two ideas. One idea is that young children bring parents great joy. The other is that young children are a big responsibility for parents. Both ideas should not be in the same topic sentence.

> **Correct:** *Young children bring great joy to parents.*
>
> **Correct:** *Young children bring parents tremendous responsibility.*

2. **Broad Enough.** The topic sentence must be broad enough so that it can be supported by details. A topic sentence that is really just a detail has no place to go.

> A. **Detail:** *Baking soda absorbs household odors in carpets and kitchens.*
> **Detail:** *Lemon juice lightens stains and cuts grease.*
> **Topic:** *Natural household products can be used for effective cleaning.*

The third sentence is broad enough to be supported by the details of the first two sentences. However, the first two sentences are too specific to be discussed in a paragraph. The same is true of the next example.

> B. **Detail:** *Genetic engineers have succeeded in cloning farm animals.*
> **Detail:** *Lawyers use DNA tests in criminal court cases.*
> **Topic:** *In recent years, genetic research has produced astounding, yet practical, results.*

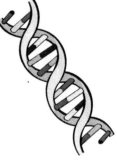

3. **Invites Discussion.** A good topic sentence makes the reader want to continue reading. It usually begins the paragraph and should invite the reader to consider the writer's topic.

> A. **Weak:** *I went to Florida last year.*
> **Good:** *Florida is the ideal place to go for a winter vacation.*

10 Copyright © American Book Company

The weak topic sentence doesn't have any energy or movement. There's no clear direction to go in writing, and the reader may not want to follow anyway. A good topic sentence makes the reader ask questions and want to read more, as in the following two examples.

B. **Weak:** *My uncle drives a black Nissan 300 ZX.*
   Good: *People often choose a particular car as a reflection of their personality.*

C. **Weak:** *Autumn leaves are often multicolored.*
   Good: *I love how the leaves on the trees explode into color each fall.*

> **A good topic sentence must be a single idea that is broad enough to invite discussion.**

Practice 3: Choosing a Topic Sentence

For each group of sentences, decide which is a good topic sentence. Then, describe why the others are not as effective.

1. a. I had never seen so much trash in all my life! _____

   b. The trash began piling up. _____

   c. Last summer, I worked for a trash collection company. _____

2. a. It's time to plant the garden and start watching baseball again. _____

   b. Irises and azaleas are beginning to bloom in the garden. _____

   c. The fresh smell of a newly planted garden is the best part of spring. _____

3. a. Bobby Knight is a demanding and controversial coach. _____

   b. Bobby Knight is a unique personality in college basketball. _____

   c. Bobby Knight lost the respect of many when, in the
      middle of a game, he threw a chair across the basketball court. _____

4. a. This has been a dry summer. _____

   b. Rainfall in the metro region is two inches below normal. _____

   c. This summer's drought may put water supplies in danger. _____

5. a. Modern rap is rooted in traditional African music. _____

   b. Modern rap has led to creative innovations in music. _____

   c. My brother listens to rap music all the time. _____

SUPPORTING DETAILS

An effective topic sentence starts your conversation with the reader, but it is up to you to continue the conversation by providing a clear, logical explanation of the main idea. **Supporting details** are specific statements that are related to the topic of the paragraph, but they do more than just restate the main idea.

1. **Supporting details are more than restatements of the topic sentence.** They provide reasons and examples that show why the main idea is true. Look at the following two examples.

Example 1: *Researchers have proven that smoking is bad for your health. Many researchers have determined smoking is unhealthy. In addition, researchers have publicized smoking's harmful components.*

In Example 1, the underlined topic sentence is *not* supported with details. Instead, the next two sentences simply restate the topic sentence in different words.

Example 2: *Researchers have proven that smoking is bad for your health. The American Medical Association has issued several warnings about the increased risk of lung cancer linked with smoking. In addition, the* New England Journal of Medicine *has issued its own separate findings verifying this same link between smoking and lung cancer.*

In Example 2, the same underlined topic sentence is supported by details. The writer cites the American Medical Association and the *New England Journal of Medicine* as providing examples of research that have shown the relationship between lung cancer and smoking.

2. **Supporting details are related to the topic.** If the details digress from the topic, these unrelated ideas can weaken the coherence of the paragraph and confuse the reader.

Example 3: *It is easier than ever to learn a new language. Sometimes it's hard to find someone who speaks another language. It's also fun to learn martial arts. Sometimes I just can't learn how to memorize things.*

Each of the sentences in Example 3 may have one or two words in common, but they all refer to different topics. Each sentence should relate to the idea "It is easy to learn a new language."

Example 4: *It is easier than ever to learn a new language. Right now, you can learn a language by taking an elective course in high school. Then, if you go to college you may have the opportunity to live in a foreign country as an exchange student. All along, you can join chat rooms on the Internet or conversation meetings in your area that will help you practice speaking your new language.*

In Example 4, the supporting sentences in the paragraph explain and relate to the underlined topic sentence. The sentences provide specific examples of ways you can learn a foreign language.

3. **Supporting details are specific, not general, statements.** The topic sentence is a general statement, but you should explain it in detail. Be as specific as you can.

Example 5: *Opinion polls question small samples of the population in order to indicate larger trends. An important part of polling is making sure that different kinds of people are represented. Even though this country is made up of many different kinds of people, opinion polls are pretty accurate.*

All of the sentences in Example 5 discuss opinion polls, but each one is general enough to be a topic for its own paragraph. They are related to the same idea, but they don't focus on one aspect of that idea.

Example 6: *Opinion polls question small samples of the population in order to indicate larger trends. Pollsters must be careful to select people of different age, gender, occupation, location, and ethnic background. In this way, a sample of as few as 200 people can give a good indication of public opinion throughout the country. Despite the small sample, the margin of error is usually between four and six percent.*

The author of Example 6 chose one general statement as the topic sentence (underlined) and supported it with specific details that emphasize the accuracy of polls based only on small samples of the population. Each supporting sentence elaborates on this one idea.

> **Supporting details are specific statements that are related to the topic of the paragraph, but they do more than just restate the main idea.**

Practice 4: Supporting Details

Read each group of sentences below. If the group forms a well-developed paragraph, write "Correct." If the group restates the topic sentence, contains unrelated ideas, or uses general statements instead of specifics, state the problem, and rewrite the paragraph on a separate sheet of paper.

1. Swimming is really the healthiest exercise anyone can do. Jumping rope is also healthy, and it's a lot of fun. Sometimes just talking on the phone with friends can be fun, but you don't get much exercise. Going to the movies can be amusing, and if you walk there, it might be healthy. Just don't get butter on your popcorn because that's not healthy.

2. Something should be done about the cafeteria food because it tastes bad. Every time I gobble a mouthful, the taste is foul. Everyone agrees that the food tastes bad, and they bring in sack lunches instead. The food just does not taste good.

3. Scientists have a new theory to explain the mass extinction of aquatic life 186 million years ago. Using chemical analysis, researchers have determined that a large amount of methane gas was released from ocean floor sediment about that time. The methane combined with oxygen in the ocean and formed carbon dioxide. Without oxygen available, marine life could not breathe. Researchers believe this was the cause of death for many ancient underwater creatures.

4.   I enjoy the smell of the air after a good rain. The air smells very good when the rain ends. After the water comes down from the clouds, the air smells very clean. Everyone enjoys the smell outside after a long soaking downpour. Nothing refreshes the air like a spring rain.

5.   Many people wonder whether there is life on other planets in the universe. All around the world, people claim to see UFO's. The idea of creatures from other planets visiting Earth has been the topic of many books and movies. Science fiction clubs are very popular and often have large annual meetings.

DEVELOPING SUPPORTING DETAILS

A good way to develop a list of details to support your main idea is to consider what questions a reader might ask about your topic sentence. Here is an example:

Topic Sentence: Florida is the ideal place to go for a winter vacation.

Reader May Ask: Where in Florida?
How do you know it's ideal?
What makes it ideal?
What kinds of things can you do there?
What if I like to go snow skiing?

By answering these questions, you can develop a list of supporting ideas for your topic.

Possible Answers: Panama City
went last year for annual vacation
good seafood, great night life, beautiful beaches
swimming, snorkeling
water skiing

From this list, you can develop a paragraph like the following:

Panama City, Florida

Florida is the ideal place to go for a winter vacation. Last year, our family spent its annual vacation on the white beaches of Panama City. During the day, we snorkeled, swam, and water skied in the clear, warm waters of the Gulf of Mexico. In the evenings, we enjoyed fresh seafood at the small local restaurants. At night, we joined other vacationers from around the world in various festivities sponsored by our hotel. Every year we travel to a new vacation spot, but the beauty and excitement of Florida will bring us back next year.

> **Supporting details provide answers to questions the reader may have about a topic sentence.**

Practice 5: Developing Supporting Details

For each of the following topic sentences, develop a list of at least 3 supporting details. The first topic is completed as an example.

1. The fresh smell of a newly planted garden is the best part of spring.

    a. *smell of new growth contrasts long months of dead winter*

    b. *early budding flowers have gentle fragrance*

    c. *freshly tilled earth has unique smell*

2. Parents have a tremendous responsibility in raising young children.

    a. _____

    b. _____

    c. _____

3. Computers in classrooms provide a wide range of learning opportunities.

    a. _____

    b. _____

    c. _____

4. Refugees who come to the United States face many difficulties if they don't speak English.

    a. _____

    b. _____

    c. _____

5. Professional baseball players get paid too much for the work they do.

    a. _____

    b. _____

    c. _____

ORGANIZING PARAGRAPHS

Now that you have a topic sentence and a list of supporting details, you must decide how you want to organize your paragraph. Just like the table we discussed at the beginning of this chapter, a paragraph is not put together haphazardly. It has structure and organization to make it stand. And just like there are different types of tables, there are different ways to organize paragraphs, such as **time order**, **spatial order**, **order of importance**, and **contrasting ideas**.

Time Order

Time order is especially important when you are writing a narrative. A story doesn't make sense when the events are not presented in the proper sequence. Here is an example:

> *I arrived after the speaker had begun her presentation. As I was running down the hill, I remembered that I had left my car keys on the kitchen table. When I started the car, I saw the clock, and I knew I was going to be late. I had to go back and get my keys.*

The lack of organization in this paragraph makes it very difficult to follow the story line. See below how organizing the passage in a time sequence makes it much easier to read and understand.

> *As I was running down the hill, I remembered that I had left my car keys on the kitchen table. I had to go back and get my keys. When I started the car, I saw the clock, and I knew I was going to be late. I arrived after the speaker had begun her presentation.*

You can also use time order to organize other types of writing, including writing to explain why. Review the paragraph on page 14 about vacationing in Florida. Notice how the details are organized according to time order.

Spatial Order

When you describe a scene or a location, you can sometimes use **spatial order** to arrange your ideas in a paragraph. Imagine yourself holding a camcorder and moving it in every direction. You can order your observations from **top to bottom**, **left to right**, **clockwise**, **near to far**, **front to back**, **inside to outside**, **east to west**, **north to south**, etc., and all of these directions *reversed* (e.g., **bottom to top**). Read the following description which is organized in spatial order.

> *When I saw the horse, I knew I was looking at a creature of great athletic beauty and ability. The horse's head was finely shaped, as if sculpted by an artist. On either side of its head, the eyes were alert and far-seeing. The ears were pointed and moved attentively to the slightest sound. The horse's neck was crested in a proud arch, and its muscular shoulders tapered down to powerful legs. The spine of the horse was perfectly aligned, and the back legs were unblemished and moved freely. The hindquarters of the horse were well rounded, and the horse's tail flowed like silk in the wind. In short, this horse was a magnificent animal.*

Look at the picture of the horse on the previous page. Does it make sense from the description you just read? If not, what additional details or observations would improve the description?

In the passage, the details of the horse are organized in a front to back order. First, the writer discusses the horse's head, along with the eyes and ears. Second, the writer provides details about the neck, shoulders, and front legs. Third, the writer describes the spine and the back legs. Finally, the author tells us about the horse's hindquarters and tail.

Spatial order can also be an effective way to organize other kinds of writing, as you can see in the following example of persuasive writing.

It's time for the city to clean up Zenith Park. As visitors enter the park, they are greeted by a broken sign that is smeared with graffiti. Next, they pass the pond where they must hold their noses because of the smell of decaying trash. If visitors make it past all of this, they reach the playground in the middle of the park. Here they find swings with ripped seats hanging limp beside slides with broken steps. The park, in its current state, is a hazardous waste area that must be cleaned up.

Order of Importance

The most common way to organize a paragraph is in **order of importance**. All of the details you include in your paragraph should be relevant to the topic and important to the reader. Some details, however, you will want to emphasize more than others. You can emphasize a certain idea by placing it either at the beginning or at the end of a paragraph. The following letter provides a good example.

Dear Aunt Jenny,

    I would really like to spend the summer with you because I have never spent much time in Oregon. Also, I am interested in earning some extra money for my college savings, and many jobs are available in your area. Most importantly, I really enjoy our short visits when we get together over the holidays, and I want to spend more time with you so we can be closer.

    Please write back soon, and let me know what you think.

Love,
Sandra

In this letter, Sandra begins with a simple wish that may be of some interest to her aunt. Aunt Jenny would be more likely to respect Sandra's second reason. However, Sandra's desire for a closer relationship will make the greatest impression upon her aunt's decision.

Of course, the letter could be arranged so that the most important idea comes first.

Dear Aunt Jenny,

  I would like to spend the summer with you because I really enjoy our short visits when we get together over the holidays, and I want to spend more time with you so we can be closer. I am also interested in earning some extra money for my college savings, and many jobs are available in your area. Besides, I have never spent much time in Oregon.

  Please write back soon, and let me know what you think.

Love,
Sandra

  Sometimes you will want to start off with the most important idea. Other times you will want to "save the best for last." The decision is yours based upon your audience, topic, and personal preference.

Contrasting Ideas

Sometimes writing assignments require that you choose one side of an issue or topic and convince the reader of the validity of your position. One good way to do this is to **contrast** your position with its opposite. In this kind of contrasting, you will point out differences and show why your position is better. For example, look at the paragraph below in which the writer is trying to convince his or her family to get a cat as a pet, instead of a dog.

  Since our family spends a lot of time traveling, a cat is definitely a better choice than a dog for a family pet. Dogs need to be let outside several times a day, while a cat knows how to use a litter box. Dogs also need to be fed regularly, whereas a cat can snack on one bowl of food for a few days. Dogs are very social animals and get lonely if they don't have people or other dogs to play with. Cats, on the other hand, are affectionate sometimes, but they can also get along just fine by themselves. A dog would not be treated well enough in our busy household. A cat would be much happier.

  In this example, the writer contrasts the qualities of a dog with those of a cat. The writer points out the reasons why a cat would fit better in the family that likes to travel. Someone with a different family situation could write a paragraph like the one on the next page.

For our young family, a dog would be a much better choice for a family pet than a cat. Dogs are social animals who love to be around people, especially kids. Cats, on the other hand, avoid crowds and often run from children. Dogs require regular feeding, which is a great opportunity to teach children responsibility. Cats require much less regular care. A dog offers great security for a home and family by barking when strangers approach. A cat can do little more than hiss at someone it doesn't like. A cat just doesn't offer our family the benefits a dog would offer.

This second paragraph shows how **awareness of audience** is important in writing. The writers know that each of their families have different needs and interests. Therefore, the writers choose reasons and examples that are appropriate for each family's unique situation.

Paragraphs can be organized according to space, time, importance, or contrasting ideas.

Practice 6: Organizing Paragraphs

Look at the pictures below. On a separate sheet of paper, write one paragraph for each picture. Make sure the sentences follow the order listed above the picture.

Time Order

Order of Importance

Spatial Order

Contrasting Ideas

Practice 7: Organizing Paragraphs

Return to the list of supporting details you developed in Practice 5 on page 15. Put each list in order according to time, space, importance, or contrasting ideas. Save these lists for Practice 9.

WRITING A CONCLUDING SENTENCE

As you learned in the last section, the beginning and end of a paragraph are very important. Sometimes a topic sentence will end a paragraph, but often it comes at the beginning, in order to alert the reader to the main idea. In this case, the paragraph will end with a **concluding sentence**. The concluding sentence brings closure to the paragraph by providing a summary of the topic and the supporting details. It may also suggest what action the reader should take. If another paragraph follows, the concluding sentence serves as a link between the two paragraphs.

As we compare a paragraph to a table, we see that the concluding sentence is like the floor which provides a stable base on which the table can stand. A paragraph that lacks a concluding sentence may leave the reader hanging, as if in midair, wondering if the author left out something. Read the example below to understand the importance of concluding sentences.

Example: *The federal government should continue to increase spending for defense. Now that the war on terrorism has started there is a need to keep this country well-armed. Currently, the United States spends more for defense than all other countries in the world combined! Congress continues to approve larger amounts of money for defense.*

This paragraph lacks an ending. The paragraph begins with an opinion about the amount of money spent for defense, and supporting details follow to back up this point. However, the lack of a conclusion leaves the reader wondering whether the paragraph is finished.

The addition of a concluding sentence like the following would make a big difference.

Concluding Sentence: *Write to your representatives to say the terrorist attacks have justified every penny spent on defense and more.*

This one sentence ties the paragraph together by summarizing the main idea and supporting details and urging the reader to take action. The reader may agree or disagree with the writer's ideas, but the reader has no doubt that the writer has brought the paragraph to a close.

> **A concluding sentence may achieve one or more of the following:**
>
> > **Emphasize an important point,**
> > **Provide a summary of the topic and details,**
> > **Suggest a response for the reader, or**
> > **Link one paragraph to another.**

Practice 8: Concluding Sentences

Read the following paragraphs. In the space after each, write a concluding sentence that best completes the topic. If the paragraph has a concluding sentence, write "Correct."

1.   The global economy is moving toward the East. By 2020, China is projected to have an economy that is roughly 11 times as large as the economy of the United States! In addition, Japan, India, and Indonesia will have production levels that rival those of the United States. Only four nations in Europe will even make the top twenty list of the world's largest economies.

_____

2.   The dancing craze is back in full force in the United States. After years of obscurity, swing music has made a rapid comeback. Also, the Latin rhythms of salsa, merengue, and cumbia can be heard in many cities. Two-stepping in clubs playing country music is also popular with the younger generation. In addition, the clubs playing techno, hip hop, and R&B music continue to draw larger crowds.

_____

3.   At the church pot luck dinner, each family competes to bring in the best entree and dessert. Mrs. Collin's chicken cacciatore was a fierce challenge to Mr. Ewing's homemade barbeque. Miss Laramie brought in two scrumptious apple pies that were gone in seconds, and everyone marveled at Miss Jenkin's homemade ice cream. This pot luck dinner was deliciously serious business.

_____

4.   Lifting weights is both mentally and physically demanding. It takes a great amount of concentration to lift large weights safely. Every lifter knows that form is crucial. The lifter must understand and visualize what he or she is doing during every second of a lift. People who do not exercise their mind in this manner end up with strains, sprains, and back and neck injuries.

_____

5.   The National Public Radio station in your city is a great educational resource. Because it receives funding from listeners, not big businesses, the station can offer diverse programming. You can hear informative and entertaining presentations about science, history, cultural movements, business trends, and film. In addition, the news programs provide longer, in-depth reports about major issues. Best of all, you can listen to all these great programs without those annoying commercials. Tune in to public radio today, and feed your mind with some high quality programs.

_____

Practice 9: Writing Paragraphs

Use the topic sentences and supporting details from Practices 5 and 7 to write four well-organized paragraphs. Be sure each paragraph has a concluding sentence.

CHAPTER 1 REVIEW: WRITING PARAGRAPHS

On a separate piece of paper, rewrite each unorganized group of sentences (1–5) in the form of a well-organized paragraph. Each group contains an unrelated idea that you must eliminate. Also, each group is missing a *topic sentence*, so you will need to create one and include it in your re-written paragraph.

1.   A. Neither the Republicans nor the Democrats are eager to tackle this issue.
     B. When considering the environment, most people think only about their own little world.
     C. They have to start going beyond the "What's in it for me?" attitude.
     D. The decisions we make have a big impact on the rest of the world.
     E. Citizens of this country need to realize that we are all part of a global community.

2.   A. The owner of the resort had breakfast ready downstairs.
     B. To our right, three deer were drinking out of a small stream.
     C. Straight ahead, the colorful valley opened up for us.
     D. To our left, the sun pierced through the tall trees.
     E. We were deeply impressed with everything we saw from our cabin.

3.   A. Our friends took the day off with us, so we could go to the mall.
     B. The editors also warned us that we would need to find some place else to work if we ever did that again.
     C. Unfortunately for us, we did not know that ACME motors advertised in our newspaper.
     D. The editors pulled every copy from the newsstands before the public saw them.
     E. The story concerned the bad performance of ACME transmissions.

4.   A. Something needs to be done, and soon.
     B. The problem is that costs keep skyrocketing while service is plummeting.
     C. Doctors used to make house calls.
     D. Meanwhile, patients spend more and more time waiting, and less and less time talking with the doctor.
     E. Doctors order more and more high-tech tests that increase medical bills.

5.   A. In addition, you are the first person to be unhappy with our product.
     B. We found, however, that the product you sent to us was in perfect working condition.
     C. The letter you sent said that the product was broken.
     D. Have you ever considered selling those gadgets yourself?
     E. Based on these reasons, I am sure you can understand why there is no possibility of a refund.

On a separate piece of paper, rewrite each group of sentences (6–10) in the form of a well-organized paragraph. For each group, you will need to eliminate one unrelated idea and create a *concluding sentence*.

6. A. Donna aimed the shot high and swished the basketball through the hoop.
   B. She passed the ball to Donna the first chance she had.
   C. Donna and Jenna want to go to the same college.
   D. Jenna certainly gave Donna an assist on the first play of the game.
   E. Next, Jenna shielded the other players from Donna as she took her shot.

7. A. Calligraphy is one of the most difficult forms of art I know.
   B. Each stroke of the pen has to be perfect.
   C. For example, the ink runs if the stroke is too slow.
   D. Also, the letters have gaps if the stroke is too fast.
   E. Because of the precision required, it can take many months to master a single alphabet in calligraphy.
   F. I hope to open a business selling calligraphy pens and ink supplies.

8. A. Some parents don't have time to coach sports for children.
   B. They said the boy wasn't getting enough playing time.
   C. This may be extreme, but how often do some parents start screaming at officials who make a bad call?
   D. Recently, the father and uncle of a football player in California beat up the boy's coach.
   E. Sometimes parents get carried away by the competition of children's sports.

9. A. The dome's shape is especially resistant to storms and earthquakes because the foundation supports all portions of the structure.
   B. A few nonconformists are building dome-style homes because of their stability and energy efficiency.
   C. The lack of walls in a dome-shaped house allows more equal distribution of heating and cooling, making it more energy efficient.
   D. Other people enjoy traditional four-sided brick homes.

10. A. This move brings Nuke-Clean closer to one of its big customers—the nuclear plant down the river.
    B. It also brings Nuke-Clean closer to my neighborhood.
    C. Some people in the neighborhood don't mind, but I think we should take action now.
    D. Nuke-Clean wants to move its operation to Smith County, so it can clean clothes that are contaminated with radiation.
    E. The nuclear plant in Chernobyl was shut down recently.

The paragraphs below (11–15) may be missing a topic sentence or a concluding sentence. Also, they may contain supporting details that restate the topic or describe unrelated ideas. For each paragraph, identify the problem. Then, on a separate piece of paper, rewrite the paragraph to make it complete.

11.   Getting the right tennis shoe for school can be an important decision. Getting blue jeans to fit is difficult sometimes. Whenever I try to tie-dye my t-shirts, they always turn out brown! My skin feels better after a long dip in the swimming pool. In summary, comfortable tennis shoes are vital for school survival.

12.   Exercising will improve blood flow to the brain and condition the muscles and bones to support the body under stress. In addition, a proper diet will ensure that the brain and other parts of the body are supplied with the proper nutrients. Third, a proper amount of sleep will keep the receptors in the brain connected for maximum efficiency. These three life activities in proper balance will keep the body and mind in shape for each day.

13.   Misha Patel enjoyed his visit to Disney World in July. The July visit to Disney World was very enjoyable for Misha. Disney World provided Misha with many interesting experiences. In conclusion, Misha was very happy experiencing many of the attractions offered at Disney World.

14.   Global warming is a very real and measurable phenomenon. Over the past century, glaciers near the poles have receded. In addition, the polar ice caps have thinned up to 40% from their previous thickness. Finally, air temperatures have warmed over 1° Celsius.

15.   The world now produces more than enough food to feed every man, woman, and child currently living. However, land useful for farming is not evenly distributed. Another challenge lies in lack of transportation to areas where there is no arable land. Furthermore, many nations lacking the arable land also lack the resources necessary to purchase the food they need. Together, these factors point to a problem in food distribution, not a lack of food.

ADDITIONAL ACTIVITIES: WRITING PARAGRAPHS

Topic Sentences

1. Review photographs, advertisements, paintings, or cartoons in books or magazines or on the Internet. Make copies of four of these visual expressions. Then, write topic sentences based on these examples. Seek feedback on your topic sentences from your teacher or from other students. Do the topic sentences focus on a single idea? Are they broad enough to be supported by details and examples? Do they invite discussion?

2. Write four topic sentences based on topics of your choosing. You can also use any of the following topics to help you get started.

school buses	**losing weight**	**tattoos**	**drinking**
favorite food	**nose rings**	**pet peeve**	**cure a cold**
girlfriend	**gossip**	**ideal job**	**favorite entertainer**
boyfriend	**my dream**	**worst job**	

   Exchange your topic sentences with your teacher or with other students. Do the topic sentences focus on a single idea? Are they broad enough to be supported by details and examples? Do they invite discussion?

Supporting Details and Organizing Paragraphs

3. Choose four of your best topic sentences from the first or second activities listed above. Write four to six sentences that support these topic sentences. Make sure your details relate to the topic, are specific, and avoid restating the topic sentence.

   Use a different way to organize each paragraph. In other words, use time order for one paragraph, spatial order for your next paragraph, order of importance for another paragraph, and contrasting ideas for your last paragraph.

Concluding Sentences

4. Write a concluding sentence for each of your four paragraphs. Make sure that your concluding sentence summarizes the topic sentence and supporting details in each paragraph.

Final Activity

5. Turn in your completed paragraphs for feedback from your teacher or tutor. Revise them as needed. For further practice in writing paragraphs, repeat steps 1-5, using different topics.

Note: For more instruction and practice for various aspects of writing, visit the Web sites or check out the books listed in Appendix B (pages 234-238).

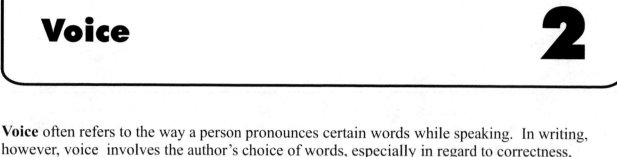

Voice

2

Voice often refers to the way a person pronounces certain words while speaking. In writing, however, voice involves the author's choice of words, especially in regard to correctness, clearness, or effectiveness. The words you choose to describe and explain your ideas greatly influence how readers receive your ideas. To choose the best words, you need to consider your purpose for writing and the audience who will read your work. Then, you can choose a language and tone that is appropriate for your readers. This chapter will help you choose correct, clear, and effective words by discussing the following topics:

- **Author's Purpose**   - **Audience**   - **Language and Tone**

AUTHOR'S PURPOSE

Everyone who writes is an author, and each author writes for different reasons. Think of the reasons why you write: you write essays for English class because the teacher requires it; you may write a note in a birthday card to your mother to express your love; or you may send e-mails to Internet friends just to say "hello." Every author writes for a specific purpose. Often, the **author's purpose** is revealed in the way the author writes. See if you can determine the author's purpose in the following two paragraphs.

Example 1:   *The common opossum is the only kind of opossum found in the United States. This species grows about as big as a house cat. It has rough grayish-white hair, a long snout, dark eyes, and big hairless ears. This opossum has a long tail that does not have much hair on it. The animal can hang upside down by wrapping its tail around a tree branch. Its teeth and claws are sharp.*

'possom

Example 2:   *One warm fall evening, our son Tom went out to the garage to feed the cat. Suddenly we heard him yell out, "A rat! A Texas-sized rat!" His older brother Joey went to investigate and reported back, "Sure enough, Mom. It is a rat!" Finally, Barb and I went to look at this "rat." When the little critter turned around to see us gawking, we realized that it was a 'possum . . . a fat 'possum.*

Both paragraphs discuss opossums, but they do so in very different ways. **Example 1** provides basic information about the physical features of one type of opossum. Though the paragraph contains descriptive words, there is no dialogue and no action. This paragraph would fit well in a science textbook. The author's purpose is **to inform**.

Example 2, on the other hand, describes characters and events with expressive words and interesting dialogue. It is part of a brief story about a surprising and funny event. Perhaps you would find it in a book of short stories. The author's purpose is **to entertain**.

26

Examples 1 and 2 show how authors can use a different style of writing depending on the purpose for their writing. The words they choose reflect a certain feeling or direction. The ability to determine the author's purpose for writing enhances your reading comprehension. In addition, being clear about your purpose as an author will make your writing more effective. Become familiar with the following list of purposes for writing so that you may better understand the reasons why authors write.

Purpose	Definition	Reading Selection
To inform	To present facts and details	"Ocean Fishes"
To entertain	To amuse or offer enjoyment	"How My Cat Turned Purple"
To persuade	To urge action on an issue	"Raise Penalties for Polluters"
To explain why	To provide clear reasons	"How Plants Grow"
To instruct	To teach concepts and facts	"Mastering Exponents"
To create suspense	To convey uncertainty	"Will Gnats Rule the World?"
To motivate	To inspire to act	"You Can Make a Difference!"
To cause doubt	To be skeptical	"Is Chocolate Health Food?"
To introduce a character	To describe a person's traits	"First Look at Captain Nemo"
To create a mood	To establish atmosphere	"Gloom in the House of Usher"
To relate an adventure	To tell an exciting story	"Lost in a Cave"
To share a personal experience	To tell about an event in your life	"The Time I Learned to Share"
To describe feelings	To communicate emotions through words	"When My Dog Died"

> **Your purpose for writing affects your diction, the words you choose.**

Practice 1: Author's Purpose

Based on the list of author's purposes, identify the author's purpose for the following reading passages. Then, discuss your choices with your class or with your instructor.

1. The fire crackled musically. From it swelled light smoke. Overhead the foliage moved softly. The leaves, with their faces turned toward the blaze, were colored shifting hues of silver, often edged with red. Far off to the right, through a window in the forest, could be seen a handful of stars lying, like glittering pebbles, on the black level of the night.

    – Stephen Crane, *Red Badge of Courage*

    A. To describe an event
    B. To create a mood
    C. To persuade
    D. To instruct

2.   Columbus' own successful voyage in 1492 prompted a papal bull (a directive from the Pope) dividing the globe between rivals Spain and Portugal. But the Portuguese protested that the pope's line left them too little Atlantic sea room for their voyages to India. The line was shifted 270 leagues westward in 1494 by the Treaty of Tordesillas. Thus, wittingly or not, the Portuguese gained Brazil and gave their language to more than half the people of South America.

A.   To introduce a character   C.   To relate an adventure
B.   To describe feelings   D.   To instruct

3.   Twelve-year-old Nadia told us a seemingly unbelievable story about her family's journey to the United States. In Romania, her father was involved in the politics of Romania, opposing the communist regime of Ceausescu. Because of death threats made against her family, Nadia and her family had to leave the country in the middle of the night. They had arranged for a boat to meet them so they could sail the Black Sea to freedom in Bulgaria. Because they left in a hurry, they took nothing with them except their clothes. The boat never came, so they swam into the sea until a boat from Bulgaria discovered her family swimming. All of them survived the swim except for Nadia's little brother, Dimitry. From that country, they obtained refugee status and traveled to the United States. Nadia is very grateful to be living here, and after hearing her story, so are we.

A.   To describe feelings   C.   To relate an adventure
B.   To explain why   D.   To persuade

4.   Hand grippers can help give your arms those bulging biceps you're after, but only if they offer enough resistance. If you can squeeze them repeatedly for one to two minutes, and your hands don't get tired, they're too weak for you. You can keep buying stronger ones or make something at home that can do the same job.

A.   To inform   C.   To describe an event
B.   To persuade   D.   To entertain

5.   My family came to America in 1985. No one spoke a word of English. In school, I was in an English as a Second Language class with other foreign-born children. My class was so overcrowded that it was impossible for the teacher to teach English properly. I dreaded going to school each morning because of the fear of not understanding what people were saying and the fear of being laughed at.

– Yu-Lan (Mary) Ying, a personal account about learning English

A.   To cause doubt   C.   To share a personal experience
B.   To entertain   D.   To create suspense

28

Practice 2: Author's Purpose

A. In a group or on your own, clip 6 articles from newspapers or magazines. Using the list of purposes for writing from this section, identify the author's purpose in each selection. Exchange your passages with a classmate to see if he/she identifies the same purpose. Then, discuss your findings with the class or with your teacher.

B. Choose two or more purposes listed in the chart of purposes for writing. Write paragraphs that emphasize each purpose. Without revealing your purposes, share your paragraphs with your classmates or teacher. See if they can identify your intended purposes.

AUDIENCE

Once you are clear about your purpose for writing, you must consider your **audience**—the person(s) who will read what you write. Unless you are writing in your journal or taking notes in class, you are always writing for a particular audience. It may be your teacher, a friend, your parents, or a manager at work. Knowing your audience gives you important information including the following:

the audience's interest: what topic or information is of interest to the audience (so you can capture the interest of your readers),

the audience's prior knowledge: what the audience already knows (so you don't tell the readers something they already know, and you can draw on that prior knowledge),

the audience's vocabulary: words that the readers understand (so you don't use words that are too easy or too difficult),

what the audience needs to know: information or explanations that you want the audience to know (so you can make a unique presentation for each audience).

This valuable information helps you write more effectively.

Read the following two paragraphs written by the same person. Try to develop a picture of the audience that the writer had in mind.

Example 1:

Since you're in the market for a new car, I wanted to tell you about mine. My new car is the best one I've owned. It's a 2005 Mustang™. It's got a 5.0 L overhead cam engine with multi-port fuel injection. It can do 0-60 mph in 5 seconds. With that much engine, passing cars on the highway is a breeze, but handling corners on back roads is a little trickier than with my old Honda CRX™. I love the rush I get when I'm cruising around with my new wheels. You should consider buying one, too.

Example 2: *Since you're in the market for a new car, I wanted to tell you about mine. My new car is the best one I've owned. It's a 2005 Mustang™. This sporty two-door is canary yellow with electric blue racing stripes and silver mag wheels. It has cordovan leather seats and a Bose™ sound system. The sunroof is the perfect canary yellow with electric blue racing stripes and silver mag wheels. It has cordovan leather seats and a Bose sound system. The sunroof is the perfect finishing touch. You should see the looks I get when I'm cruising around with my new wheels. You should consider buying one, too.*

In both paragraphs, the author is telling someone about a new car, but each paragraph includes very different details about the car. Based on these differences, how would you describe the intended audience of each paragraph? What evidence is there for your description?

Audience Interest

How does the writer try to catch the audience's interest in each paragraph? Clearly, the first paragraph is intended for a reader who is interested in a car's power and performance. So, the writer describes the car's engine, as well as the car's speed and handling. The second paragraph, on the other hand, mentions nothing about performance. The writer assumes that the audience is concerned with appearance and style, so the description focuses on colors and high-priced options.

Audience Knowledge

What does the writer assume that the audience already knows? Since the reader of the first paragraph is interested in performance, the writer assumes that the reader knows what a Ford Mustang™ is and that going 0–60 mph in 5 seconds is fast. The reader of the second paragraph may need the author to describe the Mustang as a "sporty two-door," but the reader understands well the stunning colors and fine accessories of the new car.

Audience Vocabulary

What kinds of words will the audience be familiar with and understand easily? The writer expects the reader of the first paragraph to know technical terms like "5.0 L" and "multi-port fuel injection." While these terms may speak loudly and clearly to the reader of the first paragraph, they may mean nothing to the reader of the second paragraph who appreciates "cordovan leather" and a "Bose™ sound system." Likewise, the reader of the first paragraph may have no use for these terms since they have nothing to do with power or performance.

What the Audience Should Know

What does the writer want the audience to know? In both paragraphs, the writer wants to share excitement about a new car purchase in order to encourage readers to purchase the same kind of car. The writer shares information that will be of interest to two kinds of audiences and that will encourage readers to purchase a Ford Mustang™.

> **When considering how to convey what you think your audience needs to know, consider the audience's interests, prior knowledge, and vocabulary skill.**

Various writing assignments or "real-life" writing situations will require you to address a particular audience, such as parents, teachers, other students, or the editor of a local newspaper. Considering your audience will help you write more effectively.

Practice 3: Audience

For each of the following topics, describe the interest, knowledge, and vocabulary of the given audience, as well as what you think the audience should know.

1. Topic: parental advisory stickers on music CDs   Audience: parents

Audience Interest _interested in the welfare of their children_

Audience Knowledge _unfamiliar with specific artists, but aware of rude music_

Audience Vocabulary _some knowledge of teen vocabulary, but mostly not_

Audience Should Know _parents, not record companies, need to take responsibility_

2. Topic: parental advisory stickers on music CDs   Audience: students

Audience Interest _____

Audience Knowledge _____

Audience Vocabulary _____

Audience Should Know _____

3. Topic: high salaries of professional athletes   Audience: baseball player

Audience Interest _____

Audience Knowledge _____

Audience Vocabulary _____

Audience Should Know _____

4. Topic: high salaries of professional athletes   Audience: stadium worker

Audience Interest _____

Audience Knowledge _____

Audience Vocabulary _____

Audience Should Know _____

5. Topic: using lottery to fund public education   Audience: church pastor

Audience Interest _____

Audience Knowledge _____

Audience Vocabulary _____

Audience Should Know _____

6.   Topic: using lottery to fund public education   Audience: governor of state

Audience Interest _____

Audience Knowledge _____

Audience Vocabulary _____

Audience Should Know _____

7.   Topic: importance of a high school diploma   Audience: high school dropout

Audience Interest _____

Audience Knowledge _____

Audience Vocabulary _____

Audience Should Know _____

8.   Topic: importance of a high school diploma   Audience: employer

Audience Interest _____

Audience Knowledge _____

Audience Vocabulary _____

Audience Should Know _____

LANGUAGE

No, not the foreign kind . . . In regard to writing, **language** refers to the words that a writer uses to present ideas. From your own experience, you know that the way you speak to your friends is different from the way you speak to a teacher or a parent. Also, the words you use in a conversation with a teacher are different from the words you would write in a composition for that teacher. See two different types of language in the examples on the next page.

Example 1:   An honest man has hardly need to count more than his ten fingers, or in extreme cases he may add his ten toes, and lump the rest. Simplicity, Simplicity, Simplicity! I say, let your affairs be as two or three, and not a hundred or a thousand; instead of a million count half a dozen, and keep your accounts on your thumbnail. In the midst of this chopping sea of civilized life, . . . he must be a great calculator indeed who succeeds. Simplify, Simplify. Instead of three meals a day, if it be necessary eat but one; instead of a hundred dishes, five; and reduce other things in proportion.

– Henry David Thoreau, *Walden*

Example 2:   Sometimes life gets so crazy. You've got cell phones ringing, T.V.'s blaring, cars honking, and everybody talking at the same time. You've got to simplify these days, or you just won't make it. Do you really need three beepers and two cell phones? One cell phone is <u>more</u> than enough—trash the rest. When things are getting out of control, try to focus only on the important things. Forget everything else. Take one day at a time, and use the KISS principle: Keep It Simple Stupid.

The authors of the two examples above use very different words to describe similar ideas. Example 1 uses **formal language** which includes complex sentence structure and a higher level of vocabulary. Example 2 uses **informal** language, including simpler vocabulary and sentence structure.

The differences between formal and informal language are sometimes small, but often very important. These differences are presented in the table below.

Formal Language	Informal Language
Characteristics	
broader vocabulary	simple words
more complex sentence structure	simple sentences
strict attention to proper grammar	loose following of grammar rules
Appropriate Uses	
written assignments for school	conversations with friends or relatives
business letters	personal letters, e-mail

As indicated in the table above, you should use formal language for any writing assignments in school or for any standardized tests. Formal language is also appropriate for business letters or letters to people who hold a particular office, such as superintendent, mayor, or editor of a newspaper.

Each pair of sentences below use different language to express the same idea. Read each sentence, and decide whether the sentence uses formal or informal language.

Example 3:	Danny's mom told the other kids to go away.
Example 4:	Danny's mother told the other children to leave.
Example 5:	He did not like our offer.
Example 6:	He didn't like our deal.
Example 7:	I've just about finished my homework.
Example 8:	I have almost finished my homework.

Examples 3, 6, and 7 contain contractions and other simple words, which are characteristic of informal language. Examples 4, 5, and 8 are somewhat different, and they do not contain contractions. They also replace the words *mom, kids*, and *deal* with *mother, children*, and *offer*. These changes make the language formal, which is more appropriate for most writing assignments.

While informal language can be grammatically correct, formal language is more appropriate for writing assignments, including standardized tests that require written responses.

Practice 4: Formal and Informal Language

Read each sentence below. Write on the line next to the sentence whether it contains formal or informal language.

1. You must consider the feelings of each person before making your decision. _____

2. How long has he been having trouble with his wrist? _____

3. The Web is a great place to get lots of cool information. _____

4. Would you like to join me in seeing a movie Saturday night? _____

5. Make sure you stop by while you're in town. _____

6. We anticipate future success due to our investment strategy. _____

7. Stay on the right track, and you'll be a winner. _____

8. She's never gonna go for that. _____

9. The principal presented an unusual award to one member of the faculty. _____

10. We'll have a great trip, as long as the RV doesn't break down. _____

TONE

While growing up, you have probably heard a parent or other adult say, "Don't use that tone of voice with me!" And you have probably responded, "What tone?!" **Tone** is the attitude or feeling that underlies words. You know that the same words can be said in many different tones. Just think of the many different ways You can say "No" or "Hi." In writing, tone is the way a writer uses words to present a certain attitude or feeling to the reader. A writer can use the same type of language to convey very different tones. For example, compare the two letters which follow (one is on the next page).

Mrs. Barbara Jones
15 Oak Lane
Flagstaff, Arizona 86001

Acme, Inc.
Customer Service
10 Main Street
Phoenix, Arizona 85040

May 16, 2005

To Whom It May Concern:

    I am very displeased with the service I have received from your company. In fact, it would be more accurate to say the "disservice" which I have received from your company. On three separate occasions (May 11, 14, and 15), I have dialed your so-called "Helpline" and been left on hold for over twenty minutes. You may find it hard to believe, but I have much better ways of spending my time than listening to sleep-inducing music while I'm waiting for your service personnel. Therefore, I am writing this letter so that you may waste your time contacting me at the address and phone number below. If I do not hear from a representative by the end of this week, I will cease doing business with your company.

Sincerely,

Barbara Jones

Barbara Jones (1-555-IAM-MADD

Acme, Inc.
10 Main Street, Phoenix, AZ 85040

Mrs. Barbara Jones
15 Oak Lane
Flagstaff, Arizona 86001

May 27, 2005

Dear Mrs. Jones,

Please accept our apology for the inconvenience you suffered because of our Helpline. In general, we try to respond to customers within 45 seconds of their call. At times, the volume of calls we receive prevents us from doing that. I am sending this letter to let you know that I have asked one of our representatives to call you this afternoon. If you do have not received this call by the time you receive this letter, please use the number below to reach me directly, and we will solve your problem immediately. Thank you for working with Acme, Inc., and we look forward to serving you in the future.

Sincerely,

Zhong Li

Zhong Li
Customer Service Director (1-800-IAM-SORI)

The authors of both letters use formal language to express their ideas. However, the tone which each author uses is very different.

In Example 1, the author is clearly frustrated about being left on hold. She states directly that she is "displeased with the service" she has received. She adds a slightly sarcastic twist in the second sentence by calling the company's service "disservice." The author states her problem and uses stronger sarcasm in the sentence which begins "You may find it hard to believe . . ." The last sentence is called an **ultimatum**, that is, a challenge for someone to do something or else suffer certain consequences. This shows that the author is ready to take serious action. Therefore, the author's tone could be described as angry, sarcastic, or serious. However, **frustrated** is the most accurate description of the author's tone.

The author of the second letter is responding to a frustrated customer. The author wants to solve the customer's problem and make her feel better so that she will still be a customer. He begins his letter by apologizing. He tries to offer an explanation without making excuses. He states the action he has taken and gives the customer direct access to his phone. This action shows that he, too, is serious about solving her problem. The tone of his letter may be called **apologetic**, expressing sorrow for his part in doing something wrong.

There are many different tones which you can use in your writing. Some tones are listed in the table on the next page. Use a dictionary to learn what these words mean.

Different Types of Tone

angry	stiff	dramatic	optimistic	sad
anxious	relaxed	fearful	pessimistic	tragic
rude	hysterical	happy	humorous	satirical
calm	expectant	lofty	threatening	serious
frustrated	apologetic	sarcastic	sympathetic	lighthearted
neutral	cynical	excited	relieved	doubtful

In your writing, pay attention to tone—the feeling or attitude you present with your words.

Practice 5: Tone

Based on the list of types of tone, identify the author's tone for the following passages. Then, discuss your answers with your class or teacher.

1.   Doctors are a regular set of humbugs, and most of them are quacks. They go off to school and learn some recipes for curing diseases. Then they manage in one way or another to get the teachers in their school to give them a certificate, and then they'll go out into some town or village or city and rent some space over a drugstore and get some bones and an old skull and a lot of books and spread them around the room and call it an office. They put up a sign and call themselves doctors. Then they guess what your illness is and collect their money.

–from *Shams* by John S. Draper

What is the tone of this passage?

A.   happy

B.   neutral

C.   sympathetic

D.   cynical

2.   I ain't never seen nothin' like it all my life. There we was just walkin' down the street when two guys came runnin' out of Joe's Store shootin' up everything in sight. We hit the pavement fast as we could. Thank God nobody got killed or nothin'. It's not like I ain't seen it before, but this time was too close for comfort. Ya know what I mean. That's the last time I'm takin' that short cut home from school. I'll take the long way next time. I bet you should do the same.

What kind of tone does the author use in this passage?

A.   relieved

B.   rude

C.   anxious

D.   threatening

3.

During Napoleon's war with England, both England and France seized neutral ships and goods. In addition, they were conscripting United States merchant sailors into their navies, enraging the people of the United States. In August 1810, Napoleon publicly repealed his previous decrees and declared that neutral ships could freely trade in France without risk of confiscation or conscription. President Madison believed Napoleon's words. When Britain refused to promise the same thing, Congress declared war on England and began invading Canada, starting the War of 1812.

What is the tone of this paragraph?

A. cynical   C. ironic
B. expectant   D. neutral

4. Suddenly, the boat capsized. "Felix, where are you?" I screamed. All I could see was the overturned boat and pieces of our shattered picnic lunch being tossed on the waves. I swam around to the other side of the boat, but there was no sign of him. "He's gotta be under the boat!" I thought as panic began to grip me. I dove under the boat and found Felix. His eyes were closed, but his arm was wrapped around the seat of the boat. I grabbed him and pulled him up for air. As I tried to get him breathing again, I kept shouting, "Wake up, Felix! Wake up!" Luckily, I was able to get him breathing again. Our picnic was ruined, but it wasn't a tragedy. Thank God!

What is the tone of this paragraph?

A. pessimistic   C. humorous
B. dramatic   D. relaxed

5.

The traffic began moving again. Josh was glad to be finished building houses in Washoe county. Now he was ready to relax for a couple of weeks in the Great Basin National Park. The drive home would take about two hours on the Interstate. When Josh got home, he'd pack the tent, sleeping bags, food, and cooking gear in the truck. Then he'd pick up his son, David. They'd be together for the whole weekend in a secluded woodland with no one around for miles. They'd fish the streams and lakes with fly rods. The cool air and water would refresh his mind and spirit. Josh could already smell the freshly caught fish sizzling over an open fire.

The tone of this story is

A. expectant.   C. sarcastic.
B. sad.   D. humorous.

LANGUAGE AND TONE

Language refers to the words a writer uses. **Tone** is the way the writer uses those words to present a certain attitude or feeling to the reader. Language (what is said) and tone (how it is said) are determined both by the **author's purpose** and the intended **audience**. For example, the way you ask someone for a favor is very different from the way you tell someone to leave you alone. Also, the language and tone you use with your friends at the lunch table probably would not be appropriate in the principal's office. To see how language and tone can differ in respect to the audience, read and compare the letter below with the e-mail that follows.

May 17, 2005

Sally H. Jones
621 North Main Street
Tucson, AZ 85710
Dear Sir:

Because of my great love for animals, I am very interested in working at Purrfect Pets. I visit your store frequently as I purchase food and supplies to care for my several cats and dogs. I am always impressed by the cleanliness of your store and the care you show the animals.

This summer I will be available to work full-time. Once school begins in the fall, I will need to reduce my hours to part-time, but I will still be available to work on nights and weekends.

Please find enclosed my application and a list of references. I look forward to hearing from you soon.

Sincerely,

Sally H. Jones

Sally H. Jones

Hey Jack,

What's up?! I'm really psyched about workin' at the CD Emporium with you this summer. I mean I don't have the job yet, but why wouldn't they hire me? By the way, can you stop by the CDE on your way to school tomorrow and pick up a job application for me? Thanks!

Does your sister still want to work at that stupid pet store? That would gross me out! Cleaning out all those cages with all the animal stuff in it. No thanks! Give me some cellophane-wrapped CDs any day. Catch you later. Thanks again.

T.J.

Do you see the similarities and differences between the two letters? Both writers are seeking jobs for the summer, and they want to work where they will enjoy what they will be doing. The authors share a similar purpose, but their audiences are different.

Writing is similar to giving a speech—writers need to keep their audiences in mind. Sally's writing to the owner of the pet shop where she wants to work. She has chosen the language of a business letter to address her potential employer. She avoids dialect and slang terms, and her tone is formal and respectful. The language and tone of T. J.'s e-mail, however, is very different because he is writing to a good friend, and he is asking a favor. Along with an informal tone, he uses slang terms and abbreviations that Jack will easily understand. Assuming that Jack will recognize T. J.'s style of language, T. J. uses neither his full name nor a salutation such as "sincerely" or "your friend."

The type of language and tone you use in writing greatly affects how readers will interpret your idea.

Practice 6: Language And Tone

Using the terms you have just learned, describe the language and tone you would use in writing to each of the following audiences.

1. **School principal**   Tone _____

    Language _____

2. **Other students**   Tone _____

    Language _____

3. **Good friend**   Tone _____

    Language _____

4. **Editor of the local newspaper**   Tone _____

    Language _____

5. **Manager at work**   Tone _____

    Language _____

Practice 7: Language And Tone

You are running as a representative for your class on the student council. You want to write a short announcement to your friends and to your principal that explains why you are running for this office. How would your language and tone differ for these two audiences? Explain why you chose this answer. Then, write a short announcement for each audience.

CHAPTER 2 REVIEW: VOICE

Read the following two articles. Then, on your own paper, answer the questions below, using complete sentences.

Article 1

The results of a recent survey conducted by the NIH (National Institutes of Health) indicate that substance abuse had increased in the Manhattan area since September 11. During the months of October and November, researchers randomly phoned residents of New York City, carefully screening for those living in the Manhattan area. Answers to questions about alcohol, cigarette, and marijuana use before and after September 11 revealed a 25 percent increase in alcohol consumption, a 10 percent increase in tobacco use, and 3.2 percent increase in marijuana use.

The data collected during this survey will help researchers find more effective ways to treat substance abuse in people coping with severe stress. This research has revealed that people who admitted to an increase in substance abuse were most likely suffering from post-traumatic stress disorder and depression. Substance abuse did not differ significantly among ethnic groups or gender. Age, marital status and income seemed to play a more integral role in determining whether the trauma of September 11 caused an increase in substance abuse.

Article 2

Did you know that you could die from smoking that cigarette or taking that last drink for the road? You are killing your children right now with that cancer stick, and you could kill them or someone else by drinking and driving. Smoking causes lung cancer and heart disease: there ain't no butts about it. Alcohol causes cirrhosis of the liver and birth defects: go ahead and toast *that*. Smoking and drinking aren't cool; they are a subtle form of terrorism that kills you and your family. Don't look to the HOMELAND SECURITY POLICE to protect you. You have got to protect your own home and your family against this threat. So, go home and be a hero—lose the booze and the smokes!

---

1. What is the purpose of each report?

2. Examine the language of each report. What kind of tone is used in each?

Read the following excerpt, and complete the writing exercise that follows.

> There was a proposition in a township there to discontinue public schools because they were too expensive. An old farmer spoke up and said if they stopped the schools they would not save anything, because every time a school was closed a jail had to be built. It's like feeding a dog on his own tail. He'll never get fat. I believe it is better to support schools than jails.
>
> —Mark Twain's *Speeches*

3. Write a paragraph, on your own paper, analyzing the effectiveness of this passage. Discuss the use of language and tone.

Read the following two letters which discuss censorship in the public school libraries. Then, complete the writing exercise that follows.

Dear Fellow Students,

There is a quiet, hush-hush censorship happening in our schools that administrators were hoping we wouldn't notice. Did you know that the library won't order certain books they think we shouldn't read? Do they think we're too young to understand the facts of life, such as the prejudice against the immigrants who helped build this country or the social problems of the "haves" vs the "have-nots" with political double dealing and business scandals? Are they afraid we'll be brainwashed by the authors? Do they think that we are a second generation of slackers and just don't care! Many of these books are considered to be classics, and we should be required to read them, not restricted from reading them. I am really insulted by the heavy-handed censorship happening in our very own school. Help me take a stand against this ignorance forced on us by school officials, and write to your school board telling them how ticked off you are about this whole thing.

Thanks,

Ricky Mondego

Dear Members of the School Board,

    I am writing to express my disappointment that the library will not order books they deem too controversial for our school. As a member of the 11th grade and a soon-to-be contributing member of this community, I should be encouraged to read quality literature and to think critically about the issues these books represent. I feel that my right to access information of my choice has been violated by this censorship.

    Allowing, and even encouraging, the students of this school to read this material will help us to develop the kind of analytical skills that we need to become productive citizens. Through reading these books, we will be reassured that the very issues we face today have been plaguing the minds of great writers for centuries. Sheltering us from these issues accomplishes nothing. I ask that you reconsider your decision to ban these books from the school library and renew your faith in the developing minds of the younger generation.

Sincerely,

Ricardo Mondego

Ricardo Mondego

---

4.   Although the same student wrote these letters to accomplish the same goal, the tone and language are very different. Write a paragraph explaining how the audience has influenced the author of these letters. Discuss the differences in tone, language, and audience.

5.   Look at the first letter on the previous page. Notice the vocabulary differences in this letter. Is it more informal than the second letter? Why? Change some of the vocabulary in the letter to sound as though it were aimed at an adult audience. How did you choose the words to change, and what did you change them to?

ADDITIONAL ACTIVITIES: VOICE

1. Put yourself in someone else's shoes. Imagine you are running for mayor of your town. Write three paragraphs: one a press release for the local paper, one a letter to your opponent, and one to your best friend. Here are some possible topics with which you can agree or disagree.

school vouchers	**school uniforms**
new licensing laws for ATV operators	**restricted internet use**
amusement park safety	**hybrid cars**
mandatory community service	**restriction on concerts**

   Share these paragraphs with your teacher or classmates. Is the language effective for the audience? Why? Why not?

2. Your younger brother or sister is taking Algebra I with the school's toughest math teacher. In one paragraph, offer him or her advice on passing the class.

3. Write two letters from a pet's point-of-view. The first should be a list of demands; the second a thank you note for the things your owner does for you. Don't reveal what kind of animal you are; let your audience guess.

4. Compare the language on the front page of your local paper to the language in one of your textbooks. Both are intended to inform, but the audience for each is different. Discuss how this affects the language.

5. You just bought a CD by your favorite band, and you can't wait to listen to it. Once you open it, you discover there is a huge scratch in the disc. Write a letter of complaint to the company. Once you are finished with the letter, exchange complaint letters with a classmate. Now write a response to your friend's letter of complaint as if you were the president of the company.

Creating Ideas and Content 3

In the last two chapters, you practiced writing paragraphs. In this chapter, you will expand your writing skills to compose a five-paragraph essay. You will learn about the following:

- **The Basic Structure of an Essay**
- **The Writing Process**
- **Generating Ideas**

- **Focusing Ideas**
- **Making a Plan for Your Essay**

BASIC STRUCTURE OF AN ESSAY

A five-paragraph essay should include three main parts: **introduction**, **body**, and **conclusion**.

Basic Structure of an Essay

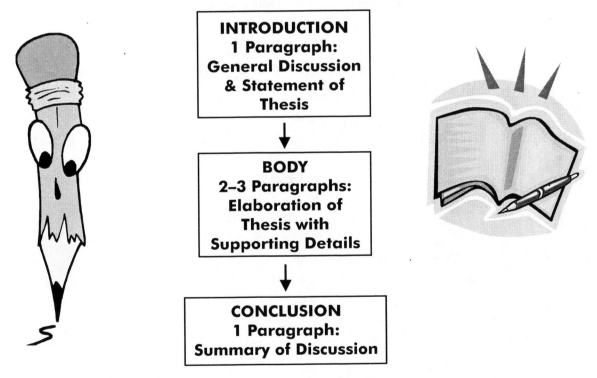

INTRODUCTION
1 Paragraph:
General Discussion
& Statement of
Thesis

↓

BODY
2–3 Paragraphs:
Elaboration of
Thesis with
Supporting Details

↓

CONCLUSION
1 Paragraph:
Summary of Discussion

The **introduction** is the first paragraph of your essay. It gets the reader's attention, prepares the reader for what will follow, and states the **thesis** of the essay. The thesis of an essay is much like the main idea of a paragraph.

The **body** consists of three paragraphs which support the thesis. Each paragraph is focused around a topic sentence which can be drawn from the key points of the thesis. In turn, the topic sentence of each paragraph is supported by the details explained in the rest of that paragraph.

The **conclusion** is the last paragraph of your essay. It reinforces the thesis of your essay with a vigorous summary of your argument. It ties everything together and convinces the reader of the rightness of your position.

THE WRITING PROCESS

Whether you are composing a letter, an in-class essay, or a lengthy homework assignment, your writing does not appear magically. You must follow a process. You have to **think**, **write**, **review**, and then repeat these steps. Study the writing process described below.

The Writing Process

THINK

1. **Read the Writing Prompt Carefully.** Make sure that you understand what question the writing prompt is asking and who your audience is.

2. **Generate Ideas.** Make a list of every idea that comes into your head regarding the topic. Don't judge the ideas as good or bad yet.

3. **Focus Your Ideas.** From your list, choose some ideas that you can use for your essay, and make a plan for how you will present them.

WRITE

4. **Write.** Write a draft based on your plan. Use complete sentences to develop your ideas into paragraphs.

REVIEW

5. **Revise.** Check over your draft for coherence, transitions, and sentence variety and structure. Delete any unnecessary words, phrases, or sentences.

THINK

6. **Think** about any other ways you can improve your essay.

WRITE

7. **Write** the final copy of your essay clearly on the lined paper.

REVIEW

8. **Proofread.** Neatly correct punctuation, spelling, capitalization, word choice, grammar, and sentence formation.

It may seem like there are many steps to follow when you only have a limited amount of time to write an essay. For now, go through the steps slowly, learning each one thoroughly. As you practice, these steps will become like second nature to you. Then, you will be well prepared for any writing assignment you face, including timed essays on exams.

Practice the writing process: think, write, and review.

READ THE WRITING PROMPT CAREFULLY

The first step in writing a good response is to read the writing prompt carefully. Make sure you understand the **question** you are to answer. It is also important for you to identify the **audience** to whom you are writing, such as the principal, other students, or readers of the local newspaper. Read the following sample writing prompt carefully.

> A recent survey has shown that teens aged 12 to 17 watch an average of eleven hours of television each week. However, children between the ages of 2 and 5 watch an average of thirteen hours of television each week. Your teacher has given you the homework assignment: discuss with your family the amount of television watched in your home. Decide what you think about young children watching nearly two hours of television each day.
>
> As a way of introducing the topic of children watching television, you will write an essay answering the following question: "Does television affect young children positively or negatively? Explain your answer." Once you finish the essay, you will give it to your parents to "look over." This will start your family's discussion.

1.   What question does this writing prompt ask?   ⟶   "Does television affect young children positively or negatively?"

The writing prompt does not ask you to address whether your family watches too much television, or why teens watch less television than younger children. The prompt asks whether television affects young children positively or negatively. Stick to this issue.

Watching television may affect young children in both positive and negative ways. You must decide if, overall, the effects are positive *or* negative. **For persuasive writing, it is important to choose one side of an issue.** Though it is helpful for you to acknowledge and/or answer possible objections to your position, don't try to argue both sides of the issue at the same time. Since your purpose is to persuade readers, you must first be clear about your own position.

2.   Who is the audience?   ⟶   Your parents

Of course, the teacher will be reading this sample essay, but you will also share it with your parents. This dilemma of a dual audience is similar to testing situations or writing homework assignments in which you are asked to address a certain audience, but the essay will be graded by a teacher or professional reader. In response to this sample writing prompt, you must use more formal language and tone for your teacher, while at the same time being aware of comments or objections your parents may have.

> **Answer the correct question for the proper audience.**

GENERATING IDEAS

Once you clearly understand what the writing prompt is asking, you can begin generating ideas to use in your response. You may have many good ideas, but they aren't useful until you get them out of your head onto the paper. **Brainstorming** and **freewriting** are two methods of getting your ideas out of your head, so you can work with them.

Brainstorming

One way to explore possibilities for your essay is through **brainstorming**. Begin writing down whatever comes to mind regarding the topic and questions provided by the writing prompt. Do not worry about grammar or spelling, and don't make any decisions about the ideas as you write them. Just let them flow freely from your thoughts. Your purpose is to create a list of ideas and details that you can use to develop your essay. For example, look at the brainstorming list below which is based on the following prompt:

Does television affect young children positively or negatively? Explain your answer.

What's wrong with television?
learn new information
kids are quiet
kids need exercise
they should be out playing
safe places to play?
educational programs
Barney, Sesame Street, NYPD Blue
see lots of commercials!
sex is used in commercials
kids like TV
Too many hours in front of the tube
tv is violent
sitting around playing video games
what if parents aren't home
kids watch too much TV

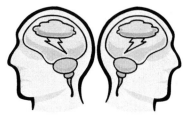

As you can see from the list above, the process of brainstorming helps you generate ideas for your essay, but it also can help you clarify your thoughts. As the ideas flowed freely onto the page, the student who wrote the above brainstorming list developed an opinion about the effects of television on young children.

Practice 1: Brainstorming

Create a brainstorming list for each of the following topics:

1. Should prayer be allowed in public schools?

2. What are the effects of having metal detectors at the doors of your school?

3. Agree or disagree with the following statement: "All teenagers should be required to complete a driver's education course before they are approved for a driver's permit."

4. Air pollution is increasing in your area. How should your community respond?

Freewriting

Freewriting is another way to write down ideas that you can use for an essay. When some people are asked a question, they just start talking to help them think out loud. Sometimes, this is how people find out what their thoughts are. When you freewrite, you simply start writing and see what happens. Don't worry about grammar and spelling. If you get stuck and don't know what to put next, write "I don't know what to write." Just keep writing, and let the ideas flow. Look at the following freewriting sample about the topic of school uniforms.

> *school uniforms are stupid. I want to wear what I want to wear. Can you see me in one of those silly skirts? Those colors are always so bad. Who woudl want unifiorms anyway? How much do they cost. I couldl never get a date if I were wearing a uniform. I don't know what to write Schoool uniforms stifle student individuality. Everyones an individual we don't need to look the same. What are the benefits. As long as clothing is clean and respectable, why do we all have to wear the same thing? Think of the added expense of buying two sets of clothes. Clothes that can conly be worn at school and closthes t home, I wouldn't be caught dead in one of those schoool uiformns otuside fo school*

Obviously, the student who wrote this has some strong opinions that could lead to a good essay.

To generate ideas for your essay, write down whatever you think, without making judgments about it.

Practice 2: Freewriting

Try freewriting about each of the following topics:

1. The need for improved public transportation in your area.

2. Life contains many joyful moments. What was the happiest day of your life?

3. School activities such as field trips, plays, and concerts can be fun and educational. What was your favorite school activity last semester?

4. Cheating in school is the wrong way to get an education. How should students who are caught cheating be punished?

FOCUSING IDEAS

Obviously, you cannot create an essay directly from a brainstorming list or a freewriting sample. The ideas don't follow any logical order. Also, there are too many ideas. You can't use them all. You need to choose a group of related ideas that you can develop into a coherent, well-organized essay. **Clustering** can help you organize your thoughts and develop the thesis for your essay.

Clustering

Clustering is one helpful way to start organizing your ideas by grouping related thoughts together. In the clustering process, you put the main question of the writing prompt in the center of the page, and draw a circle around it. Then, you draw branches off from this circle to add topics and supporting details.

Sample Clustering for Effects of Television on Young Children

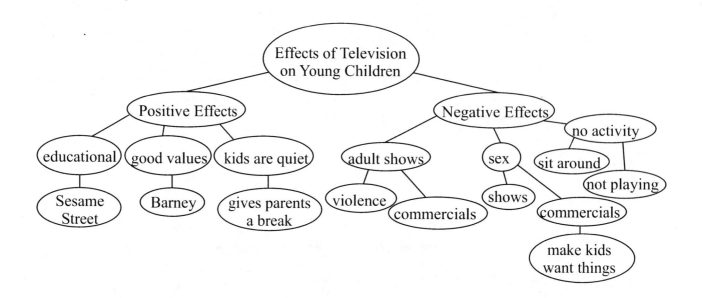

The clustering process can help you narrow your ideas, but these ideas still need to be limited further. You can choose only one portion of your cluster to develop your essay. For example, in the cluster diagram above, there are more ideas grouped around the negative effects of television. This indicates interest, enthusiasm, and support for this idea, and would, therefore, make a good focus for an essay.

Practice 3: Clustering

Choose four of the topics from Practice 1 or Practice 2, and create a clustering diagram for each one. (You will use these diagrams for Practice 5, so keep them in a safe place, like your portfolio or writing folder.)

THESIS OR MAIN IDEA

Your response to each writing prompt will be focused around the **thesis** or **main idea** of your essay. The thesis is the main point—the idea you are trying to prove. It is what *you* want to say. The thesis must be broad enough to invite discussion but narrow enough to be manageable in four to five paragraphs. It summarizes the topic and purpose of your essay in one sentence and includes the general topic, your focus, and supporting points. Look at the example below:

General Topic	Focus	Supporting points
Television affects young children	in a negative way	showing them adult programs commercials make kids want things takes from playtime activities

A sentence which states the thesis would look like this:

Television has a negative effect on young children because they can watch programs that are not meant for their age, see commercials for products they don't need, and miss out on playtime they do need.

The statement of the thesis for your essay is similar to the topic sentence of a paragraph. It provides the reader with valuable information about what is to come, and it gives you a kind of compass to keep your essay on track. As you will see in the next section, you can use each of the supporting points from your thesis to form topic sentences for the body paragraphs.

> **Use clustering to help you develop the thesis for your essay.**

Practice 4: Thesis or Main Idea

A. **Below are three topics that have been focused in a specific way. Choose another way to focus each topic, and provide three supporting points.**

	General Topic	Focus	Supporting Points
1.	School uniforms	not good idea	look bad limit individuality more expensive
	School uniforms	*good idea*	*less distracting dress* *promote professional attitude* *large families pass down to younger kids*

General Topic	Focus	Supporting Points
2. Part-time jobs for students	unrewarding and time consuming	decrease study time pay low hourly wages interfere with social life
Part-time jobs for students	_____ _____	_____ _____ _____
3. Driver's education	teens should be required	parents can't teach they feel invincible everyone should be required
Driver's education	_____ _____	_____ _____ _____
4. Metal detectors at school doors	should be installed when principal decides necessary	increases safety in schools invasion of privacy worth it airports do the same thing
Metal detectors at school doors	_____ _____	_____ _____ _____

B. **For 2, 3, and 4 above, choose the position you support. Then, write a statement of the thesis for three different essays in which you will defend your position.**

1. _____

_____

2. _____

_____

3. _____

_____

MAKING A PLAN

Your thesis is like the destination you have chosen for a journey. The ideas you have gathered in your clustering diagram are the stops you want to make along the way. You still need to decide how you will get to your destination, putting your stops in the proper order. An **outline** helps you plan your journey.

Outline

An **outline** lays out the plan for your essay in a very structured way. It is the road map you will follow in writing your draft. You will get to your destination more easily if your road map looks like the following:

I.   Introduction: General discussion including statement of controlling idea
II. Body
    A. Paragraph 1: Topic 1 (from statement of controlling idea) and supporting details
    B. Paragraph 2: Topic 2 (from statement of controlling idea) and supporting details
    C. Paragraph 3: Topic 3 (from statement of controlling idea) and supporting details
III. Conclusion: Summary of discussion

An outline for the essay about the effects of television on young children might look like this:

I.   Introduction: Television affects young children negatively because they can watch programs that are not meant for their age, see commercials for products they don't need, and miss out on playtime they do need.

II. Body
    A. Television exposes children to adult programs.
        1. Theft
        2. Murder
        3. Sex
    B. Commercials increase children's wishes for needless products.
        1. Children find it difficult to tell reality from pretend
        2. Products bring happiness
    C. Television takes away from children's playtime.
        1. Lack of play with others
        2. No fresh air and movement

III. Conclusion: Young children should watch less television

Outline Shortcut

An outline can be very helpful for organizing an essay when you have more than 90 minutes to complete the assignment. However, sometimes you must complete writing assignments within a class period or other limited testing time.

One way to save time is to use your clustering diagram to create an **outline shortcut** in place of a complete outline. You can look at the clustering diagram you have already produced, and write "CI" next to the circle that will be your controlling idea. Then, choose two or three circles from which you can form your body paragraphs, and put them in order by writing 1, 2, or 3 next to them. You may even want to group a few ideas for one paragraph by circling them. With this shorthand notation, you have made a kind of outline that will help you write your introduction around the thesis and support it with the body paragraphs according to the order you have chosen. Then, you can summarize your key ideas in your conclusion.

See below how the clustering diagram from page 50 can be used in this way.

Sample Outline Shortcut for Effects of Television on Young Children

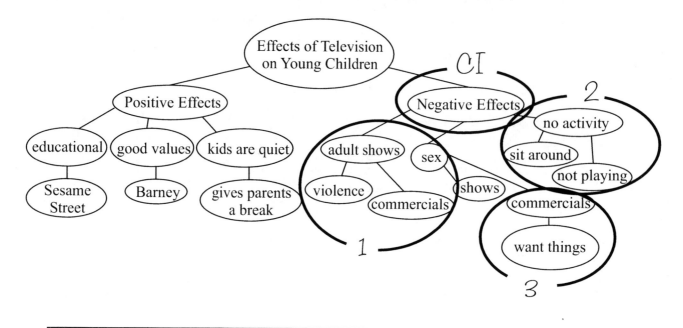

Use an outline or your clustering diagram to make a plan for your essay.

Practice 5: Making a Plan

A. Choose two of the topics for which you have generated ideas, and develop outlines for each one.

B. Choose two of the clustering diagrams you have made, and organize each one into an outline shortcut.

CHAPTER 3 REVIEW: CREATING IDEAS AND CONTENT

Note: Keep your papers from this Chapter Review in your portfolio. You will use the work you have done here in the Review for other chapters in this book.

A. Read the sample brainstorming list for the writing prompt below. Then, on a separate sheet of paper, write down your brainstorming ideas surrounding the topics in prompts 1, 2, and 3.

Sample writing prompt:

This year the Parent Teacher Association (PTA) is planning an extended field trip for the junior class. The parents and teachers want to make sure the trip is educational, but they also want it to be entertaining. In order to make a good choice, the PTA is seeking input from the students. What do you think would be a good place for an entertaining and educational field trip?

Sample Brainstorming List:

Disney World	*Innovations*	*Parade of Lights*
Epcot Center	*Living Seas*	*Disney Quest*
exhibits	*technology displays*	*computer simulators*
cultural showcases	*unlimited video games*	*interactive exhibits*
native food	*Space Ship Earth*	*computer software*
native workers	*bumper cars*	*custom-designed roller coaster*
native animals	*Disney characters*	*Magic Kingdom*

Prompt 1: Many students today work while they are in school. While some people cite the heightened sense of responsibility and discipline it brings to students in their academics, others believe the hours spent working interfere with the time needed for studying and doing homework. Is it an advantage or disadvantage to have a job while you are in school?

Prompt 2: Many school districts are now considering the idea of school vouchers. In the voucher system, parents who do not want to send their children to public schools will receive a voucher which can be used to pay for tuition at any accredited private school. Is this initiative a good idea or not? Why?

Prompt 3: Your local newspaper is sponsoring a contest with a $10,000 prize. The contestants must write a two-page essay which answers the question, "If you were granted one wish to change the world, what would you change?" Write a convincing essay for the judges.

Note: If you would rather brainstorm about a different topic, choose one or more from the several writing prompts in Appendix A (pages 225-233).

B. **Read the freewriting example below that creates ideas about the sample prompt for Part A. Then, on your own paper, freewrite your ideas surrounding prompts 4 and 5.**

Freewriting Example: *Members of the PTA, I think we should go to Orlando, Florida, to have our field trip. We would have a great time. I remember going into Disney Quest, we could play video games for free all day. In Epcot, you can tour many important countries of the world and eat their food, too. I remember going to the Magic Kingdom. You see, at night they do this special show called Parade of Lights. It's pretty fun. Of course, they have the Disney characters over there too, Oh yeah, did I forget to mention that Epcot has all of these special attractions where you get to explore and experience some great technological innovations. They seem to have new attractions there every year!*

Prompt 4: Your parents have informed you that they will be moving to another state during the middle of your senior year in high school. One of your relatives, however, lives in the area of your school. Write a letter to your parents either convincing them to let you stay on at the high school or convincing them that you would be better off moving with them to another state.

Prompt 5: Your school district is considering changing to a year-round school schedule with month-long breaks in December and July. Many students are in an uproar because they enjoy having a long summer vacation to take extended trips. However, many teachers and parents support the proposal because students would remember more information. Which do you think is a better school calendar? Why?

Note: **If you would rather freewrite about a different topic, choose one or more of the several writing prompts in Appendix A (pages 225-233).**

C. **On a separate sheet of paper, take each of the ideas from Part A, and organize them by clustering. From these clusters, notice common details, and write a controlling idea. See the sample below taken from the sample brainstorming list in Part A.**

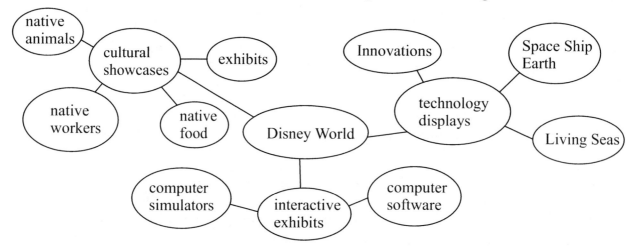

Thesis: *Walt Disney World will provide the best educational and entertainment opportunities because of its cultural showcases, technology displays, and interactive exhibits.*

D.   **Use your clustering diagrams from Part C to create outline shortcuts for prompts 1, 2, and 3.**

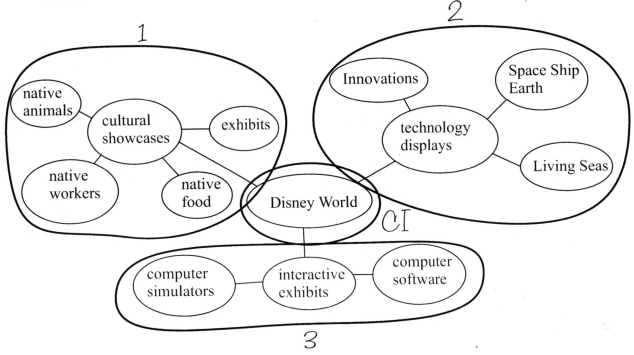

E.   **On a separate sheet of paper, create an outline for prompts 4 and 5 based on the clustering diagrams you designed in Part C.**

Example:

   I. Introduction: *Walt Disney World will provide the best educational and entertainment opportunities because of its cultural showcases, technology displays, and interactive exhibits.*

   II. *Body*
         A. *Cultural showcases*
               1. *Exhibits and food*
               2. *Native workers*
               3. *Native animals*
         B. *Technology displays*
               1. *Innovations*
               2. *Space Ship Earth*
               3. *Living Seas*
         C. *Interactive exhibits*
               1. *Computer simulators*
               2. *Computer software*

   III. *Conclusion: Disney World is the best place for this special field trip.*

Note: **Keep your papers from this Chapter Review in your portfolio. You will use the work you have done here in the Review for other chapters in this book.**

ADDITIONAL ACTIVITIES: CREATING IDEAS AND CONTENT

1. As a class, choose one of the following topics to discuss.

    raising the driving age to 18   **offensive bumper stickers**
    voting on the Internet   **sex before marriage**
    using cell phones while driving   **praying in school**
    no homework policy for high school students **race prejudice in school**
    benefits of studying a foreign language **your favorite cars**

    Once your class has chosen a topic, each student, individually, should create a brainstorming list of ideas regarding that topic. Then, students should gather in small groups to share, compare, and further develop their lists. The class should then create a large brainstorming list by writing ideas on the chalk board. Finally, the class should choose which ideas would make the strongest essay.

2. Choose another topic from #1. On your own, freewrite on this topic for about 10 minutes. Then, gather in small groups to share, compare, and further develop your freewriting. Finally, as a class, create one extensive freewriting sample on the board or overhead projector. Then, choose the ideas that would make the best essay.

3. In #1, you developed a brainstorming list, and in #2, you created a freewriting sample. Now, choose either one, and develop a clustering diagram. Then discuss your clustering in a small group. Finally, contribute your best ideas to a clustering diagram for the entire class.

4. Review your clustering diagram from #3. Then circle and label the part of your cluster that would be an outline shortcut. Use the sample outline shortcut on page 57 as a guide.

5. Based on your outline shortcut from #3, create a thesis for your essay. Write it down, and then compare it with the thesis from other students in the class. Make sure it includes your topic, your focus, and your supporting ideas.

Organizing and Drafting The Essay

4

Once you have generated ideas, focused the ideas, and made a plan for your essay, you are ready to start writing a **draft**. A draft is an attempt to put all of your ideas and planning onto paper in the form of an essay. You develop this draft by organizing complete sentences into paragraphs.

Some people like to write several drafts, changing and improving each one significantly. Other writers spend more time being precise the first time and may write only two or three drafts. For in-class writing assignments, you usually have only enough time to write one draft, revise it, and proofread it. That is why it is important for you to practice writing essays now, so it will be easier for you to do when you only have a limited amount of time, like on an exam.

This chapter will help you improve your writing skills by providing practice in the following areas:

- **Improving Word Choice**
- **Developing Coherence**
- **Writing Introductions and Conclusions**
- **Using Transitional Words**
- **Writing the Draft**

IMPROVING WORD CHOICE

Your draft is an attempt to convey your ideas accurately and in an interesting way to the reader. Once you have identified your audience and decided which tone and language would be appropriate, you will select certain words and phrases to reflect these decisions. Your **word choice** is an important way to interest the reader, accurately convey your ideas, and provide convincing reasons for your position on a topic. Improving word choice involves **selecting specific words**, **using a dictionary and thesaurus**, **being aware of connotations and denotations**, and **avoiding clichés and sweeping generalizations**.

Select Specific Words, Not General Words

One aspect of good word choice is selecting specific and concrete words rather than general or abstract words. Avoid vague, overused words like *thing*, *nice*, *great*, *bad*, *good*, and *a lot*. These words have many meanings, but none are very clear or specific. Specific words provide the reader with a clear image of what you are describing. For example, compare the two passages below which describe the same event.

Example 1:   *As we rode down away from the hill, the lightning kept flashing and flashing. One thunderclap followed right after another, but each sounded very strange. The lightning made it hard to see, and hail hit the windshield as I continued to drive.*

Example 2:   *A moderate incline runs towards the foot of Maybury Hill, and down this we clattered. Once the lightning had begun, it went on in as rapid a succession of flashes as I have ever seen. The thunderclaps, treading one on the heels of another and with a strange crackling accompaniment, sounded more like the working of a gigantic electric machine than the usual detonating reverberations. The flickering light was blinding and confusing, and a thin hail smote gustily at [the windshield] as I drove down the slope.*

– H. G. Wells, *The War of the Worlds*

As you can see from Example 1, general words provide a bland description, while in Example 2, concrete words paint a vivid picture. A good way to improve your word choice is to try to answer the questions *who?*, *what?*, *where?*, *when?*, *why?*, and *how?* in as much detail as you can. Take, for example, the following sentence:

Example 3:   *When he hit the home run, the crowd cheered.*

The sentence tells the basic facts, but it could be improved significantly with a more detailed description. Consider the following questions: Who hit the ball? How did he hit it? Where did it go? How did it get there? In what way did the crowd cheer? To answer these questions, one might write the following sentence:

Example 4:   *When John's mighty swing sent the ball hurtling over the rightfield fence, the crowd leapt to its feet and burst into wild cheers.*

In this sentence, the writer gives detailed answers to the above questions and provides a vivid picture of what happened. Good descriptions are more interesting and more persuasive.

Practice 1: Using Specific Words

Fill in the blanks with the appropriate words. The first two are completed as examples.

	General	**More Specific**	**Very Specific**
1.	athlete	football player	wide receiver
2.	food	fruit	banana
3.	animal	_____	cocker spaniel
4.	_____	pop music	hip-hop
5.	car	S.U.V.	_____
6.	_____	pop-music star	Norah Jones

7.	_____	below freezing	12° F
8.	young	school age	_____
9.	tree	_____	pine
10.	government official	_____	George W. Bush

Practice 2: Using Specific Words

On your own paper, rewrite the following sentences using specific words to create more vivid descriptions.

1. The dog barked all night long.

2. The strong wind caused a tree to fall on our house.

3. It was so hot, we had to jump into the pool.

4. He almost cried when he saw his son graduate.

5. That book was boring.

Use a Dictionary or Thesaurus

A dictionary and thesaurus are valuable tools to help you improve your writing. Even if you are not allowed to use them for in-class writing assignments, using them for your practice essays will greatly improve your vocabulary and your writing skills.

When you are unsure of the meaning of a word, look it up. A good **dictionary** will provide you with the most exact meaning of the word. For example, try looking up the words "flammable" and "inflammable." You may be surprised at what you find.

When you can't find just the right word to express the idea or picture you want to convey, go to a **thesaurus**. A thesaurus provides many different words that have similar meanings. For example, if you look up the word "see," you will find many interesting alternatives such as *observe, behold, examine, inspect, stare, notice, scan, spy, catch sight of, survey,* or *contemplate.*

Practice 3: Using a Dictionary and Thesaurus

In a thesaurus, look up these common words: *eat, sleep, drink, short, big.* **For each word, list three similar words that you find in the thesaurus. In a dictionary, look up the definitions for each of the words you found in the thesaurus. How are the words similar to and different from each other?**

Be Aware of Connotations and Denotations

One important part of word choice is knowing the difference between the **denotations** (dictionary meanings) and the **connotations** (emotional associations) of words. For example, the words *slender* and *skinny* both mean "thin." However, if you called a person *slender*, that compliment might get you a date. On the other hand, calling the same person *skinny* might be offensive. In a similar way, the words *determined* and *stubborn* both refer to persistence and an unwillingness to be moved from a particular position. However, *determined* carries a positive connotation, while *stubborn* is usually considered a negative word.

Practice 4: Connotations and Denotations

Use a dictionary to help you describe the connotations and denotations of the following words:

1. watch, glance, stare
2. walk, stroll, meander
3. run, sprint, scurry

4. shivering, trembling, quaking
5. strong, sturdy, tough

Avoid Clichés and Sweeping Generalizations

Avoid using **clichés** in your writing. These overly familiar expressions include popular phrases such as "busy as a bee" and "to make a long story short." These dull, overused expressions interfere with your message. Simple, straightforward language is often more effective. For example,

Clichés	**Simple Language**
busy as a bee	very active
to make a long story short	to summarize
cute as a button	endearing
stop beating around the bush	get to the point
save it for a rainy day	save it for when you need it

Also, avoid **sweeping generalizations** like the following: "No one ever calls me." Unless used for dramatic effect in a story, words like *always, never, ever, no one, everybody*, and *everywhere* are most often not true and show an overly simple understanding of the topic being discussed. Replace these unrealistic claims with accurate descriptions. For example,

Sweeping Generalization	**Accurate Description**
No one ever calls me.	I rarely get phone calls.
It always rains on my birthday.	It seems like every year it rains on my birthday.
Everybody knows that Cincinnati has the best team.	Many people believe Cincinnati will win the championship again.

Practice 5: Clichés and Sweeping Generalizations

The passage below expresses strong patriotic feelings, but the writer has weakened the impact of the argument by using sweeping generalizations and worn-out phrases. Rewrite the passage by improving the language used.

The United States has always been the most patriotic country. From the beginning, people worked day after day to do the right thing and make this country free. Everyone knows that the United States is the best place in the world to live. You'll never see the good life until you come to the Land of the Free and the Home of the Brave. Nobody can ever deny that our country is Number One.

Practice 6: Word Choice

On your own or with others, review some of your previous written responses, looking for inappropriate word choices. Revise them, using more effective word choices. (This is a good opportunity to use a dictionary and a thesaurus.)

Practice 7: Sweeping Generalizations

On your own paper, rewrite the following sweeping generalizations with a more accurate description.

1. Today's movies are better than movies of the past.

2. I always get up early on Saturday mornings.

3. I never get to watch the shows I want to watch.

4. We always laugh at every joke.

5. Airplanes are not safe anymore.

6. Tall people like to play basketball.

7. That dog follows me everywhere I go.

8. None of the people in wheelchairs can ever play sports again.

9. No one here can ever get a phone call because Mary is always on the Internet.

10. Old people always complain about their aches and pains.

WRITING INTRODUCTIONS

In Chapter 1, you learned that the beginning and the end of a paragraph are important. The same is true of an essay, where the **introduction** and the **conclusion** should each consist of one paragraph. In this section, you will learn **how to write an introduction** and about **different types of introductions**. In the next section, you will learn to write **conclusions**.

How to Write an Introduction

The **introduction** is the first paragraph of your essay. Usually, it is shorter than the body paragraphs, but it serves an important purpose. It tells readers where you are going and invites them to join you. It should catch the readers' interest and clearly describe the thesis of the essay. The introduction may also inform readers of the order of support for the thesis.

You probably have seen stores that try to attract customers by placing a huge, flourescent-colored sign outside, advertising an incredible sale. This catches the interest of potential buyers and leads them into the store. Then, the sales people can show the customers other merchandise that is of higher quality, but is also higher priced. This is what the store managers really want to sell.

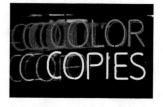

This approach to sales is somewhat similar to how you want to lead readers into your essay. You want to catch the readers' attention, lead them into your essay, and then, explain the purpose of your essay. A simple way to build an introduction is by using the following three components: **lead**, **tie-in**, and **thesis**.

Lead

Sometimes you can start your essay by stating the thesis of your essay, but often, that type of beginning is too abrupt. You need to grab the reader's attention first, and make the reader want to read further. You can do this with the first sentence, called a **lead**. The lead may be one of the following:

- **statement of your position on the topic**
- **problem or riddle**
- **surprising statistic or fact**
- **question**
- **brief story**
- **quotation**
- **catchy remark**
- **general, thought-provoking statement**

Tie-In

Once you have captured the readers' attention with your lead, you need to draw their attention to the thesis of your essay. You need to consider the audience, the topic of your essay, and your personal preference in developing a creative link between the lead and the statement of your thesis.

Thesis

You practiced developing a thesis in the last chapter. The first paragraph is a good place to state the thesis because it lets the reader know the topic of the essay, your position on the topic, and how you are going to order your supporting points.

Different Types of Introductions

Below, you will find examples of introductions that use different types of leads followed by a tie-in and a statement of the thesis. The first example is labeled for you. For the other examples, circle the lead, [bracket] the tie-in, and underline the statement of the thesis.

State Your Position on the Topic

Panama City, Florida, is the ideal place to go for a winter vacation.
[You may want to ski the snow-capped peaks of the Rocky Mountains, but I have enough cold weather all winter long. When Christmas break arrives, I want a taste of the warm summer sun. A wool blanket and a roaring fire may do it for some people, but I want more than a cup of hot cocoa to warm my chilled bones.] I want to go someplace where I can choose from a wide assortment of water sports, enjoy the mouth-watering taste of fresh seafood, and run through the cold waves hitting the shoreline at night.

Here, the writer's position is stated directly and emphatically in the first line. This emphatic declaration is an attention-getter. As discussed in Chapter 1, this topic sentence invites discussion. The author briefly comments on a possible objection to the topic sentence, and then states the thesis in the last sentence of this brief introduction.

Problem or Riddle

Dentists recommend brushing your teeth with it. House cleaners use it to scour counter tops. You can add it to your laundry detergent to freshen your clothes. And, of course, it is an essential ingredient for many baking recipes. Sodium bicarbonate, popularly known as baking soda, is the most useful item in your household. It is especially helpful for cleaning, eliminating odors, and maintaining personal hygiene.

Unlike the introduction that states your purpose right off, the "riddle" introduction holds back one piece of information while teasing the reader to guess what it might be. Notice how this introduction gives examples that support the thesis, even before stating that idea in the final sentence. More examples are needed for the body paragraphs, but these are good starting places.

Surprising Statistic or Fact

In one year, firearms killed 0 children in Japan, 19 in Great Britain, 57 in Germany, 109 in France, 153 in Canada and 5,285 in the United States. In the "land of the free and the home of the brave," we cling to our right to bear arms. However, the frightening numbers that result should make us reconsider the effects of this "right." If I could change any law in the United States, I would make a sensible gun law that includes licensing of handgun owners, registration of handguns, and limiting gun purchases to no more than one a month. A law like this would protect our children, make society safer, and secure liberty for those who want guns and those who fear guns.

A statistic or fact is only surprising if it contradicts common views or beliefs. Regarding gun violence, people who read or watch the news know that people using firearms often tragically kill children. What they may not know is that the United States is unique in this area among its primary political allies. This statistic will catch the attention of readers and make them want to continue reading.

Question

> *Isn't coin collecting for nerds, old people, or wealthy investors? Coin collecting stirs up images of shy, lonely people locked away in a room seeking comfort from some shiny coins. When I tell people that my favorite hobby is collecting coins, they ask if it isn't really old-fashioned and boring. Well, maybe it used to be boring, but not since the United States mint began circulating the new state quarters. They are full of history, fun to collect and trade, and they are not expensive.*

Beginning an essay with a question automatically engages readers and makes them start thinking. It also creates curiosity about how you will answer the question, making the readers wonder if you will agree or disagree. In the example above, notice that the answer the author gives is surprising.

Brief Story

> *When I walked into the Fairlawn Nursing Home for the first time, I had an uneasy feeling in my stomach. I didn't know what to expect when I entered the circular Activities Room. I found a dozen elderly people, each staring out the floor-to-ceiling picture windows that framed a variety of unique bird feeders. The Activities Director had assured me that my visit would be a great help, but I didn't know what to do. I walked over to one of the windows and spotted a small, dark gray bird with white underparts and black on top of its head. I whispered to myself, "I wonder what kind that is?" Next to me, a gray-haired, frail-looking woman smiled and said in her gravelly voice, "That's a nuthatch, my dear." Our conversation continued from there and continues each Tuesday when I visit Mrs. Joblanski. I consider my time at the nursing home to be my most rewarding after-school activity because the staff is happy to have some help, I have a new friend in Mrs. Joblanski, and I learn so much from the wisdom she has gained during her years of life.*

The key to beginning an essay with a short story is to keep it *brief*. The story is not the focus of the essay, it is only a lead-in to your topic. You can increase the effectiveness of this type of introduction by including details in the story that relate to the thesis. Notice in the story above that the author describes examples of a resident who loves to see visitors, a welcoming staff person, and the wisdom of an older person. These details not only help introduce the thesis but also help to support it.

Quotation

"April is the cruelest month," wrote T. S. Eliott. Most people wonder why he wrote this, but I don't. Many people spend the winter months longing for the tiny buds and lengthening days of spring. Others consider the summer the high point of the year because they can escape to their cabin on the lake for fishing and mosquito dodging. Some people spend all year waiting for the fall foliage to explode in brilliant color. These people are missing the best season of the year. For me, winter could last all year long, and I would be happy. So what if you can't swim in the lake, and you have to go to school everyday. When else can you enjoy unique outdoor sports, warm, cozy nights by the fire, and the wonderful holiday season?

Any interesting quote that can be easily related to your topic will make a good lead for your introduction.

Catchy Phrase

For some students, taking a standardized test is almost as daunting as fighting a major economic depression, but as Franklin D. Roosevelt said in 1933, "We have nothing to fear but fear itself." With these words, the President encouraged the people of the United States not to despair of the bank closings and job losses. He believed the American people, with the help of their government, had the resources and talent to restore their economic well-being if they did not let fear stop them. In a similar way, students must overcome "test anxiety" in order to succeed. Through adequate preparation, good health practices, and simple relaxation techniques, students can improve their performance on standardized tests.

This introduction uses a catchy phrase followed by a quotation. The striking contrast between taking a test and fighting a Depression sparks interest, and the quote from Roosevelt continues the metaphor. The writer may choose to use allusions to fighting panic later in the essay to help connect the ideas.

General Thought-Provoking Statement

Almost 40 years since Martin Luther King's "I Have a Dream" speech and nearly 140 years after Abraham Lincoln's Emancipation Proclamation, the scourge of racism still undermines the great principles of this nation. It has become obvious that legislation cannot erase the fear that prevents people from seeing their common humanity. Racism is the biggest problem in the United States precisely because many people don't think it's a problem, it contradicts the very principles upon which this country is founded, and it is an international embarrassment in an age of increasing global diversity.

Large issues attract large audiences. By stating a general principle, idea, or situation at the beginning of the essay, you allow readers to connect with a familiar idea. Then, you can direct them to the specific issue or approach you want to discuss in your essay.

> **Build your introduction with a lead, tie-in, and statement of the thesis.**

Practice 8: Writing Introductions

For four of the topics listed below, use brainstorming or freewriting to develop a thesis and three supporting points. Next, write an introduction. Use a different type of lead for each introduction. (Save your work for other Practices in this chapter.)

1. What is your favorite type of weather: sunny and fine or stormy and dramatic? Explain why you like this type of weather.

2. What do you think is the best way to deal with the energy crisis? Why is your solution the best one?

3. If cost were not an issue, what music concert would you want to attend and why?

4. How do your dreams affect your life? Give reasons why dreams are important to you or why they are not.

5. What class would you choose if you could pick any elective for the next semester? Why?

6. What play would you want your school to perform with you in the lead role? Why?

7. What way do you prefer to communicate with your friends when you are not with them: letter, phone, cell phone, e-mail, or Instant Messenger™? Why?

8. If you could choose whatever you wanted, how would you choose to celebrate your birthday? Why?

WRITING CONCLUSIONS

The ending of a composition is just as important as the beginning. You don't want to end your composition by running out of ideas. You want to bring your essay to a logical **conclusion**. You can imagine your essay is like taking someone for a ride in a taxi. When you get to your destination, you don't want to slam on the brakes and tell your passenger, "Get out!" You want to announce that you are nearing the destination, ease on the brakes, and say "good-bye" when your passenger steps out of the car. This increases your chances of a good tip.

The concluding paragraph should be similar. You want to let the readers know that they have reached the end of the composition. Then, remind them about the points you have discussed along the way, but don't restate the controlling idea. Finally, leave the readers with a thought to ponder. In writing the conclusion, you can use many of the same strategies as you do for writing the introduction, but instead of saying "hello," you are saying "good-bye."

Summarize, But Don't Restate, Your Controlling Idea

The last thing you want to do in a conclusion is to introduce a new idea. Instead, summarize the information and reasons that you have already provided. This does not mean to repeat the introduction or to restate the thesis. Before you say "good-bye," remind the reader of some highlights you've covered along the way, as in the example on the next page.

In summary, collecting the new state quarters has provided me with hours of enjoyment. I have been researching the history of the states, collecting and trading the coins with my friends, and enjoying this hobby without hurting my bank account. The value of these coins may never reach an out-of-sight amount, but the personal satisfaction, learning, and friendship that I have found through this hobby is invaluable to me.

Conclusion as Introduction in Reverse

One effective way to write a concluding paragraph for an essay is to write an introduction in reverse. In other words,

(1) briefly remind the readers of your topic sentence,
(2) tie-in the thesis to your final "good-bye," and
(3) instead of a lead, use a "good-bye" statement.

The conclusion below uses this model.

Panama City gives me everything I want in a vacation spot, and more: exhilarating water sports, fresh seafood, and moonlit beach walks. Year after year, my family escapes the cold northern climate by traveling south, but we never tire of the fun, the food, and the relaxation that this great vacation spot provides. However, in case you still have questions about where to go for your next winter vacation, just consider your packing list: bathing suit, towel, sun screen. Sounds good to me!

Give the Audience a Question to Ponder

In the conclusion, you want to summarize the information and reasons that you have already provided. Though you don't want readers to have questions about your position or choice, you may want to leave readers with a question that invites them to ponder their own positions. The following conclusion is an example.

Citizens of the United States fiercely protect their right to individual freedom. Independent-minded people formed this country telling Great Britain to leave them alone and to stop interfering in their lives. This rich tradition of liberty should be protected, but not at the expense of our children. Sensible gun laws place reasonable limitations on the purchase of fire arms. These laws do not abolish the "right to bear arms"; they simply protect our children. How many more children must die before we make reasonable laws to protect them?

> **In your conclusion, summarize your main points and say "good-bye" to the readers.**

Practice 9: Writing Conclusions

Using your ideas from Practice 8 on page 68, write conclusions to match the introductions you wrote. Experiment with different types of conclusions. (Save your work for Practice 13.)

USING TRANSITIONAL WORDS

In Chapter 3, you saw how an outline is like a road map guiding you as you write your essay. As you write your draft, remember that your readers do not have a road map. It is not enough for you just to write a series of ideas. You need to lead the readers through your composition by showing how the ideas are related to each other. **Transitional words** help the readers see the relationship between your ideas. These relationships include **time order**, **order of importance**, **cause and effect**, **comparison**, and **contrast**.

Time Order

You can use transitional words to show **time order**, that is, when events happen in relation to each other: one event before another, one after another, or both at the same time. Read the following example to see what happens when transitional words are missing.

Example 1: *Our family has a daily routine to get us to work and school. My father leaves the house. He wakes up my brother and me. I get up and take a shower. My brother takes a shower. I get dressed. My mother gets our lunches ready. We eat breakfast. We jump in the car and drive to school. Mom drops us off on her way to work.*

Example 1 is choppy because it is missing transitional words to clarify the order of events. Without these words, the reader wonders how the father can leave the house, and then wake up his sons. Below is a corrected example with transitional words underlined.

Example 2: *Our family has a daily routine to get us to work and school. <u>Before</u> my father leaves the house, he wakes up my brother and me. I get up <u>first</u> and take a shower. <u>Then</u>, my brother takes a shower <u>while</u> I'm getting dressed. <u>Meanwhile</u>, my mother gets our lunches ready. <u>After</u> breakfast, we jump in the car for the drive to school. <u>Lastly</u>, Mom drops us off on her way to work.*

Using transitional words is a simple and effective way to present your ideas and descriptions clearly. The chart below provides you with examples of transitional words that show time order.

Transitional Words for Time Order			
after	again	and then	as
as long as	as soon as	at the same time	before
currently	during	eventually	finally
first	gradually	immediately	in the future
later	meanwhile	now	second
soon	suddenly	then	third
until	when	whenever	while

ORDER OF IMPORTANCE

In Chapter 1, you saw how to structure ideas in a paragraph according to their **order of importance**. Transitional words help show which idea you want to emphasize as more important than others. The example below lacks these transitional words.

Example 3: *You should always be aware of your surroundings in parking lots at night. Look over the lot carefully for potential danger spots, for example, areas of low visibility and areas which do not have parking attendants. Be sure you have a defensive weapon, such as pepper spray or a loud noisemaker, in your hand as you walk to your vehicle. Before entering your vehicle, look through the windows to make sure no one is hiding inside.*

Notice how in Example 3 the writer did not use transitional words to indicate whether one of the steps is more important than another. Below is a corrected example with underlined transitional words showing the order of importance.

Example 4: *You should always be aware of your surroundings in parking lots at night. <u>First</u>, look over the lot carefully for potential danger spots, for example, areas of low visibility and areas which do not have parking attendants. <u>More importantly</u>, be sure you have a defensive weapon, such as pepper spray or a loud noisemaker, in your hand as you walk to your vehicle. <u>Above all</u>, before entering your vehicle, look through the windows to make sure no one is hiding inside.*

As you can see, using these transitional words helps to rank the steps required to reduce the potential danger of parking lots at night.

Transitional Words for Order of Importance		
above all	especially	first
in fact	in particular	of highest importance
more importantly	most importantly	

Cause and Effect

Linking **causes and effects** is an important aspect of writing a convincing persuasive essay. You can use transitional words to make these connections clear. Read the example below.

Example 5: *Local graffiti "artists" are becoming more brazen. Two weeks ago, they sprayed paint across three community centers. Last week, several businesses found their buildings "decorated" against their wishes. Last night, some graffiti writers took their work inside, painting the twelfth floor of the Baxton building. The city council announced a special hearing for Thursday of next week to discuss possible responses to this problem.*

The cause and effect relationship in Example 5 is not clear because the paragraph is missing a crucial transition. Read Example 6, and notice how just one transitional phrase (underlined) can bring clarity to this paragraph by signaling the effect of the graffiti writers' activities.

Example 6: *Local graffiti "artists" are becoming more brazen. Two weeks ago, they sprayed paint across three community centers. Last week, several businesses found their buildings "decorated" against their wishes. Last night, some graffiti writers took their work inside to the twelfth floor of the Baxton building. <u>As a result</u>, the city council announced a special hearing for Thursday of next week to discuss possible responses to this problem.*

Because the writer added one transitional phrase in Example 6, the whole paragraph is clearer. The phrase "as a result" shows that the city council's announcement is an effect of the graffiti writing.

Transitional Words for Cause and Effect				
as a result	because	for this reason	if, . . . then	since
whenever	so that	therefore	thus	so

Comparison

Transitional words help a writer show **comparisons**, that is, how certain ideas or subjects are similar. Example 7 lacks these transitions.

Example 7: *The United States and the USSR did not want to enter World War II. They had been forced to enter the fighting because of sneak attacks. The Soviets were caught off guard when Hitler broke his non-aggression treaty and invaded the Soviet Union on June 22, 1941. The United States suffered a surprise attack when the Japanese struck the US naval base at Pearl Harbor on December 7, 1941. From that time on, the two countries were allies in fighting the Axis powers of Germany, Italy, and Japan.*

Due to the lack of transitional words in Example 7, the similarities between the United States' and the Soviet Union's entry into World War II are not as clear as they could be. In fact, the first sentence is awkward. The few well-placed transitions shown in Example 8 make the passage much more effective and easily understood.

Example 8: *<u>Neither</u> the United States <u>nor</u> the USSR had wanted to enter World War II. <u>Both</u> countries had been forced to enter the fighting because of sneak attacks. The Soviets were caught off guard when Hitler broke his non-aggression treaty and invaded the Soviet Union on June 22, 1941. <u>Similarly</u>, the United States suffered a surprise attack when the Japanese struck the US naval base at Pearl Harbor on December 7, 1941. From that time on, the two countries were allies in fighting the Axis powers of Germany, Italy, and Japan.*

"Neither" and "nor" may not sound like comparison words, but they point to negative similarity. The other underlined transitional words make the comparisons between the US and the USSR clearer. Also, note the importance of "from that time on" in the last sentence to show the order of events.

Transitional Words for Comparison

also	as well as	at the same time
both	equally important	in the same way
likewise	neither/nor	similarly

Contrast

Transitional words also help a writer make **contrasts**, or differences, clearer. Read the example below to see how a contrasting paragraph needs transitions.

Example 9:   *You may consider caves and mines the same kind of holes in the ground. They are really quite different. Underground streams and rivers form caves over millions of years through erosion. Humans use machines to dig mines over the course of only a few months. The rapid removal of rock during the mining process requires the use of supports to prevent a mine's ceiling from collapsing. The slow, natural formation of caves makes these supports unnecessary. The slow process of cave formation allows natural gases to escape slowly and safely. Miners must be cautious of the explosive and poisonous gases that are rapidly released as the earth is blasted open. As you can see, human development of the earth is often rapid and dangerous. Nature's development can be gradual and peaceful.*

Example 9 makes sense without transitional words, but it does not flow well. The writer lists ideas but does not connect them. Read Example 10 to see how transitional words can help the flow of the ideas in the paragraph.

Example 10:   *You may consider caves and mines the same kind of holes in the ground, <u>but in reality</u>, they are quite different. Underground streams and rivers form caves over millions of years through erosion. <u>In contrast</u>, humans use machines to dig mines over the course of only a few months. The rapid removal of rock during the mining process requires the use of supports to prevent a mine's ceiling from collapsing. <u>However</u>, the slow, natural formation of caves makes these supports unnecessary. The slow process of cave formation <u>also</u> allows natural gases to escape slowly and safely, <u>whereas</u> miners must be cautious of the explosive and poisonous gases that are rapidly released as the earth is blasted open. As you can see, human development of the earth is often rapid and dangerous, <u>while</u> nature's development can be gradual and peaceful.*

73

Transitional Words for Contrast

although	and yet	but	despite
even so	even	though	however
in contrast	instead of	in spite of	nevertheless
whereas	while	rather than	still
on the one hand		on the other hand	

Use transitional words to help readers see the relationship between your ideas. These relationships include time order, order of importance, cause and effect, comparison, and contrast.

Practice 10: Transitional Words

Read the paragraphs below. Decide how each paragraph would be best organized, whether by *time order*, *order of importance*, *cause and effect*, *comparison*, or *contrast*. Then, rewrite the paragraph on a separate sheet of paper, inserting the correct transitional words or phrases.

1.   There are many things to remember as you get ready to go back to school. Develop a positive attitude about the upcoming school year. Make sure you understand your class schedule. You know your classes. You should buy plenty of school supplies such as pens, paper, notebooks, and a calculator. Take time to inventory your clothes, and make sure you have the clothes you need. These tasks are completed. You will be ready for the new school year.

2.   Both your beliefs and your actions are important in leading an exemplary life. Your beliefs should guide you to knowing how to act in all situations. If your actions do not match what you believe, people will not listen to what you say. If you act in a way that seems good to others, but you have no beliefs to explain your actions, people may label you as shallow. Be certain and careful with both your beliefs and your actions in order to be an example to others.

3.   Watching television at my grandmother's house was always a family event. Her TV was so old it didn't even have remote control! My family fought over what show to watch. We were used to watching two or three channels at the same time, while using the remote control. Grandma didn't have cable. We had to twist and turn the antenna and our bodies, just to get a decent picture. Two of us were on the sofa watching TV and somebody else sat in the recliner. The TV screen would get all fuzzy. We all had to pile onto the sofa. We could avoid these problems with the television and the family fights. We bought Grandma a new television (with remote control!) and a year's cable service. Our visits to Grandma's are much more peaceful, though, in a way, we miss the wrangling.

4.   I like to prioritize the duties I feel towards those around me. I feel duty-bound to care for and protect my parents, brothers, and sisters. I try to take care of my extended family and close friends. I consider it necessary to serve my country in the case of foreign attack. These three circles of obligation complete the priorities I feel in my social and civic life.

5.   Ordering something as simple as a pizza requires several steps. You should look through the tower of coupons that has grown from daily advertisement mailings. You must endure the arduous process of finding out what everyone wants on their pizza. Call the pizza place and wait on hold. You are ready to hang up and make your own pizza. Distract your mind from the growing hunger in your stomach by getting your money ready. The delivery person arrives, run out to the car, grab the pizza, and shove the money in the person's hand. You can enjoy the lukewarm pizza that you earned with all your hard work.

6.   The preparation required for a test is quite similar to the preparation needed for a sports event. Training for any sports event requires daily practice to keep the athlete's body in good condition. Test preparation requires daily practice and review to keep the scholar's memory up to date. The night before a sporting event, the athlete must get plenty of rest. A scholar must rest his or her mind, so it will be fresh for the big event of the test. A good athlete will take pride in a nutritious diet that provides the building blocks for a strong body. A scholar must feed the mind with nutritious food to increase mental skill. Test-taking may not have the same glamour as athletic competition, but both activities require preparation in order to achieve success.

Practice 11: Transitional Words

A.   **On your own, or in small groups, skim through articles in newspapers, in magazines, or on the Internet. Find paragraphs that contain transitional words based on each of the following: *time order*, *order of importance*, *comparison and contrast*, or *cause and effect*.** Share these paragraphs with your teacher or other students. Do the transitional words improve your understanding of the paragraph? Why or why not?

B.   **On your own, or in small groups, write four different paragraphs. Each paragraph should include transitional words from the different categories discussed in this chapter: *time order*, *order of importance*, *comparison and contrast*, or *cause and effect*.** Return to the lists of these words to help you. Then, exchange your collection of paragraphs with your teacher or with another group, and grade the paragraphs by evaluating how well the transitional words are used within each paragraph.

Here are some possible topics for each of your four paragraphs:

Time Order
Your first driving lesson
A time you got lost

Order of Importance
Prioritize your duties for today
Who are the three most important people in your life? Why?

Comparison and Contrast
Do you prefer pizza or hamburgers? Why?
Which is better on a Friday night–watching television at home or going out to a movie?

Cause and Effect
Why is a high school diploma important?
What are the effects of sports programs on high school students?

DEVELOPING COHERENCE

Coherence means to stick together. You want the ideas of your essay to "stick together," that is, to be connected and to lead from one to the other. Tying your ideas together is an important part of helping readers understand your writing. Three ways you can link the ideas and paragraphs in your essay are **planning an order**, **using transitions**, and **repeating key words and phrases**.

Planning an Order

In Chapter 1, you practiced four different ways to organize ideas: spatial order, time order, order of importance, or contrasting ideas. Organizing your ideas in a certain order is the first step to developing a coherent essay.

Using Transitions

In the last section, you saw how transitional words link ideas from one sentence to another. They also link ideas between paragraphs to make the whole essay "stick together." Without these transitional words and phrases, the writing becomes less interesting or even less understandable.

Repeating Key Words and Phrases

While you don't want to say the same thing over and over, repeating certain key words and phrases can improve the readers' understanding of the topic. By including key words or ideas from your controlling idea in the topic sentences of your paragraphs, you will make it easier for readers to follow your train of thought. These repeated words are like landmarks along the road of your essay, reminding the readers where you have been and where you are going. For example, look at the following plan for an essay in which the topic sentences repeat key words from the controlling idea:

Controlling Idea: *Citizens of the United States could greatly improve the country by obeying the law, protecting the environment, and being kind to other people.*

Topic Sentence: *The first and most basic step to <u>improving the country</u> is to <u>obey the law</u>.*

Topic Sentence: *In addition to <u>obeying the law</u>, <u>citizens</u> can make this country even more beautiful by <u>protecting the environment</u>.*

Topic Sentence: *A third way to <u>make the United States a better place</u> to live is for <u>citizens</u> to reach beyond their own self-interest and <u>be kind to one another</u>.*

You can also repeat key words or phrases throughout the essay, not only in topic sentences.

> **Develop coherence (link the ideas and paragraphs) in your essay by planning an order, using transitional words, and repeating key words and phrases.**

Practice 12: Developing Coherence

A. <u>Read</u> the following essay. Decide how the writer ordered ideas in the essay. Then, (circle) transitional words, and <u>underline</u> repeated words.

In this era of the global community, more and more of us enjoy discussing different philosophies. Presently, there are as many different philosophies as there are cultures. One philosophic-type topic of unending interest is the question of whether or not animals have souls. Of course, most organized religions and philosophies have opinions on this question. One way to keep your balance when discussing it is to keep an open mind and heart. You never know when a new viewpoint will change your thoughts around. Or at least, listening allows you to understand someone else's perspective.

A different approach to the question of whether or not animals have souls is found in the philosophy of Taoism: a Chinese belief system which includes the concepts of the *yin* and *yang* energies. Taoism holds that embracing the natural flow of these energies, balanced and open to the path of life, creates harmony. Instead of making a definite statement about the existence of animal souls, the way of Tao would look to the natural world for instruction.

There is a story in the writings of Chuang Tzu, a spiritual leader in China, called "The Joy of Fishes" which begins with two men walking along a river, where they see fish leaping in the water. One of the men remarks on the happiness of the fish. The other man asks how, since the speaker is not a fish, can he know the fish are happy. The first man answers this way: "I know the joy of fishes in the river through my own joy, as I go walking along the same river." The concept is that all beings truly share the walk along life's river experiencing the same kinds of joys and sorrows even though they are different beings.

A tale from the city of Edinburgh in Scotland, for example illuminates this idea. Long ago in the 1850s, a little dog, Bobby by name, devoted himself to guarding the final resting place of his master—this was a grave in Greyfriars Kirk graveyard. This he did for 14 years. The people of the city, likewise, noticed the dog's devotion and felt a connection with the loss and sorrow the dog experienced. They recognized the sorrow that comes to us all.

In the happier days of Bobby's life, he belonged to John Grey (Jock), a policeman in the city of Edinburgh. Bobby, a Skye terrier, was Jock's steady companion in the city, walking up and down the cobbled streets or standing at the policeman's post. Together, they braved the infamous Scottish weather, which was often damp and freezing.

Then, sadly Jock fell ill with tuberculosis and passed away in 1858. Bobby followed his master's funeral procession. After the service, Bobby was taken to the Grey's home to stay. However, that Bobby would not do. He followed the route back to the graveyard, and for the next 14 years, the graveyard was where he stayed.

Meanwhile, people of the city took notice. James Brown, the groundskeeper of the graveyard, took care of Bobby, while another townsman who admired Bobby's devotion to his lost master paid for the license that was needed, to keep Bobby out of the pound. The news of the little dog spread through the city and beyond, bringing visitors who wanted to see and experience Bobby as the living monument to his master.

Finally, after his 14 year vigil, Bobby died. For the first time ever, the city leaders voted to allow a dog, Bobby, to be buried beside his master in the graveyard. Moreover, a statue of Bobby was placed at the entrance to the graveyard. We all respond to feelings of loss as well as those of joy. For many, Bobby symbolizes true gratitude. For followers of Tao, this is an important virtue. Subsequently, not only did Bobby, a mere dog, possess this virtue, in fact he brought a city to share in this gratitude to John Grey. Did Bobby have a soul? You may want to find the balance of this question soon in your own heart.

B. Read the composition below. Identify and evaluate the introduction and conclusion. Then, (circle) transitional words, and underline repeated words.

Tiger at the Door

A Jewish author wrote "The Lord created people because He loves stories." That must be why snow falls so heavily north of Flagstaff, Arizona; it gives us a lot of time to tell stories and to hear stories and to argue about the best stories. In my opinion, the best ones always involve animals and their bond of love with people. Really, the very absolute best stories are about my family and my cat, Tiger. I have trouble choosing which story to tell about Tiger, for she and I have grown up together. So, I will tell the stories about loss and gain: Tiger's history and mine.

First, our story's beginning is familiar. Tiger's loss when she was abandoned was our gain. My father and brother had gone to a local river to fish. As they were casting, a tiny kitten crawled into the worm bucket turning it over. When my father went to bait his hook again, he found only this dirty-faced kitten with a nightcrawler hanging off one ear. My father, a practical man, began threading his hands through the grass trying to retrieve his lost worms. My brother scooped up the kitten and fed it bologna slices. "Can we keep it, please?" my brother pleaded. "If it's a boy, we can name it Moses, like the baby in the Sunday school story." How could my father say no to saving a lost Moses from the river? Later learning she was female, my brother lost interest, so she became mine. I named her Tiger, an exotic creature. She had a taste for bugs and worms, not mice. Our family often sat watching her trap moths and mosquitoes on the screen door. Tiger brought us into her world, and we brought her into our family circle.

As she grew in size and gained in confidence, Tiger took great delight in pushing my parents' patience, while my brother and I secretly laughed with her. She gave birth to her two litters of kittens in our fishing boat. After one litter, my father covered the boat. When Tiger managed to tear the cover and to give birth again in there, my mother, discovering the crime, reacted quickly. She took Tiger and family for a one-way car ride without telling me. (This family story was a secret for years!) Many lonely weeks dragged by; I had only memories and stories of my lost friend, Tiger. And then she was at the door. Muddy, skinny, and bruised, she made it home, but she didn't remember us. Instinct alone brought her back, and she was so changed that my father took her from me believing she had rabies. Thankfully, he quickly realized she was acting oddly because she had lost her memory—cat amnesia! So, he let me sit near Tiger to tell her stories about herself. I did this every day for weeks. With the time together, good food, and a chance for her bruises to heal, Tiger became her affectionate self again, regaining trust in us.

Later, there would be more healing for Tiger in the loss of her child-bearing days. My parents had her "fixed." Now, my father and brother could go fishing without checking for new life in the boat. They left one July morning, my father retelling old fish stories, until they got to the next county. There, he glanced back to see Tiger jumping from the boat. Screeching to a stop, he managed to call Tiger to him and took her to a nearby bait shop. Shushing my brother's protests, he asked the shop owner to keep Tiger for the weekend and warned him about her yen for worms and such. Tiger stayed with this kind soul, however, he hadn't understood the warning thinking he should feed Tiger only worms. The bill for food wasn't outrageous, and my father, regaining a happy cat, thought the price of family peace was well spent.

Finally, stories are priceless, and Tiger has more to share. These days, though, Tiger has gained a place to sleep inside the door instead of outside. We, as a family, unite to guard her and keep her safe. You may ask: Why all the concern over a cat? Well, Tiger's story is my story, and it is my family's story. She is a big part of my history, and what I have learned in life about love, about gain and about loss, has often come through our door with Tiger.

WRITING THE DRAFT

After practicing the many different aspects of drafting, you are ready to write your own draft. Remember, when you write a draft, it does not have to be perfect on the first try. You have time to revise and proofread later. Focus on getting your ideas onto paper. As you write, leave wide margins, as well as space between each line, so you have room to make changes later. As you practice writing, you can develop your own personal writing process. Some writers follow their clustering directly. Other writers begin writing the body paragraphs, write a strong conclusion, and then go back and write an introduction. There are no rules for this part of writing. Find the best way for you to get your ideas on paper.

Before you get started, let's return to the essay topic about the effects of television on young viewers. As you will recall, the thesis or controlling idea was stated as follows:

Television has a negative effect on children because they watch programs that are not meant for their age, see commercials for products they don't need, and miss out on playtime they do need.

Based on this thesis and the outline that appeared in Chapter 3, a student wrote the following draft.

Television has a negative effect on children because they watch programs that are not meant for their age, see commercials for products they don't need, and miss out on playtime they do need. Little kids watch a lot of television. Television can be great for teaching kids numbers and letters and sometimes even manners. Kids learn other things from television, too. Besides that, they could be doing a lot of other good things other than watching television.

People get killd all the time on TV, children are watching Sesame Street or Barney or some other cartoon, and on comes a commercial for an adult show that will be on later that night. In those few seconds, children exposed to theft, murder, and sex that they shouldn't see.

Another important question to ask about TV and small children is what they are <u>not</u> doing while they are watching television. Children especially between the ages of two and five are growing very quick and need to exercise their growing muscles. They learn by doing, not by sitting. When children sit in front of a televsion, they are not running or jumping. They are not exploring the world outside or learining motor skills developed through puzzles or blocks. Further, therye not learning the social skill of playing with other children. Children may watch tv together, but it does not require them to actually play togetherr.

Commercials are another problem with television. Commercials advertise other shows with adult content in them, commercials tell kids to buy all this stuff theat they don't need. Thats' how television pays for itself. Companies pay to put commercials on tv and they hope kids will buy their stuff. The commercials tell kids that they will be happy if they buy the stuff. They will be like other kids and they will be liked by other kids if they have this stuff. It is difficult enough for addults to tell the difference between reality pretending in commercials. How is a three-year-old supposed to do that?

79

Some shows on television may be educational or entertaining for children, but libraries and schools are much better places for kids to learn. Kids can learn a lot from computers, too. Although some problems with television are the same for computers. Violence, sex and commercials are important problems with television. Little kids shouldn't watch much television. They should be outside playing.

This draft has many errors that you can detect easily as you read. These errors are typical of any draft. That is why revising and proofreading are so important. In the next two chapters, you will practice these skills. For now, let your ideas flow from your outlines onto the paper as you write your drafts for Practice 13.

> **As you write a draft, leave wide margins, as well as space between each line, so that you have room to make changes later.**

Practice 13: Writing The Draft

A. **In Practice 8 and Practice 9, you created an introduction and a conclusion for four different essays. Return to your introductions, conclusions, and brainstorming lists and develop outlines for two essays on the four topics. Then, draft the body paragraphs. Remember, your essays don't have to be perfect. However, pay attention to the skills you practiced in this chapter.**

Use the following checklist as you write each essay.

☐ I used specific words.

☐ I avoided clichés and sweeping generalizations.

☐ I used active voice.

☐ I developed a clear introduction.

☐ I wrote an appropriate conclusion.

☐ I used transitional words to link ideas together.

☐ I wrote a coherent essay.

☐ I left wide margins and space between each line, so I can make corrections more easily.

B. **Return to Practice 5: Making a Plan on page 54 in Chapter 3. In this exercise, you developed outlines and clustering diagrams for four different topics. Now, use these plans to draft an essay for one or more of the topics. Use the checklist above to help you.**

C. **For further practice and instruction in writing, visit two of the Web sites, or consult one of the books listed in Appendix B: Writing Resources.**

CHAPTER 4 REVIEW: ORGANIZING AND DRAFTING THE ESSAY

For the Chapter Review in Chapter 3: Creating Ideas and Content, you prepared brainstorming lists, freewriting samples, clustering diagrams, outlines, and outline shortcuts for five different writing prompts. Based on these prewriting activities, write a draft of an essay for one or more of the writing prompts. Use the skills you practiced in this chapter. You may also use this checklist from page 80.

☐   I used specific words.

☐   I avoided clichés and sweeping generalizations.

☐   I used active voice.

☐   I developed a clear introduction.

☐   I wrote an appropriate conclusion.

☐   I used transitional words to link ideas together.

☐   I wrote a coherent essay.

☐   I left wide margins and space between each line, so I can make corrections more easily.

Note: You will revise these drafts in the Chapter 5 Review, so keep them in a safe place, such as your portfolio.

ADDITIONAL ACTIVITIES: ORGANIZING AND DRAFTING THE ESSAY

1. Rewrite the following paragraph, using vivid images and concrete words to enhance the description.

   The trees line both sides of the street, giving shade to all who pass by. The trees also shade the houses in the neighborhood. Birds play in the air and make their usual noises. Woods surround the neighborhood, and in these woods there is a small pond. Sometimes children will swim there, or sail toy boats across the pond. There is usually a breeze blowing across.

2. This paragraph below contains clichés and sweeping generalizations. Rewrite the paragraph in Standard American English.

   I have a bone to pick with Lindsey Savage. Two shakes of a lamb's tail after his election, he is raising a ruckus. "The county roads need fixing," he says, "so let's add 1% to the sales tax." Lindsey Savage is so crooked he has to screw on his socks. The extra money for road improvements will just go to line the pockets of his sidekicks in the road construction business. Then they'll just piddle around and waste our money. If you hate more taxes, make a beeline for the county commission meeting next Tuesday night. Voice your opinions, or we're up the creek without a paddle.

3. On your own or in a group, skim through 3–4 articles in magazines such as *Time, Newsweek, People, Sports Illustrated*, etc. Find an article that has an effective introduction and conclusion. In 3–4 sentences, explain why they are effective. Then share your findings with your class or instructor.

4. Use the same articles from number 3, and describe how the articles develop coherence. List 3–4 examples of how the author uses transitional words and repeats certain key words or phrases. Also describe how the author ordered his or her ideas. Share your findings with the class or instructor.

Revising The Essay For Sentence Fluency

5

Even if you plan your essays very carefully and try to write your drafts precisely, you will still have room for improvement. Your teacher or the professional readers who grade your essay will look only at your final product. You want them to see your *best* effort, not your *first* effort. Remember, writing is a process of thinking, writing, and reviewing. Once the drafts are finished, it is time for reviewing which includes **revising** and **proofreading**. This chapter will help you with revising, and the next chapter will show you how to proofread.

Revising is looking again at the drafts of your essays with the intention of making changes to improve them. Revising involves the steps shown below.

- **Adding Clarifying Information**
- **Deleting Unrelated Sentences**
- **Eliminating Unnecessary Words**
- **Correcting Shifts in Tense or Person**
- **Checking for Parallel Sentence Structure**
- **Developing Sentence Variety**

HOW TO REVISE

Before revising your drafts, you may want to take a short break of a minute or so to think about something else. Then, return to your essays, and read them as if you were the audience. Put yourself in the place of the people who will be reading them, and read as if you were seeing the essays for the first time. Make your changes by using the spaces in between the lines and in the margins. While you read your essays during the revising stage, ask yourself the following questions:

1. **Is the introduction a good preview of the rest of the essay?**
2. **Does my statement of the thesis give my essay a clear purpose?**
3. **Do the body paragraphs support the controlling idea with logically arranged supporting details?**
4. **Will my audience clearly understand how my ideas fit together?**
5. **Is there any irrelevant or repeated information that I can cut out?**
6. **Is there information that I need to add to make my ideas clearer?**
7. **Do my sentences fall into a repetitive and uninteresting pattern?**
8. **Have I used transitional words appropriately?**
9. **How can I improve my word choice?**
10. **Are there unexpected shifts in person or tense?**
11. **Are there unnecessary words that I can delete?**
12. **Does my conclusion tie the essay together and leave the reader with an action or thought to consider?**

Return to the draft of the essay about how watching television affects young children (pages 79–80), and consider the questions above.

As you looked over the draft, you probably noticed the following:

In the **first paragraph** of the sample essay, the thesis is clearly stated. However, an introduction is stronger when it begins by getting the reader's attention and leads up to a statement of the controlling idea, usually in the last sentence of the first paragraph.

The **second paragraph** begins with a broad generalization that does not provide a good connection with the first paragraph. The details which follow are a good start, but they could be improved with more description.

The **third paragraph** and **fourth paragraph both** have some significant grammar and spelling errors that need to be corrected. More significantly, the fourth paragraph, which addresses commercials, should follow the second paragraph, which also deals with commercials. Rearranging ideas, even paragraphs, is appropriate for the revising step in the writing process.

The **conclusion** strays away from the topic by introducing subjects that haven't been discussed in the essay, such as libraries and computers. The conclusion should not introduce new ideas or information but tie previously developed arguments together into a strong ending. You want to leave your readers with something they can remember easily.

Considering these improvements, a revised essay might look something like this:

"Hey kids, let's count to ten! One, two, three . . ." Sure television can be great for teaching children numbers and letters. Some tv shows even teach children manners. But what else do children learn from TV? Does television harm children? And what could they be doing instead of watching TV? Television has a negative effect on children because they can watch programs that are not meant for their age, see commercials for products they don't need, and miss out on playtime they do need.

Even though children may be watching shows appropriate for their age, there is still a chance that they will see programs that are meant only for adults. A young child may be enjoying Sesame Street, but in changing the channel to watch Barney, he or she sees commercials for adult shows that will be on later that night. Two teens run up to car, throw the driver out, jump in themselves and drive away. Next, mean looking faces shout angry words, guns flash and person lies dead. Finally, a man and a woman being taking off each other's clothes. In these few seconds, the children is shown theft, murder, and sex that children shouldn't see.

Commercials are another problem with television. As well as advertising shows with adult content, commercials persuade children to buy products theat they do not need. Thats' how television pays for itself. Companies pay to put commercials on television and they hope children will buy there stuff. The voice on commercials tell children that they will be happy if they buy a certain toy or cereal. They will be like other children. And other children will like them if they have those products. It is difficult enough for adults to tell the difference between reality pretending in commercials. How are a three-year-old supposed to do that?

Another important question to ask about TV and small children is what they are not doing while they are watching television. Children especially between the ages of two and five are growing very quickly and need to exercise their growing muscles. They learn by doing, not by sitting. When children sit in front of a television, they are not running or jumping. They are not exploring the world outside or lerning motor skills developed through puzzles or blocks. Further, therye not learning the social skill of playing with other children. Children may watch television together, but it does not require them to play togetherr.

Some shows on television may be educational or entertaining for children. Hoowever, inbetween these shows their commercials with adult situations and violent images. In addition, other commericals teach children the false idea that byying all kinds of products will make them happy. And even if children could only watch educational shows without commercials, they would learn more and be more heathy if they went outside to play with their freinds.

There are still some errors in the essay which the next chapter will address. For the rest of this chapter, you will practice some revising skills.

ADDING CLARIFYING INFORMATION

When you write your drafts, *you* know what you mean, but you want to be sure it will be clear to your audience. As you revise your essays, imagine that you are the intended audience reading the essays for the first time. You want to make sure the readers have enough information so that they have no unanswered questions. Ask yourself if added information, more details, or another example would make your writing clearer. The following sentence provides a good example.

Example 1:   *At its next meeting, the school board will consider the proposal.*

The writer may have provided enough information for someone who is familiar with the situation described. However, another reader might ask, *"Which school board?" "What proposal?"* or *"When's the next meeting?"* The writer must add information to make the description clearer, as in the following sentence.

Example 2:   *Next Thursday night, the city school board will consider the proposal to expand the recycling program in all schools.*

With this sentence, the readers don't have to be members of that particular school district in order to understand what the writer is describing. All the necessary information is provided. You want to write the same kind of sentences for the reader of your essays.

> **Make sure you provide the audience with enough information to understand your ideas.**

Practice 1: Adding Clarifying Information

Revise the following sentences by adding clarifying information.

1. I went with Rafael and Scott to our favorite hang out, and we saw Priscilla.

   _____

   _____

2. The plants withered because of the drought.

   _____

   _____

3. Few people have big families these days.

   _____

   _____

4. Trees clean the air.

   _____

   _____

5. I bought a new lens to take better pictures.

   _____

   _____

DELETING UNRELATED SENTENCES

In some cases, you may want to add information, ideas, or examples to your sentences. In other cases, you will want to eliminate information, ideas, or examples if they do not relate directly to the topic of your essay. Look at the paragraph below.

> *I got a lot of great deals at the Clothing Mart. All the shoes were 50% off, so I bought two new pairs. I bought four new shirts because they were on sale–buy one, get one free. I'm so glad my friend Chris was there to help me pick out clothes. The pants were reduced by only 10%, but I really liked a green pair, so I bought it. I've never seen such a great sale.*

Each sentence in the paragraph relates to the writer's purchasing new clothes at a big sale. The author's appreciation of Chris' help, however, does not fit well in the paragraph. This sentence is not related closely enough to the other sentences, so it weakens the coherence of the paragraph. Deleting the fourth sentence will make the paragraph more concise and coherent.

> **Delete sentences or phrases that are not directly related to the paragraph or essay.**

Practice 2: Deleting Unrelated Sentences

Read each of the following paragraphs, and draw a line through the unrelated sentence.

1. Out of all the classes I took in high school, it seems that Social Studies dealt most with real-life situations. For example, we studied current events and discussed how what's going on in the world affects us right here at home. We also learned some of the historical reasons why certain conflicts continue to this day. That teacher really knew what was going on! We were shown how to read newspaper and magazine articles about current events and evaluate them for facts versus opinions. Since having that class, I've been able to "read between the lines" much better.

2. My first day in high school was pretty challenging. For the first time, I changed to a different class every fifty minutes. The school was huge, and I got lost during every move. I showed up to every class late. To top it all off, the combination to my locker didn't work, so I had to carry all of my books the entire day. I was not looking forward to going home, either, because I had to mow the lawn. My only consolation was that the other students in my classes were really friendly, and the teachers were understanding of what happens that first day.

3. When Leah turned the corner and entered the perfume shop at the mall, she got more than she bargained for. The most horrid smell in the world assaulted her nose. Customers and sales associates in the store were coughing and gagging! Leah quickly pinched her nose and ran for her life. After running for about fifty feet, holding her nose, she released her nose and breathed some fresh air. There's nothing like fresh air to increase your mental functioning. After that incident, Leah thought it would be best to go home. Then, the next morning, she read about someone placing a stink bomb in the store as a prank.

4. I look forward to a solution to the problem of the super-sensitive security motion sensor. Once that type of motion sensor is activated, the slightest movement can set it off. A flying moth or even my cat scratching the litter box after a large dinner can send loud sounds pulsating through my house. I know the sensor needs to detect the sounds and motions of a thief, but how many thieves are actually as small as a moth or as silent as a cat? A home security system is very expensive.

5. Jorge pulled his car over to the side of the road when he reached the bridge spanning the Ohio River from West Virginia to Ohio. This 451 mile southern boundary of Ohio which started near East Liverpool at the junction of Ohio, West Virginia, and Pennsylvania had great memories for him. As a teenager working on a tugboat, he had traveled the river to its end just west of Cincinnati at the junction of Ohio, Kentucky, and Indiana. Jorge checked his tires. He had great memories of boating, fishing, sailing, and water skiing on this river. He leaned over the railing and watched a tug boat push some coal barges upstream. The early morning sun glistened on the water below. It was exciting to be home again where his memories had their beginning.

ELIMINATING UNNECESSARY WORDS

Along with unrelated sentences, you want to eliminate unnecessary words. Good writing does not necessarily involve lengthy sentences full of big words. Good writing expresses ideas clearly through effective words—the fewer the better. As an example, read the following sentence.

Example 1: *As I was reflecting the other day, I thought about the very great number of people who, as of yet, have had very little experience of their own with using the Internet by going on-line.*

This sentence includes various words that do not help Readers understand the writer's intended idea. In fact, these extra words cloud the meaning. Read the following sentence without the extra words.

Example 2: *Two days ago, I thought about the many people who have never used the Internet.*

This shorter sentence provides the same information, but it does so more directly and clearly.

As you write your drafts, don't worry too much about extra words. Let the ideas flow. However, when you are revising, eliminate unnecessary words, and replace them with a simpler way of expressing the same ideas. Use the chart below to help you.

Unnecessary Words	Simple Language
due to the fact that	because
with respect to	about
hurried quickly	hurried
at that point in time	then
conduct an investigation	investigate
circular in shape	circular
there are many students who join	many students join
has a preference for	prefers
it is my belief that	I believe that
she is the kind of person who doesn't tolerate rudeness	she doesn't tolerate rudeness
In Nathaniel Hawthorne's novel *The Scarlet Letter*, he writes about	In *The Scarlet Letter*, Nathaniel Hawthorne writes about

Good writing expresses ideas clearly through effective words—the fewer the better.

88

Practice 3: Eliminating Unnecessary Words

Rewrite the following sentences, and eliminate the unnecessary words.

1. I received various and many compliments while attending the cast party due to the fact that the peers of my own age have a preference for acting that is less formal in style.

   _____

   _____

2. At this point in time, the county commissioners are taking into consideration the reasons for or against pursuing formal and official charges against the sheriff.

   _____

   _____

3. These are the issues that will determine who will be elected President.

   _____

   _____

4. In my mind, I was thinking that the class's poor results on the tests that were administered in physics class were due in large part to the short amount of preparation time.

   _____

   _____

5. There are many people who have homes in the urban downtown area due to the fact that they can live in close proximity to work.

   _____

   _____

CORRECTING SHIFTS IN TENSE OR PERSON

Remember the image on page 68 of giving the reader a taxi cab ride through your essay? While you are "driving," you don't want to shift gears abruptly. You want to keep the ride smooth, not giving the readers any unexpected surprises. One way to do this is to avoid shifts in **tense** or **person**.

Shifts in Tense

It is important to keep **one verb tense** throughout your essay. Once you choose present or past tense, stay with it. Read the following passage, and notice how the underlined verbs shift from present tense to past tense.

Example 1:   *It is the last game of the championship. Tamara, the girl who is always picked last when forming teams, sits on the bench and cheers her team, the Rockets, against the visiting team, the Panthers. Earlier in the game, Louise, the star pitcher of the Rockets, sprained her arm in the opening pitch. Now, in the last inning with a one run Rockets advantage and bases loaded, her replacement, Jenny, also sprained her arm. In a desperate move, Dalia, the coach of the Rockets, told Tamara, "Try your best honey. Just try not to break your hand when you throw the ball."*

The shifts in tense make the readers unsure about how the narrator is related to the action. See how much more smoothly the passage below reads because it keeps the same tense.

Example 2:   *It was the last game of the championship. Tamara, the girl who was always picked last when forming teams, sat on the bench and cheered her team, the Rockets, against the visiting team, the Panthers. Earlier in the game, Louise, the star pitcher of the Rockets, sprained her arm in the opening pitch. Now, in the last inning with a one run Rockets advantage and bases loaded, her replacement, Jenny, also sprained her arm. In a desperate move, Dalia, the coach of the Rockets, told Tamara, "Try your best honey. Just try not to break your hand when you throw the ball."*

Example 2 reads much more smoothly because the tense is consistent. The last sentence contains a quotation which creates a situation where a shift to present tense is appropriate. Also consider the following example.

Example 3:   *When the teacher said, "We will now turn to page 103," we all laughed because of the funny picture we knew was there.*

In this sentence, the shift in tense is clear and appropriate. The quotation marks the shift in tense, so it does not come as an unexpected surprise to the readers. Be sure to pay attention to verb tense in order to improve your writing.

Shifts in Person

"Person" refers to the point of view of the writer, as outlined in the chart below.

Point of View		
Person	**Use**	**Pronouns**
first person	the writer speaks	*I* or *we*
second person	the writer speaks to the reader	*you*
third person	the writer speaks about someone or something	*he, she, it,* or *they*

Shifts in person have a similar effect to shifts in tense. They can cause confusion by making the readers unsure of the writer's perspective. Consider the following passage.

Example 4:   *When I saw the water bubbling up from the ground, I knew there was a pipe leaking under there. I started digging slowly because you never know if you might hit the pipe or an electrical cord. You just have to be careful. As I dug deeper, I found the leak. You can just imagine how happy I was to find it.*

In everyday speech, shifting from *I* to *you* is quite common. However, this practice does not follow the rules of Standard English. In Example 4, the writer tells a personal story about an underground water leak. The writer begins speaking from the perspective of the first person, then shifts to the second person, then back to first and finally, back to second. These shifts interfere with the clarity and flow of the passage. Compare the revised passage below.

Example 5:   *When I saw the water coming up from the ground, I knew there was a pipe leaking under there. I started digging slowly because I knew I might hit the pipe or an electrical cord. So, I dug carefully. As I dug deeper, I found the leak. I was very happy to find it.*

Example 5 gives the readers a clear sense of where the narrator stands in relation to the story. The narrator maintains the first person point of view, rather than shifting points of view.

> **Keep person and tense consistent in your writing.**

Practice 4: Shifts in Tense or Person

Rewrite the following sentences, making sure that tense and person are consistent.

1.   A person who wants to learn how to play piano must be dedicated because you have to practice every day.

_____

_____

2. I was walking to the laundromat when I saw Philip, and I would talk with him.

   _____

   _____

3. Typically, first-year students have trouble adjusting to a new schedule, but after a while, you learned your schedules.

   _____

   _____

4. I went to the bank to make a deposit, but I couldn't because you know how long the line gets.

   _____

   _____

5. Students need to take out huge loans since it takes a lot of money for you to finish college.

   _____

   _____

6. It was the first of October, and I am planning on driving into the mountains to see the leaves change color.

   _____

   _____

7. I am an athlete who trains hard, but you never knew when an injury can happen.

   _____

   _____

8. So many children go hungry every day, while other people threw food in the trash.

   _____

   _____

9. People don't think it will happen, but a bad illness can made you lose your job.

_____

_____

10. Because a growing baby is so small, any drugs a pregnant mother took affected the baby greatly.

_____

_____

CHECKING FOR PARALLEL SENTENCE STRUCTURE

Parallel sentence structure means that the parts of the sentence which are equally important are also similarly expressed. In other words, verbs match with verbs, adjectives with adjectives, prepositional phrases with prepositional phrases, and so on. Note the parallel structure in the following famous sentences.

I came; I saw; I conquered.   – Julius Ceasar

Ask not what your country can do for you; ask what you can do for your country.   – John F. Kennedy

For I was hungry and you gave me food; I was thirsty and you gave me something to drink; I was a stranger and you welcomed me.   – Jesus Christ

These sentences have a rhythm and power because they are written in parallel structure. Writing that is not parallel can be difficult to read, and it is not Standard English. Carefully read the following examples, listening to the flow and logic of the words.

Not Parallel: *Billy knows how to play basketball, sing opera, and can even cook gourmet meals.*

Parallel: *Billy knows how to play basketball, sing opera, and cook gourmet meals.*

Not Parallel: *The three best things about summer are eating ice cream, swimming at the pool, and no school.*

Parallel: *The three best things about summer are eating ice cream, swimming at the pool, and not going to school.*

Not Parallel: *Sarah likes pole bending, to barrel race, and to rope calves.*

Parallel: *Sarah likes pole bending, barrel racing, and roping calves.*

> **Parallel sentence structure means matching verbs with verbs, adjectives with adjectives, and so on.**

Practice 5: Parallel Sentence Structure

Rewrite the following sentences using parallel sentence structure.

1.   The coach told us to go to bed early, to eat a good breakfast and don't arrive late for the game.

   _____

   _____

2.   The school lunches need more fresh fruit, less fried food, and there should be more choices.

   _____

   _____

3.   We searched for Tiger upstairs, downstairs, and crawled under the house.

   _____

   _____

4.   My hobbies include reading books, watching movies, and stamp collecting.

   _____

   _____

5.   In this class, we will learn to blend various colors, to use different types of paper, and how to draw realistic portraits.

   _____

   _____

6.   Did you make your bed, wash your clothes, and cleaned your room today?

   _____

   _____

7.   Statistics show that the world's population will increase rapidly while the world's resources are declining at an alarming rate.

   _____

   _____

DEVELOPING SENTENCE VARIETY

Sentence variety involves writing sentences of different structures and lengths. It includes using different types of words and phrases. These variations make your writing more interesting to readers. Three ways to develop sentence variety are by **combining simple sentences into longer ones**, **starting a sentence with something other than the subject**, and **using a question or exclamation occasionally**.

Combining Simple Sentences

Simple, direct sentences are often the best way to convey ideas. However, if these simple sentences become repetitive, they make the writing uninteresting. Compare the two examples below.

Example 1:   *We went to the basketball game. We were late. There was a huge crowd of cheering fans. The team won. Everybody celebrated in the parking lot. Then, some jubilant fans had parties at their houses. It was a great night.*

Example 2:   *After arriving late to the basketball game, we joined the huge crowd in cheering our team to victory. Hundreds of people continued the celebration into the parking lot and then on to the homes of jubilant fans. What a night!*

Example 1 is a list of simple sentences, and the repetition is boring. In Example 2, the writer has combined several of these simple sentences into a few longer ones. Both passages tell the same story, but the second one is more interesting to read because of sentence variety.

Starting a Sentence with Different Beginnings

Most sentences begin with a subject, continue with a verb, and end with an object. Adjectives and adverbs may appear along the way. This pattern works well, but your writing could get repetitive and boring. Therefore, from time to time, start a sentence with something other than the subject. Look at the following examples:

Begin with an adverb:
Replace "I found myself suddenly in a bad situation." with
"<u>Suddenly,</u> I found myself in a bad situation."

Begin with a prepositional phrase:
Replace "We stopped at the ice cream stand on the way home." with
"<u>On the way home,</u> we stopped at the ice cream stand."

Begin with a participial phrase:
Replace "The children ran into the candy store, screaming with joy." with
"<u>Screaming with joy,</u> the children ran into the candy store."

The examples above show different ways of forming sentences. They also show how a modifier is best understood when it is placed near the noun or verb it is modifying.

Using a Question or Exclamation

Finally, using a **question** or **exclamation** occasionally can provide a welcome change of pace for the reader. Compare the following two examples:

Example 3: *I didn't like it when my best friend told me he was going out with my ex-girlfriend. It was the worst feeling I've ever experienced.*

Example 4: *How would you like it if your best friend told you he was going out with your ex-girlfriend? Well, I know. It's the worst feeling I've ever experienced!*

Examples 3 and 4 show how to use a question or exclamation to add variety to your writing. Example 4 also shows how a shift in person can be used effectively.

> **Vary your sentences by combining simple sentences into longer ones, starting a sentence with something other than the subject, and using a question or exclamation occasionally.**

Practice 6: Sentence Variety

On your own paper, rewrite the following paragraphs by varying the sentences.

1.   My friends and I went to the Great Western Forum to see professional wrestling. There was a huge crowd. Everybody was screaming and yelling. All the fans were cheering for their favorite wrestlers. My favorite wrestler won all her matches. She flipped one of her opponents off the mat. She flew into the crowd. I was scared that she was going to land on me. She fell right next to me. I saw her up close. I saw that she was very big.

2.   My best friend is a guy. We've known each other forever. Other girls ask me about him. They ask me why we are good friends. I tell them he is funny. He thinks of weird stuff. He tells me this stuff to hear me laugh. Sometimes I just tell him that he is too strange. He will listen to my opinion. He says that he is glad that he knows someone who will both laugh and tell him different.

3.   You never know what effect you can have on other people. Sometimes it can be a big effect. Our school held a talent show. My friends and I did a lip sync to a song by 'N Sync. The crowd cheered. Everyone thought it was great. After the show, everyone wanted to tell us how great we were. I shook everybody's hand. I had a little fever that day. I found out later that I had strep throat. A lot of students were out sick the next week.

4.   There's a new student in our school. His name is Omar. Most of his friends are in the chess club. He wasn't very popular. He wanted to run for student council. There was another student who was coming up for re-election. Her name is Theresa. Omar's friends were excited about his campaign. They put up a lot of posters all around the school. Omar gave a good speech. He had some good ideas. This was the first time he did something like this. He won by a small margin.

Practice 7: Revising

A.   **Based on the skills you learned in this chapter, revise the following paragraphs.**

1.   The first and primary duty and responsibility of an American citizen is to support and uphold the government, the United States, and the Congress. In particular, a citizen can become a member of the local school board. I enjoy eating that old American favorite, the hot dog. You could be an active part of public education. You could influence the lives of children in your community. Another way to support the government is to serve on a jury in a public trial. We could keep criminals out of society. You must be an active citizen. Then our government will be stronger because of the active participation and involvement of all citizens.

2.   At first, do not be scared when people in public tried to communicate with you. We Americans are much more outgoing than I saw in Britain. They are the kind of people who are more subdued. They put smile on their face that is polite. People were very emotional here in the United States. When Americans are happy and cheerful, they will show it. When they are unhappy and sad, they are not embarrassed to cry in front of the other many people.

3.   Becoming popular in life has one big part of people getting into groups. To become popular may cause a person to join a group because they want to prove themselves to someone. This happens usually to new students at a new school. Becoming popular and well-known in the working area is about the same as school. This happens when someone gets a job they would like to keep. They try to impress the boss. People also join groups to become popular to be cool, so other people around them will like them.

B.   **Return to Practice 13: Writing the Draft, on page 80 in Chapter 4. In this practice exercise, you wrote 2 essays on some topics. Based on what you have learned in Chapter 5, revise these essays to make them better. Then, share your essays with other students, seek their input, and incorporate their suggestions to improve your essays.**

Use the following checklist to help you.

☐ I added clarifying information.

☐ I corrected any shifts in tense or person.

☐ I deleted any unrelated sentences.

☐ I checked for parallel sentence structure.

☐ I eliminated any unnecessary words.

☐ I used sentences of different lengths and structures.

Note: You will proofread these essays in Chapter 6: Proofreading the Essay.

CHAPTER 5 REVIEW: REVISING THE ESSAY FOR SENTENCE FLUENCY

> Write a letter to your school counselor explaining what career field you wish to enter and why you have chosen that field. Include details and convincing information to show your counselor that you are serious about your career choice.

Dear Counselor Billings,

I would like to show you why I am now choosing to pursue a medical career. While I have been growing up I have had many doctors to inspire me. When I was diagnosed with cancer as a young four-year-old, I was very scared. However, the doctors and nurses took the time to explain how they would help me. In the end I would like to be a doctor to help others in an important way, provide an income for my family, and make important contributions to the medical field.

Most importantly, I want to be in a profession where I can help people in the way I was helped. Being a doctor would give me the ability to touch the lives of people because being there for some one when their health is at risk and being able to give them the advice they need is a great feeling. I look forward to looking at my patients as people. not cases. I want to make them laugh, as well as give them the medicine they need. I want to make their lives better by giving them real support and lending them my expertise. The best kind of knowledge to have is the kind that you can share with the world.

Secondly, providing an income for the family I will one day have concerns me. I don't want to have to work sixty hours a week in a job I hate so that I can bring in enough money, to keep my family taken care of. I want to have time to spend with my family instead of being with a company that becomes my family because I spend so much time there. I want to be able to earn enough in a regular work-week to not need to work overtime hours. Being a doctor will give me the opportunity to work the hours I want while still being able to provide for my family.

Thirdly, I want to pursue a career in medicine so that one day I can make important discoveries to help patients. I believe there are other cures to cancers waiting out there in the world. I find it hard to believe that the only way today to cure people from cancer is to inject them with poisonous chemicals. I was really scared when I was a kid and all my hair fell out. Those chemicals do things to your body that nature didn't intend. And they damage you. I want to find cures for diseases from the natural world. Our bodies are natural, so we shouldn't be surprised to find cures for diseases coming from nature. I would like to be at the front of efforts to find natural remedies to many of the diseases afflicting the people.

To tell you the truth, I want to be a doctor because I can help people in an important way, provide a good income for my future family without having to work too hard, and contribute important natural discoveries for cures for diseases. Being able to work my own hours will help have balance between future family responsiblities and work. Helping people is why I feel I have been put on this earth, and I want to help someone in the way someone else helped me. In addition, producing natural cures for diseases will help me to leave this earth feeling I have made a lasting difference while I was here.

Sincerely,

Felix Lee

B. **For the Review in Chapter 4: Drafting the Essay, you wrote drafts for several different essays based on your prewriting activities from Chapter 3: Planning the Essay. Return to those essays now. Revise them based on the skills you practiced in this chapter. You may also use the checklist below.**

☐ I added clarifying information.

☐ I corrected any shifts in tense or person.

☐ I deleted any unrelated sentences.

☐ I checked for parallel sentence structure.

☐ I eliminated any unnecessary words.

☐ I used sentences of different lengths and structures.

Note: **You will proofread these essays in the Chapter 6 Review, so keep them in your writing folder (portfolio).**

ADDITIONAL ACTIVITIES: REVISING THE ESSAY FOR SENTENCE FLUENCY

1.   **Revise the essay below. It was written in response to the writing prompt below.**

> Your school board is planning to require all people entering the school to pass through a metal detector and wants to know how the students feel about this decision.
>
> State how you feel about the use of metal detectors in school, and give specific reasons why you feel this way. Give enough details so that your readers will understand your ideas.

Now that the year is winding down, we be confronting an important issue. Do we want metal detectors in our school next year or not? This issue is complex because, you know, we have had a lot of problems with student violence on campus. At this moment anyone can walk on campus with a knife or gun in their pocket and no one would know until the person decided to display or use the weapon. At the same time, having metal detectors inhibits our freedom. Every time we want to enter the school would be having to submit to an electronic search. I believe however that the benefits of having metal detectors far outweigh the costs. Every time we have something metallic on, we will have to remove it and display it to the public. This interferes with our constitutional right to privacy. We need to protect ourselves from our own student body, visitors to campus, and adults; in the school in order to make the school a truly safe environment.

Firstly, the metal detectors will protect us from ourselves. As students, we know how easy it is for us to get our emotions up on any number of issues. It doesn't take much arguments be starting all of the time over boyfriends and girlfriends. More often than not on campus these days, students be fighting about these problems instead of discussing them. Another thing, people starting vicious rumors cause people to get angry. We have had two people on campus arrested already for assault and battery in separate incidents. As violence increases, the numbers show that the potential for weapons to come into play be increasing to. Weapons, unlike a fist, has a much higher potential to permanently disable or kill. Weapons be causing all kinds of tragedy among the student body. Needless to say, I understand how students would feel hassled by going through machines and having to remove metallic items because some of you people will probably need to change your whole wardrobe! However, students need to realize it is for their own safety that this is becoming necessary.

Secondly, metal detectors will protect us from visitors that may want to harm us on campus. Currently, people may come on campus with the permission of the administration, but they do not get searched for weapons beforehand. Let's say some intelligent, crazy person convinces to administration to let him on campus for show and tell or something, then he pulls out a handgun while we're changing classes and kills ten of us. Now who here wants that. No one of course. If visitors get offended about being having to go through a metal detector, maybe they have something to hide.

Third, metal detectors would protect us from adults within the school as well. Remember, teachers and administrators would have to go through the metal detectors just like us. Sometimes in class I have seen the students get out of control. I can just imagine how tough it is to be a teacher. There are times I imagine that if I had a gun in my desk, I just might be tempted to let off a round at some kid whose throwing spit wads or throwing balls of paper across the classroom. I'm not saying the teacher would shoot a student they might just shoot up in the air but you have to imagine that the bullet could kill somebody on the second floor. It is for our safety and for the safety of even those obnoxious jerk kids that we have metal detectors for the teachers and the administrators.

To make it short, the safety of the student body, visitors, and the school faculty is at stake in this decision. We need to complete our education in a safe environment for all, so please support the installation of metal detectors starting next fall.

Choose either writing prompt 2 or 3 below, and write an essay about it. Then do activity 4.

Prompt 2: You are entering a contest to win a new Lexus™ convertible. You must write a composition that addresses the following question; "Who is your all-time favorite entertainer?" Brainstorm about this topic, and write your draft. Try to convince the judges that your choice is the best one. Then, use the skills you learned in this chapter to revise your composition. Share the composition with the class or with your instructor.

Prompt 3: One of your friends lies about everything from how much money his family has to all of the parties he goes to every weekend. Persuade him that lying is wrong and will hurt him in the long run. Do prewriting activities (brainstorming, freewriting, clustering, outlining) on this topic. Then, write a draft for a composition. Revise this composition based on the tips and strategies you practiced in this chapter. Compare your revision with those of others in the class.

Activity 4: With a partner or in a small group, exchange your compositions from number 2 or 3 above. Provide oral or written feedback to each other. Use the checklist on page 99 as a guide. If you agree with your peers, incorporate their suggestions into an improved revision of your composition. Then, share it with the class or with your teacher.

Proofreading The Essay For Conventions

6

You've written and revised your essays, and now you are ready to hand them in to your teacher, right? Well, they are almost ready, but not even the best writers turn in a piece of writing before they do a careful **proofreading**. Proofreading is the process of checking your essays for errors in capitalization, punctuation, spelling, and grammar as well as for repeated words or omitted words. Before turning in your final copies, take time to look for these small, but costly, errors.

The essays require you to demonstrate knowledge of Standard American English through grammar and usage, punctuation, and sentence formation. Proofreading the final copies of your essays will help you demonstrate these skills. In this chapter, you will review proofreading notation, and then practice proofreading for errors in the following areas of writing:

- **Capitalization**
- **Internal Punctuation**
- **Grammar and Usage**

- **Spelling**
- **Sentence Formation**

If you or your teacher feels more practice or review of grammar would be beneficial, read the text and complete the exercises in American Book Company's companion resources, *Basics Made Easy: Grammar & Usage Review* book and software.

PROOFREADING NOTATION

Types of handwriting are not graded on writing assessments, but if your paper cannot be read, it will not be graded. So, write neatly and clearly even for your proofreading corrections. **Proofreading notation** refers to certain ways of making corrections that are standard among writers. Below is an example of how you might make corrections to the third paragraph from the essay about the effects of children watching television (on page 84).

Commercicals are another problem with television. As well as advertising shows with adult
situations, commercials persuade children to buy products theat they do not need. That is
Thats' how
television pays for itself: Companies pay to put commercials on television and they hope children
their
will buy there stuff. The voice on commercials tell children that they will be happy if they buy a
a
certain toy or cereal. They will be like other children. And other children will like them if they
and
have those products. It is difficult enough for adults to tell the difference between reality
is
pretending in commercials. How are a three-year-old supposed to do that?

102

Notice how the proofreading marks are written neatly and clearly, so they don't interfere with reading the passage. Develop standard abbreviations and notations for editing your writing.

EDITING AND PROOFREADING CHART

Symbol	Meaning	Example
sp	spelling error	They're ~~Their~~ back from vacation. (sp)
cap	capitalization error	I live in the ᴇast, but my sister lives in the ᵂest. (cap)
. ? !	end marks	Where are you going/(?)
,	comma	Hello⸴Mr. Ripley (,)
^	add	the Ray went to ^ store.
/	change	children Television teaches ~~kids~~ manners.
frag	fragment	Near Kokomo. (Frag)
RO	run-on	He tripped he fell. (RO)
t	tense error	ed Yesterday I walk ^ to school. (T)
s-v	subject-verb agreement	Keisha and I loves/ to shop. (S-v)
mod	misplaced modifier	Quickly, Sam ate the sandwich. (mod)

CAPITALIZATION

Capitalization involves the practice of using a mixture of capital letters ("A") and lower case letters ("a"). In the early development of English, writers used only capital letters. Now, in modern English, there are rules for capitalizing certain words in order to emphasize their importance. One example is the first word of a sentence, like the word "**One**" which began this sentence. Another example of words that are capitalized is proper nouns, like "**Ely, Minnesota.**" There are many other examples of times when a word should be capitalized. Think for a moment about the examples that you know.

Looking for errors in capitalization is an important proofreading skill. You will practice this skill in the following exercise.

> Certain words are capitalized to emphasize their importance. These words include the first word in a sentence, proper nouns, words in titles, etc.

Practice 1: Capitalization

Carefully read the letter below, proofreading for errors in capitalization. (Circle) all of the words with capitalization errors, including words that should have been capitalized and were not, as well as words which should *not* have been capitalized but were. *Hint:* There are forty-eight (48) words with capitalization errors to find.

july 24, 2005

dear mr. Golden,

My Family and i finally went on our vacation to the grand canyon in arizona. we got there on a Wednesday Morning. My brother, will, and I both wanted to go on the Helicopter tour first, but mom and dad said—"Later!"

When we first walked to the Edge of the South Rim, our jaws dropped, and we exclaimed "oh, wow!" at one time. Mom took a step back. "oh," She said, "I don't think I can hike this!"

Some german Tourists, hearing our english voices, stopped by us at that moment to ask about the horseback tours. We helped them find the Camp office, and we spoke with kelly o'hara, the Park Ranger on duty. after giving us information about the Canyon and reassuring Mom about the bright angel Trail, Ranger o'hara asked if we were from the south. I guess our accents are more noticeable than i had thought . . .

Since I know that you, as my english Professor, will be asking for this later, Maybe you could look over my Outline for the Annual "what I did this summer" paper.

    I.   Memorial day pool Visit
       A.   sunburn
          1.   Second degree burns

                sincerely yours,
                Leigh Harpar

INTERNAL PUNCTUATION

Internal Punctuation refers to the writing marks that are used within the structure of a sentence. They include **commas**, **colons**, **semi-colons**, **apostrophes**, and **quotation marks**. The appropriate use of these marks add clarity and logic to your writing.

Commas **,**

The action of writing an essay has a certain flow and thought process in drafting and even in revising. This flow can create an engaging paper, but it can also lead to omissions of certain punctuation. **Commas** are often forgotten in the flow of writing. Proofreading for any missing commas is important for the clarity of your paper.

Commas can signal a contrast, set off extra information, or separate items in lists. There are other uses for commas as well. Consider what you know about using commas, and then begin the next exercise.

Practice 2: Commas

Read the story below carefully, looking for all missing commas. Insert commas where they are needed, and (circle) them. *Hint:* **There are thirty-five (35) commas that are missing.**

What's in a Car's Name?

In our college library I fingered the book's jacket in disbelief. The title had to be a joke or was it? The letters stood out lemon yellow on a cobalt blue background spelling out the words *How to Name Your Car*. I told my best friend Renatta "Hey look at this!"

"Well yeah" she remarked in a bored tone "I saw a book kinda like that in my lit class by T. S. Eliot about how to name your cat. Crazy huh?" Still curious I headed to the nearest table to find out why this book would have been written and what it said.

When I began reading the book I realized that it detailed not only car names but also who would choose to name a car. Apparently Westerners who have not gone past the high school level in their education are more likely than other people to name their vehicles especially their mud-caked trucks and open-air jeeps. Sitting at that table I felt my past revealed exposed. My parents with their two semesters of college between them had named our huge maroon station wagon—had named her "Battle Axe." It was a righteous and well-deserved title. My family also according to the book fell into the common masses category by referring to this hulking machine with the pronoun "she." In her glory days she plowed into several smaller cars—usually in the shopping center parking lot where my mother vainly tried to overcome the "blind spot" that came with the car. Battle Axe always came away unscarred from the crashes but the other cars weren't so lucky.

After fourteen years we got our next car on May 17 1996. This new "she" had been pre-owned by my grandparents who lived in Fort Collins Colorado. She was a pale yellow black-topped Chevelle with a sweet 350 engine—she could move out! What did we name her? We named her "Cream Puff." She and her name lasted until the puff from her engine became a bluish-black oily cloud of smoke.

105

Colons **:** Semi-Colons **;** and Apostrophes **,**

The **colon** signals that there is a bit of information that the sentence needs. It most often sets off a list, a quotation, an appositive (renaming), an explanation, or an example. Colons are also used in number phrases like time notations or Biblical references. Two major rules about colons are

1) <u>never</u> place it right after a verb (between the verb and its object), and

2) <u>never</u> use it to separate two independent clauses with a coordinating conjunction between them.

You may use a **semi-colon** to separate two independent clauses which are closely related to one idea. (For more emphasis, you may also use a colon in this case, especially to emphasize the second clause.) Another common use of the semi-colon is to separate items in a list when the item names contain commas.

Apostrophes do not separate anything; they signal either possession or missing letters in contractions.

To improve your proofreading skill, consider the guidelines above and consider how you normally use these punctuation marks. Then, complete the following exercise.

Practice 3: Colons, Semi-colons, and Apostrophes

First, carefully read the story below and continuing on the next page, for content. Next, insert the missing punctuation marks and (circle) them. *Hint:* **There are twenty-four (24) colons, semi-colons, and apostrophes missing in the passage.**

Wild Life Unleashed!

Wildlife, exotic wildlife, is moving into a neighborhood near you, according to these types of news stories a five-foot iguana, sunning herself on a rock, startles kids at a local elementary school a large python, an abandoned pet, was found inside the mayors limo, digesting a meal and the Humane Society was called to trap imported eels, which were eating rare koi fish in a park pond.

OCELOT

Where does this exotic wildlife come from? It is imported by people who see exotic pet ownership as cool whereas, its really quite brutal. Even in the 70s, the United States experienced a craze in wild animal ownership, promoting the importation of exotic wildlife including the following ocelots, cheetahs, and Canadian wolves. The rich and famous paraded these animals with rhinestone collars and leashes down city streets. The craze lasted until the animals matured and reverted to wild habits howling at all hours, spraying walls, and shredding the owners' belongings. Reports of cruelty and neglect increased, and zoos refused to take these animals for lack of space and the high level of nursing they required. The federal customs agency mercifully stepped in, halting the importation of these wild creatures.

Nowadays, the exotic pet of choice is more likely to be a reptile or a carnivorous fish of some kind. Parents buy or allow their children to buy these creatures, believing them to be ideal companions quiet, caged, and low-maintenance. When the pets have grown too large or too worrisome, however, theyre dumped into rural areas, including local waterways, to fend for themselves.

The following letter is a possible scenario illustrating the hazards of exotic pets

Gilbert's Trout Farm

Dear Sir

I m writing to let you know about some stuff that I think I lost in your lake. On September 2, 2000, at 7 27 a.m., I was fishing with my parents when I lost the following things a flashlight, with extra batteries two rock n roll covers for CDs with tubes of Virtualglu taped inside and a fresh water eel, with huge teeth. Its cage is missing too. I am sorry for the trouble, but my family is ok with the eel being gone.

> Sincerely,
> Will Stephens

This accidental release of a wild pet is an exception it is usually done intentionally. The zoos and nature centers are again refusing to take the new form of exotic pets, and these animals are taken either to vets to be put to death or to remote areas to be abandoned. In the text of the Old Testament, Genesis 1 28, humans are given dominion over the other creatures on Earth. Isnt it time to consider a more humane philosophy of dominion where there is nurturing and care, instead of exploitation and neglectful ownership?

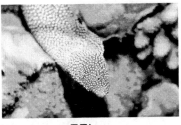

EEL

Beware! The next wave of released pets will be even smaller life forms fuzzy tarantulas, desert scorpions, and Madagascar hissing cockroaches. Dont give in to the lure of owning this bizarre form of consumerism. You might end up just being bugged.

Quotation Marks   66 99

Quotation marks are signals, framing words that belong to someone other than the author. When used in fiction, quotation marks help to keep the voices of different characters from becoming confused. There are two types of quotation marks:

> **double quotation marks (" ")** are used to signal direct quotes or some titles
> **single quotation marks (' ')** are used to signal quotes within quotes

Practice 4: Quotation Marks

Carefully read the story below, first for content. Then, look for missing quotation marks, and add the quotation marks where needed. Next, (circle) the ones you added. *Hint:* **There are eight (8) pairs of double " " marks and one (1) pair of single ' ' marks missing.**

Summer Blight

Race you to that mimosa! challenged Sophie, pointing to a slender pink-dotted tree.

You're on, dork, snorted Terrell, and the loser has to bring everybody sodas.

We took off, with me—dead last as usual. We fell under the scant shade of the tree, panting and sweating from the summer's heat. I rolled onto my back to look up through the mimosa's fern-like leaves.

Did you know that these trees were all killed by a blight years back? I asked. My aunt Beryl always talks about climbing these trees as a kid, but they were huge then. Now the blight's over and the mimosas are growing again, but they're all scrawny, like this one here. Wonder when they'll be big enough to be good climbin' trees again . . .

Sophie sat up, frowning and fussing, Don't try to change the subject. You know it's you that has to get the sodas, and while you're at it, you might as well bring food, too.

Terrell agreed with her (as usual) that as the fartherest-back-of-all-time loser I should bring anything they wanted. My speech had backfired—making them hungrier and thirstier than ever. I tried again.

With this drought going on, the worst in history even, I think we should forget the sodas. Just remember, I said raising a hand into the air, that old saying, Don't spit; you just might need it. And I think . . .

Sophie and Terrell threw dust, thistles, and rude names at me until I got up and trudged off, feeling as much a loser as Charlie Brown in the comic strip Peanuts. Then, as I got closer to our screened door, I started daydreaming about what would happen if I fell in a hole or was taken by aliens. Sophie and Terrell—well, I expect that they would just wither up and blow away like blighted mimosa shoots.

> **Use appropriate internal punctuation within your sentences, including commas, colons, semi-colons, apostrophes, and quotation marks.**

GRAMMAR AND USAGE

Grammar and usage refers to the ways that writers put together words, phrases, sentences, and paragraphs. When you are proofreading, you want to make sure that you have followed the rules for Standardized American English. Look for mistakes in your usage of **nouns**, **articles**, **adjectives**, **adverbs**, **negative words**, **verbs**, and **subject-verb agreement**.

Nouns and Articles

Nouns are words which name people, places, things, ideas, and concepts. **Common nouns** name general examples of these. **Proper nouns** name specific people, places, things, ideas, and concepts and are capitalized. Proper nouns are capitalized and common nouns are not. There is a special group of nouns called collective nouns. **Collective nouns** name single units made up of many members. Two examples are a **school** of fish and a **committee** of delegates.

Nouns may be **possessive**, showing ownership or a relationship. There are several different ways to form the possessive of a noun. Two of the guidelines are as follows: for a singular noun, add an **'s**; if the noun is plural and ends in **s**, then add only an apostrophe after the letter **s** (s').

In English, **articles** like "the" or "a" are closely associated with nouns. These small words often give the reader essential information about the noun they accompany. There are three forms of articles:

definite–"the" indefinite–"a / an" zero–no article

1. The first form, the **definite article**, is "**the**." It can be used with any type of noun. "**The**" marks a thing that is known to readers either by general knowledge, the context of the rest of the writing, or by the information in the noun phrase.

Example 1:	**The** sun rises in the morning.
Example 2:	A wildfire blazed out of control in eastern Colorado. It is **the** worst fire seen in 200 years.
Example 3:	**the** Great Basin Park, *or* **the** blizzard that shut down Yosemite in 1993

   There are three instances where "the" is always needed:

   - Before the word **same** (**the same** time zone)
   - Generally before a written (ordinal) number (**the first** star I see)
   - Before a superlative statement (**the best** music)

2. The second form, the **indefinite article**, **a / an**, does not identify a certain thing. The writer may know of the particular noun item but does not expect the reader to know it. The indefinite article **a / an** can only be used with singular nouns. The article **a** is used before a word that begins with a consonant letter or sound. The article **an** is used before words that begin with a vowel letter or sound.

Example 1:	I went to **a** concert.	He worked on **a** railroad.
Example 2:	She had **an** egg for breakfast.	They drove for **an** hour to get to the fair.

3. The third form, the **zero article**, means no article at all. No articles are used with plural or uncounted nouns. Often, vague generalizations are made with no article.

    Example 1:   We will serve <u>hot tea</u> with lunch.
    Example 2:   <u>Trees</u> give off oxygen, benefitting our atmosphere.
    Example 3:   Religious texts are founded on <u>faith</u>.

Practice 5: Nouns and Articles

<u>READ THE DIRECTIONS FOR BOTH PARTS, A and B,</u> **BEFORE reading the passage.**
The following news review involves practice for nouns and articles. Read it carefully, and follow the directions for each part:

PART A: **IN LINES 1–7 ONLY,** look for nouns and articles. Underline all <u>common nouns</u> once, underline all <u>proper nouns</u> twice, and (circle) all articles. *Hint:* There are twenty-four (24) common nouns, three (3) proper nouns, and thirteen (13) articles.

Not the Same Old Grind!

1   Have you been to the new recreational park? If not, you've got to go. It's so awesome! It's
2   called Skateboard Survivor Park. The entire complex is arranged so skateboarders have
3   the right-of-way.   The park's property is a sprawling 27 acres of convenient urban land.
4   The park's compassionate leader is J. C. Powell, a life-long educator. Mr. Powell's vision
5   for the park was that it be a safe but challenging course for serious skateboarders. After
6   only a few crises, construction was completed on schedule. The master-of-ceremonies'
7   speech was made on skateboards; an official showed off the park's unique features. There

8   are grinding railes, half-pipes, rampies, multi-level shelfs and spirals for extreme speed and
9   complicated maneuvers. Previewing the park, I saw some skateboarderes shooting around
10   like torpedos and others bailing out like dominois. A brand new skateboarding splash
11   fountain has been put in for cooling off and jumping off. The huge food court, three storys
12   high, can be reached by avenuess that are marked "Skateboard Traffic Only." When has
13   that been seen before? The walking crowd has its own pathwaies and food kioskes: set
14   around the perimeter of park only. The best wayes to reach the park include city busis
15   and the underground rail system. There is a small entrance fee that gives you run of the
16   parks' grounds for as long as you can survive or until they vote you out at closing time. I
17   don't know about you, but I'm voting to grab my boards' and head over there right now!

PART B: **IN LINES 8–17 ONLY,** look for incorrectly written possessive and plural nouns and missing articles. Neatly strike through the incorrect form, and clearly write the correct form above it. For missing articles, use the caret sign, ^ , and supply the missing word. *Hint:* There are sixteen (16) errors.

Pronouns

Pronouns take the place of nouns in a sentence. A pronoun must agree in number and gender with the noun it replaces. Some examples of pronouns are **I**, **you**, **she**, **he**, **it**, **we**, **they**, **us**, **their**, **who**, **that**, **someone**, **whose**, **none**, and **nobody**. Some of these pronouns may act as adjectives when they are followed by a noun: for example, **that**, **those**, or **these**. Also, there are pronouns which may begin a question: for example, **what**, **who**, or **whose**.

Before beginning the next practice, you may want to consider how you use pronouns or review the use of pronouns in the companion text, American Book Company's *Basics Made Easy: Grammar and Usage Review (2001)*.

Practice 6: Pronouns

Read the following essay carefully, first for content. (Note that it continues onto the next page.) After reading the passage, go back and read the directions for Parts A-B.

Part A: In this section, find and (circle) the pronouns. *Hint:* There are eighteen (18) pronouns used in this section.

Playground of Impressions

At some point in time, say in second grade, two kids meet on a playground for the first time, and if they don't beat each other up, then a friendship grows. These innocent days pass quickly, however, and soon these same kids learn to be more wary of how they react in social situations. Even young children begin to use a "public face." These two kids could be you and me or anyone we know. Everyone has some type of mask that they use in social settings to protect their private selves from ridicule, whether it, the ridicule, is real or imagined. Often a destructive mind-set of "us against them" can develop when people bond in this shallow, appearances-only, type of way. So the question is should I, or should you, trust and act upon first impressions? No, we should not. It is better for us to let a friendship grow with the passing of a few seasons.

Part B: In this section, proofread for errors in pronoun usage. **Neatly strike through the errors that you find, and then write the correct pronoun form above each error.** *Hint:* There are twenty-one (21) errors in pronoun usage.

In a first impression, the brassiest personality may mask a shy, unsure self, and a quiet, dignified approach may only be covering up a really boring personality. You can see that there are many aspects to creating a first impression, but it are all based on surface appearance. There is the tilt of the head: is the person that I are meeting looking alert, confident, interested? They may indicate only a stiff neck instead of the proud carriage that us perceive. There is the impression of eye contact to be assessed: does this person look you in the eye with steady reassuring gazes? Them could really be the peering looks of a near-sighted person whose is trying to figure out just who I are. There is the tone of the voice: is this person speaking in a pleasant tone with an elegant accent? That person could really be pretentious and smothering a God-given accent or this poor soul could be trying to disguise a sinus condition. Lastly, there is a general message sent through clothing: are the clothes, who wearer is a stranger to them, the latest fashion and worn with flair and poise? That person could be employed by the mall department store and is a walking commercial or is a person so clothes-conscious that any one else's clothes are good enough to appreciate.

All of the above positive first looks were something my best friend in high school had. Them who met she for the first time admired her beauty and dignified ways. What them did not know was that her tried to commit suicide twice before graduation. Beauty did not protect this lovely girl from emotional problems. There was also in my high school a popular football player what had all of the best first looks. However, his was taking "legal" steroids which unfortunately affected him personality; they made him act violently. Many people were hurt whose were taken in by the first impression he demonstrated.

The image that began this discussion was a playground. The playground must be expanded as us grow. We must meet people in different situations over time to begin to understand who them are and if we should put in the time and effort of building a relationship with they. Remember: First impressions are the worst impressions.

Adjectives, Adverbs, and Negative Words

Adjectives are words which modify, or describe, nouns and pronouns. Adjectives answer the questions **Which? How many?** or **What kind?** In contrast to many other languages, English almost always places adjectives <u>before</u> the word(s) that they modify. **Pronouns** and **articles** can also function as adjectives.

Adverbs are used to modify many different kinds of words. Adverbs can modify verbs, adjectives, or other adverbs. Frequently, adverbs end in **-ly**, but not always. All adverbs answer one of these questions: **Where? When? In what manner?** or **To what extent?**

Adjectives and adverbs are also used to compare or "weigh" differences. The **comparative** form of adjectives and adverbs (**-er**) is used to compare two things. The **superlative** form of adjectives and adverbs (**-est**) is used to compare three or more things.

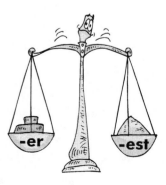

> **Note:** For words with one syllable, use the **-er** and **-est** ending. For words with two or more syllables, place **more, most, less,** or **least** in front of the comparing adjective or adverb. If the comparison is negative, use the words **worse** (two things) or **worst** (three or more things).

Two **negative words** cannot be used to express one negative idea. When they are, it is called a **double negative**. Unfortunately, it is one of the most common errors in English: for example, *I can't hardly wait for summer vacation*. There are many negative words including **nothing, not, nearly, never, hardly, neither**, and **no one**.

Practice 7: Adjectives, Adverbs, and Negative Words

Read the following story for content. Then, proofread the text for correct use of adjectives, adverbs, and negative words. When you find an error, neatly strike through the word, and clearly write the correct form above it. *Hint:* **There are thirty (30) errors.**

Cake Walk

Kelly had waited eager for months before her sixteenth birthday party. Her mother promised to hold a dance party for her at the newer city community center which was only one block from theirs apartment. Kelly's wholest family was going to be there and her tenth grade class. Aunt Marilyn, the more creative person in the large family, worked as the top cake decorator in Olgetree's Grocery, the better shop in the tri-city area. She came over weeks early to ask Kelly what cake she would like for this specialer party.

"I want two cakes," Kelly declared bold. "The firstest one is for all the girls. We want a Black Forest cake. You know the one with, like, red stuff inside and the deliciousest white icing."

"I know which one you mean," her aunt replied, smiling. "Do you know how the Black Forest cake got those name?"

"Uh, no," Kelly answered vague, thinking about the next cake she wanted.

Her aunt went on happy. "Well, it came from Germany which has the deeper and dark forests in all of Europe. The "red stuff" is really chocolate cake. The most old legends of wood sprites say that woodland spirits brought the cake to a powerful king as a peace offering. The king, however, refused the cake, and the sprites cursed him. They say that there is still magic in the most old recipes of the Black Forest Cake."

Kelly shook her head, saying, "I don't never believe in that kind of stuff, Aunt Marilyn, but that was a great story. Now about the next cake. It will be for all the guys. Make it a Devil's Food cake."

"Girl!" her aunt exclaimed. "Are you trying to make trouble?"

"Just kidding!" Kelly laughed. "I really want the kind of cake that my bestest friend likes a lot. He likes a double-fudge chocolate cake with chocolate chunks and the more bigger the better."

The cakes were baked, and the night of the party arrived with the worstest blizzard that anyone had seen. There was even lightning and thunder with the huge snowfall. In the dance room, however, there was a ton of food, a greater band, and beautiful decorations. The time for cake came, and the lights were turned out. Kelly stood by Aunt Marilyn who held the cake, and everyone sang. Sudden, there was a tremendous crash of thunder and a blinding flash of light. The vibration was enough to start the cake sliding, with all sixteen candles burning, off the plate. It landed with a mournful squish—upside down. There was the more horriblest silence for three seconds, and then Aunt Marilyn tipped the cake more or less back on the plate, exclaiming, "Whatever you wished for will come true! Kelly, all the candles are out . . ."

But there was no Kelly. Someone whispered that she must have wished to disappear in the worstest way. Aunt Marilyn thought wild about the curse of the wood sprites. Then, the lights came back on, and Kelly was standing at the threshold with the second cake firm in her hands and a smile on her face that was brightest than any amount of candles.

"Aunt Marilyn!" Kelly teased. "Remember I have never believed in none of that magic or wishes. I just do what needs doing. And tonight I am going to <u>do</u> my party quick before the lights go out again."

Verbs

A **verb** is a word or group of words which is a part of every complete sentence. A verb can describe action which the subject takes or receives. A verb can also link the subject to another word which describes it. Verbs must agree with the subject in a sentence in number and person, and verbs change tense to indicate the time of action.

Consider how you use verbs in sentences and in essays. Generally speaking, a verb tense should not change within an essay without a good, logical reason, but verbs do shift in number with the subject of the sentence. Think for a moment about how you use verbs, and then complete the following exercise.

Practice 8: Verbs

Read the following passage, first for content. Next, proofread for errors in verb form. Neatly strike through the errors, and then clearly write the correct verb above each error. *Hint:* **There are sixteen (16) errors in the text.**

Big Top Follies

Were you going to the movies soon? There is a great film in town. It's been playing at the Dollar Theater, and I saw it last night. The movie are all about a circus clown and his wild ambitions. The clown goes around trying to win weird bets. For example, he betted the elephant trainer this: he could feed an elephant a wrist watch and then find the watch in the elephants' straw, still working. He lose that bet since the animal steps on the watch before the clown can save it. The clown is tried other schemes: he sang for the flamingos, he swim in the crocodile pool, he left flowers for the bearded lady, and he tried to teach the donkey to bow. These bets do not works out. The poor clown  then go to the ring-leader of the circus. The clown asking him to think of a bet that he, the clown, can win. The ringleader cannot help but laugh. He do come up with a bet, though. He dares the clown to run for president. He sound serious, but it's a joke. The clown, however, agrees to it. Would you believed this silliness unless you saw it? The clown actually wins the election by a few votes, and he prevented a hand recount. I won't give the end away, but the movie is fueled by mix-ups and Jim Carrey-type humor. I was laughing about it right now. I thought about seeing it again, but the real election has been coming soon. I can just watch that.

Practice 9: Forms of Verbs

Carefully read the passage below. Decide how each *boldfaced* verb should be changed, and then rewrite the words on the blanks provided.

Riding Part 2: Mounting a Horse for the First Time

Some horses are elegant and mild creatures; however, some **were**[1] rough and ill-tempered. This last type of horse is an accident waiting to happen. **Did**[2] not let the accident happen to you. There are many ways to protect yourself while enjoying the ride. The first and best protection is education. A professional trainer **can taught**[3] you how to ride. Horses are intelligent, but that does not mean you **should have relied**[4] on their good sense. This basic horse care book **helped**[5] you stay in control. Riding is, above all, a lesson in the age-old communication between humans and horses. People **have rode**[6] horses successfully, for eons.

<u>Mounting</u>: Begin your approach to the horse slowly and quietly. **Spoke**[7] to the horse calmly as you are mounting, and always mount from the left side of the horse. Assuming that the horse is tacked up and held, first **have looped**[8] the reins in the palm of your left hand, and also hold the horn of the saddle with the fingers of your left hand. Second, lift your left foot and slide it through the stirrup; you **are needing**[9] to use your right hand to hold the stirrup steady. Next, reach with your right hand for the back rim (cantle) of the saddle while pushing off with your right foot. Continue that movement, and **swung**[10] your right leg over the saddle. You **are sat**[11] in the middle of the saddle. Be sure to put your right foot into the right stirrup, and **taken**[12] better hold of the reins with both hands. Take a look around before directing the horse to move.

1. _____   7. _____
2. _____   8. _____
3. _____   9. _____
4. _____   10. _____
5. _____   11. _____
6. _____   12. _____

LIE and LAY / SIT and SET

There are two sets of commonly confused irregular verbs. First, there is **lie** and **lay**. Lie is defined as "to recline," while lay is defined as "to place something." They are close in meaning, and in the past tense, lie is spelled lay. The other irregular verbs are **sit** and **set**, which have a similar problem: they are very close in meanings and spellings. See how these irregular verbs are used in the following sentences.

Raul <u>sat</u> in the café chair and <u>set</u> his cup on the table.

Marian said, "I am going to <u>lay</u> my book on the bed before I <u>lie</u> down."

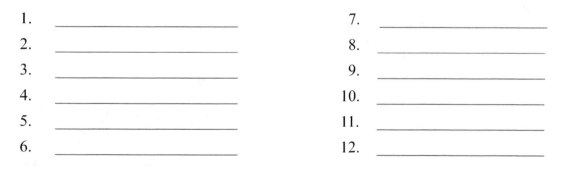

In proofreading for errors involving the verbs **lie/lay** and **sit/set**, the first step is to remember that they exist. Also, study the chart below which shows how these verbs are used in different tenses. If you are not clear about the appropriate use of these and other irregular verbs, refer to the companion text, American Book Company's *Basics Made Easy: Grammar and Usage Review* (2001) for lists of these verbs and for practice exercises in using them.

Infinitive	Present Participle	Past	Past Participle
lie (to recline)	(is) lying	lay	(have) lain
lay (to put)	(is) laying	laid	(have) laid
sit (to rest)	(is) sitting	sat	(have) sat
set (to put)	(is) setting	set	(have) set

Practice 10: Lie and Lay / Sit and Set

Read the historical account below, first for content. Then, (circle) the correct verb form in the parentheses that completes the meaning of the sentence. There are eighteen (18) pairs.

Casualty of War

During World War I, the United States Army kept many of its new recruits in training by (sitting / setting) up temporary camps in rural areas. One such area used by troops was the land (lying / laying) near Black Jack Mountain in Marietta, Georgia. Here, in the early 1900s, one could have seen soldiers (sitting / setting) on pine logs in between training sessions. Part of their training sessions involved learning how to fire weapons, including small cannons, which (set / sat) mini-bombs down upon faraway targets off the side of the mountain. These soldiers never guessed that in the future these pieces of ammunition would be found (lying / laying) on the ground, some still undetonated, and all kinds of people would collect them.

One of the more famous instances of this sort, at least in local lore, was that of a small boy whose father (set / sat) him up into a tree. Using a burlap sack, this father was harvesting pecans, which (lay / lie) under trees in the shadow of Black Jack Mountain. The child (sitting / setting) in the tree saw a hand-sized cannon shell which had (lain / laid) in that tree for decades. The child broke off a limb and tried to pry the shell away from the tree. The father heard his small son's voice calling, "Look what I found!" The next sound he heard was an explosion which echoed off the rocks (set / sit) into the side of Black Jack Mountain.

Struggling back to his feet after having been (laid / lain) flat by the shock wave and the shock, the child's father saw pieces of shattered pecan limbs (lying / laying) over blasted clods of red clay. They say that the man first emptied the sack of pecans, placing them back where they had (lain / laid) before he came, and then he gathered up his child, wrapping him in the rough burlap material to carry him home.

The family and the community (laid / lain) the child to rest in a cemetery near Scufflegrit Road, the turn-off to visit Black Jack Mountain. No memorial was (sit / set) near the place where this young war casualty fell; neither Teddy bears nor flowers ever marked the spot. The legend lives on, though, (sat / set) forever into the hearts and minds of a generation of Georgians who grew up (setting / sitting) on front porches listening to the call of whippoorwills and to the cautionary tale of the boy who (set / sat) in the wrong tree and reached beyond himself.

Subject-Verb Agreement

Subject-verb agreement means that both the subject and the verb of a sentence or clause must be of the same number and person. For example, a singular subject must be paired with a singular verb, and a noun in the first person must be paired with a verb in the first person. Consider first how you use verbs to agree with subjects, and then complete the following exercise.

Practice 11: Subject-Verb Agreement

Read the following passage, first for content. Then, proofread for subject-verb agreement. If the subject and verb do not agree, neatly strike through the error, and clearly write the correct form above each part. *Hint*: **There are fifteen (15) errors to be found.**

Bin There?

Have you ever felt that life was stacked against you? Has you sensed that there is a burden present that presses down unrelentingly? I am experiencing that right now. It are a massive, quivering stack, consisting of squished wood fibers in rectangular shapes, menacingly growing before my face.

Yes! The "To-Be-Recyled" paper collect on my desk, daring me to dislodge it with an ill-advised move. It silently dare me to reach for paper clips or a white flag of surrender. I, now, refers to the stack as the "Re-sigh-call" for help-heap. The really bad news are that no one listens to my pathetic wails drifting through the wall of paper. Neither the management nor the office staff comes to my aid at all.

Instead, the people in my office has impeccable timing. They senses just when the stack has eroded to a manageable level. Then, they marches by with all the righteous solemnity and shallow grief of failed game show contestants, piling their orphaned projects and rejected manuscripts onto my convenient desk. There go another group now. As I fix a withering glare upon the back of the offenders (who can't be bothered to take the stuff out to the bin), the slow march continue until fading into a conference room for the finger-pointing postmortem.

After wishing, vainly, that they suffer some sort of disabling paper-cut on those pointing fingers, I calls for pizza. Moments later, I watches, with a smirk that would leave the Grinch green-er with envy, as the previously preoccupied staff scurry about. Working feverishly, they all carts away enough paper, outside to the recycling bin, so to allow pizza boxes to be centrally deposited. After the meal, who will recycle the boxes?

Yeah, I've "bin" there—head-first in the recycling bin. . . .

Subject-Verb Agreement with Collective Nouns

Collective nouns name single units made up of multiple members. Collective nouns have special rules regarding agreement with verbs. If the unit is truly acting as one as in "A <u>swarm of bees</u> **lives** here," then the verb reflects the singular subject. However, if the unit's members act individually as in "A <u>swarm of bees</u> **perform** their various jobs," then the verb reflects the plural nature of the subject.

Proofreading for collective noun errors concerns the verb form used with them. Think about the logic of using the singular and plural form with the action that is occurring: is it a group or individual action? Then, complete the following exercise.

Practice 12: Subject-Verb Agreement with Collective Nouns

Read the passage below, noting the use of different collective nouns. Then go back, and decide if each collective noun is acting as a group or as individuals. (Circle) one verb in each pair to agree with the subject.

In Pursuit of Trivia

My senior class (know / knows) one thing for sure: we all love trivia. We are putting on plays showcasing our knowledge of it as well as the talents of other students.

The audience (clap / claps) when we act out animal behaviors using obscure collective nouns for groups of animals. For example, when in danger, a knot of toads (leap / leaps) into mud together; when there is a regrettable road kill incident, a murder of crows (take / takes) their favorite positions in the pecking order; and lastly, in a jungle river scene, a crash of rhinos (attack / attacks) a fishing canoe.

It is after this that the other student groups take their turns. First, the band (begin / begins) to play a thunderous medley of hits. Then, the skate club (demonstrate / demonstrates) their different special techniques, with trivial variations in moves. That is a very popular part of the show. Next, the debate team (argue / argues) about the relevancy of trivia. Lastly, the school choir (sing / sings) their favorite, though unheard-of, show tunes.

I believe all this trivia mania began when the student body (was / were) challenged to discover the origin of the school's name: Eagle Lake-Eight High School. Well, it was difficult, but our class found the secret. Apparently, the school board (has / have) some members who are avid fans of Andy Griffith: the Mayberry sheriff, you know. So they chose the name to honor him; in the 70s, he starred in a television show, "Adams of Eagle Lake." It ran for only eight days before being canceled. Now that's trivia!

> **Proofread your essay for proper usage of nouns, pronouns, articles, adjectives, adverbs, negative words, and verbs, as well as subject-verb agreement.**

SPELLING

Spelling is the process of arranging letters to form words. This may seem simple, but spelling English words can be difficult. The English language has a history of taking words from other languages and trying to make the spelling of them fit into the rules of Standard American English. These rules are rather inconsistent in the first place, so it makes spelling twice as difficult. This chapter will provide you with hints and practice in finding **homonyms** and **incorrect spellings** while you proofread.

Homonyms

Homonyms are words that sound the same, even though they have different spellings and meanings. The best way to proofread for errors in the use of homonyms is to recognize the homonyms that you tend to misuse and look for those first. You may also want to find a list of the most commonly misused homonyms. Study the list so you can recognize common errors.

ant   **aunt**

Practice 13: Homonyms

Read the following essay for content and word meaning. (It continues on to the next page.) Then, (circle) which homonym in each pair is correct for the meaning of the sentence.

Hurdles

Having a birthday can be just (plane / plain) dangerous. You don't believe me? Well, then I'd like to (advise / advice) you better because you haven't had a birthday like mine. It's like this: I had the brilliant idea to take some of my friends to the "Extreme Bike Course" for my 15th birthday. Questioning the safety of this plan, my parents all but said no. They tried to give me wise (council / counsel) and good (advise / advice) instead. However, with serious vows of allegiance to safety gear and pledges of future chores to be done, I (won / one) the day and got the go-ahead.

My friends and I were hyped up for (too / two) weeks while planning this party. We could hardly (bear / bare) the wait. (Whose / Who's) to say that we should have been worried? My parents called the course to check out (it's / its) rules and party arrangements. Finally, the day came, and my dad took us to (were / where) the course was located, over near Hoover Dam, just off the "Dam" road, US-93. I thought that we would just jump on our bikes and go. Not. (Writing / Righting) the check was the first hurdle that slowed us down, but Dad cleared that (won / one) just fine, filling in the dollar and (sense / cents) in the right places. Dad later described the next paper he had to sign as "(personnel / personal) information. You know, like the instructions on where to send your dead and broken body." He always exaggerates. It was just the usual disclaimer to relieve the bike course (personnel / personal) of any legal responsibility should I become, like, really hurt. I (blew / blue) this off by showing Dad my and my friends' safety gear; we were carrying full-body protection to (were / wear).   Out-maneuvered, Dad signed the release papers with his eyes shut. What a kidder! Well, after (hour / our) wait, you can imagine how bad we wanted to start. It was taking (two / too) long.

So we took off for the course looking cool in our backwards caps, bike shorts, and shirts with the arms cut out. Well, we wanted our biceps to be (bare / bear) didn't we? As the five of us mounted our bikes, we saw girls in the stands watching for guys; I mean they were trying to act smooth, but we could tell that we were having an (affect / effect) on them, and they were interested.

Interested! Really, they were fascinated, telling us later at the hospital, (were / where) they had followed us, that they had never seen the human body contorted in quite those positions while hurtling through the air like (plains / planes). I won't detail every crash, but you know, it <u>looks</u> easy to do those aerial moves that you see on TV. Lloyd lost a tooth–in his lip; Renaldo ripped his racing shirt and his wrist; Tito twisted and tore all the tendons in his knees; Cal careened into a corner and was concussed; and I, I got injured just where I deserved it, (write / right) in the mouth. I needed stitches inside my cheeks and in my gums: fifteen of them in three places each, or 45 to be exact.

That night, using a straw, I celebrated with mashed-up birthday cake and the taste of blood. Dad said it all when he observed that actually wearing the safety gear would have made more (cents / sense). If I make it to my next birthday, he suggested that we rent an Extreme sports video. I was deeply (affected / effected) by his concern, but because of my swollen mouth I could not speak. So, I had to (right / write) my answer—"Yeah, I'm on that."

Incorrect Spellings

Incorrect spellings of words can make your writing sloppy, confusing, or even incomprehensible. Proper spelling is an essential part of effective writing. Because so many words in English have irregular spellings, it is important to memorize commonly misspelled words. It is also helpful to follow a plan when proofreading for spelling errors.

First, consider the spelling errors that are typical for you, and look for those types of errors. **Second**, think about the basic structure of forming words, and correct any words that do not follow the structure. **Last**, use your sight memory—the memory which tells you when something just does not look right—and correct the word so it looks right. Using this plan, your proofreading for spelling should be successful.

Before you begin the practice on the following page, think about your own spelling patterns, and think about the rules for spelling that you know. In a notebook, make a list of words that you frequently misspell. Write them ten times each for practice. Be ready to use the proofreading plan (in the paragraph above) for your spelling errors.

Practice 14: Spelling

Read the following short essay carefully for meaning first. Then, proofread it for spelling errors. When you find a misspelled word, strike through it neatly, and then above the word, write the correct spelling clearly. *Hint:* **There are 42 spelling errors in the essay.**

NPR Today

Are you tring to find an intelligent, meaningful communications source? The easyest way to find what you are seaking is to swicth your radio dial to an NPR station. The National Public Radio station is a frist class educational resource, hepling schools in your city. The public radio stations rely on listeners, ordinery peple, for funding their bugdets. Becuase of that, Thy can refuse to run commercials or to counsider big buisness interests befor their audiances' interests.

In this way, public stations can offer viry differrant types of programming and can schedule the programming to meet their listeners' needs. Adults and children can unnite to support this resourse. There are shows which they can enjoiy together or individualy. The public stations, you may kow them as NPR stations, broadcast an interesting vareity of shows about sience, history, cultural movements (includeing

sports results), business trends, and film. This is just a bare sampeling of the varied broadcasts ofered to the public by the public (radio). The many station managers and jornalists, your freinds in radio, also foremat their news programs to reelly explain issues and to take time over importent events, instead of feeding their listeners sound bites from sleesy politicions' speaches.

Have you found a radio station that could offer all of this? KJZZ, the public station in Tempe, for example, is one of the best. In Febuarary, this station will be having a fund drive for new fans to jion public radio memebership, allowing them to take control of their destinys. Tune your radio in tommorow to your local public radio station and dicsover, all over again, how good radio can be.

Spelling English words can be difficult, but studying regular and irregular words will bring you success.

SENTENCE FORMATION

Sentence formation is one of the key writing elements. To demonstrate skill in this area, you must use **end punctuation** appropriately, correct any **sentence fragments** or **run-ons**, correctly identify and punctuate **phrases** and **clauses**, and avoid **misplaced** and **dangling modifiers.**

End Punctuation

End punctuation is one constant in the English language. There are three ways to end a complete sentence.

A period ends a complete statement.

A question mark ends any question.

An exclamation point ends a forceful or emotional statement.

These marks signal a definite end to one sentence and the beginning of the next sentence. End punctuation adds to the organization, variety, and tone of your writing.

Practice 15: End Punctuation

Read the following story carefully, and then add end punctuation as needed. Circle each added punctuation. *Hint:* **There are twenty-six (26) end punctuation marks to add.**

GREEN!

Has anyone out there noticed a government plot being carried out in dim grocery store aisles Yes, it's a top secret federal government plot that only certain foreign governments have paid to learn How do I know I read Stephen King novels, don't I But you, you need to look around you Look for GREEN; it's leaping out, screaming, grabbing at you everywhere you go

At one time, in years past, parents urged their children to eat green vegetables We are talking about naturally green things And just as naturally, the children turned away loudly exclaiming, "Yuck " These children are now the grownups driving SUVs Further study reveals an even deeper shame; these are the people who are voluntarily drinking–hold on–be prepared to be sickened They are drinking GREEN TEA Not only is this tea green, but it is flavored with other healthy things: peach, kumquat, lemon, and ginseng What's next, spinach-flavored green tea

Just to make sure that today's kids, those vital elements of target audiences, are not left out, the food industry has now funded research producing a truly grotesque, unnatural form of vegetable–GREEN KETCHUP The marketers using this research are based in Roswell, New Mexico They claim that kid experts chose this color over blue, yellow, and rainbow

But why toy with the artificially-enhanced natural red dye color at all Because as I said before, it is a government plot They are breaking down taboos–the natural order of the universe It is a law of nature, which Mrs. Einstein recorded: kids hate green food But if the government can break this taboo, breaching the limits of food color, think of all the other ways "Big Brother" can mold us Just watch for the acceptance of green eggs and ham Oh, no What am I saying It's too late

Sentence Fragments and Run-Ons

End punctuation errors may result in **sentence fragments** or **run-ons**. A **sentence fragment** is a phrase that is punctuated like a sentence, but it lacks a subject or a verb. To correct these, simply add the missing element. A **run-on** occurs when two independent clauses are joined with no punctuation or connecting word between them. The combining of independent clauses requires either end punctuation, a semi-colon, or a comma (internal punctuation) with a coordinating conjunction.

You have practiced using internal and end punctuation. Now, you can use commas with the following coordinating conjunctions to correct sentence fragments or run-ons: for, and, nor, but, or, yet, so. Remember these words by taking the first letter of each, spelling "**fanboys**."

When writing for a test, you may stop a sentence too soon, or make one sentence blend into the next. As you proofread, make sure each sentence is complete and correctly punctuated.

Practice 16: Sentence Fragments and Run-Ons

Read the passage below. There are both run-ons and fragments in the story. Decide how to best correct each sentence error, and write your answer on the lines that follow. If there is no error, write the word "correct" on the line. Answers may vary.

1. Betsy was not the most graceful or athletic person in our class.
2. Seemed a little klutzy and a natural-born bookworm.
3. In our 7th grade year, however, a vast change.
4. Before, the basketball coach let everyone play he decided to hold team tryouts this year.
5. Appeared to be a challenge to Betsy.
6. She had never been interested in sports now Betsy stayed in the gym after school for weeks before the tryout.
7. Practiced dribbling, passing, and shooting the ball.
8. In classes, bringing books on basketball strategy.
9. Her hard work and single-mindedness got Betsy on the first-string as a guard.
10. We elected Betsy to be the captain of the team she inspired us, on the court and off, in all our years in school.

1. _____
2. _____
3. _____
4. _____
5. _____
6. _____
7. _____
8. _____
9. _____
10. _____

Phrases and Clauses

Phrases and **clauses** are two groups of words that help form the structure of sentences. A **phrase** is a group of words that acts as a single unit in a sentence, but it lacks either a subject or a predicate or both. Phrases can function as nouns, verbs, adjectives, or adverbs. A **clause** is a group of words which includes a subject and predicate. There are two kinds of clauses: dependent and independent.

An **independent clause** can stand alone as a sentence. If another independent clause is linked to it, the two clauses must be joined by a comma and a coordinating conjunction (FANBOYS). **FANBOYS** is an easy way to remember the common coordinating conjunctions: *for, and, nor, but, or, yet, so.* A **dependent clause** relies on the controlling independent clause in a sentence. The independent clause and the dependent clause are linked together by a relative pronoun such as **which, that, whose,** or **those,** or by a subordinating conjunction like **while, because, since,** or **after.**

Being able to recognize these different sentence elements is the first step in learning how to use them in your writing. You may want to review phrases and clauses in American Book Company's *Basics Made Easy: Grammar and Usage Review (2001)* before starting this practice.

Practice 17: Phrases and Clauses

Read the following passage. In the numbered blanks on the next page, write whether the bolded group of words is a dependent clause, an independent clause, or a phrase. (For extra credit, identify type of phrase: prepositional, appositive, or participial.)

Team Spirit

All sports teams have similar ways **of celebrating exciting victories**[1]. Even swim teams have big celebrations **after they swim for six hours or longer in meets**[2]. Popular expressions of group joy, **such as head butting and team "dances**[3]**,"** however, are not seen beside the pool. Instead, **there is cheering, eating, dunking, and body art**[4] on display.

The display of body art is actually created[5] with permanent markers. Coaches write a swimmer's schedule of events on the swimmer's wrist **with the markers**[6]. During the closing two hours of the meet, **the swimmers make their own statements**[7] on their bare skin, usually their arms, and then their legs, and then their backs. (They need help with that part.) The body art at the beginning of a meet is kept to a minimum **because it shows the swimmer's race list and a "Go 'team."**[8] But when a team begins to win, the body art becomes more rowdy and silly. The teams try to outdo each other by inventing funny sayings **that won't get them thrown out of the pool area by the coaches**[9].

Although the coaches stay busy watching for any problems[10], they manage to lead the cheering and celebrating. Parents, grandparents, and other team members cheer especially loudly **when their loved ones are in the water**[11]. Coaches often order fresh pizza to celebrate **before the last race has been swum**[12].

They do this **when their teams are winning by a gazzilion points**[13]. There is one other big difference between swim teams and other types of sports teams **which involves the party aspect of the sport**[14]. While other teams throw water on their coaches after a big win, swimmers throw their coaches into water.

1._____   8._____

2._____   9._____

3._____   10._____

4._____   11._____

5._____   12._____

6._____   13._____

7._____   14._____

Misplaced and Dangling Modifiers

A **modifier** is a word, phrase, or clause that helps clarify the meaning of another word by describing it in more detail. However, if a modifier is positioned incorrectly in a sentence, it can confuse and frustrate the reader.

A **misplaced modifier** is positioned in the sentence too far from what it is modifying. This confuses the meaning, as in the following example.

Example 1: *The painting had visible brush strokes that I was selling.*

In Example 1, it is unclear whether the dependent clause, "that I was selling," describes the painting or the brush strokes. The clause "that I was selling" is a misplaced modifier. To correct this problem, place the modifying clause closer to the word that it describes, as in Example 2.

Example 2: *The painting that I was selling had visible brush strokes.*

Dangling modifiers are words that modify nothing in particular in the rest of the sentence. They often seem to modify something that is suggested or implied but not actually present in the sentence. They dangle or hang loosely from the rest of the sentence. They frequently appear at the beginnings or ends of sentences. See Example 3.

Example 3: *Dangling from a hook, our bird dove for the worm.*

Does this sentence make sense to you? What is dangling: is it the bird or the worm? Obviously, the worm would be dangling from the hook, not the bird. "Dangling from a hook" is a dangling modifier because its position in the sentence makes it look like it is describing the subject, "our bird." However, it should be describing "the worm." Correctly wording this sentence would mean changing the position of the modifier, so it is closer to the object it is describing, the worm. Notice this correction in Example 4.

Example 4: *Our bird dove for the worm dangling from a hook.*

Your writing must be clear and logical. Using modifiers incorrectly will confuse your readers. Consider how to make your writing easily understood while using modifiers that adddetail and color to your writing. Be aware of the position of modifiers when proofreading.

Practice 18: Misplaced and Dangling Modifiers

Read the following short passage carefully. Then, on the lined spaces below, rewrite the passage, correcting the modifiers that are misplaced or dangling.

Family Time?

1. We often lose track of each other being such a large family on trips.
2. So I knew what would happen before we went to the craft show.
3. That's right; we lost someone after we arrived.
4. The booths had a maze of walls where we were looking.
5. Our parents forgot to meet us for lunch running to see everything.
6. Those of us who met for lunch ate hotdogs after looking and calling for them.
7. After taking a boat ride across the lake, too late, our parents remembered the missed lunch.
8. They ate stale chips and a pickle standing up.
9. Sitting together on the fountain, we found them feeding some ducks.
10. We suggested a new plan for our next trip, which will be flawless.
11. Tuning us out, our parents formed their own plans for a no-kids-allowed date.
12. Yelling loud approval, our fists pumped up and down, while insisting that we should have a kids-only party with our friends at the same time.
13. So far, our plans have been left dangling; our hopes have been misplaced: family time rules.

1. _____
2. _____
3. _____
4. _____
5. _____
6. _____
7 _____
8. _____
9. _____
10. _____
11. _____
12. _____
13. _____

> **To demonstrate skill in sentence formation, you must use end punctuation appropriately, correct any sentence fragments or run-ons, correctly identify and punctuate phrases and clauses, and avoid misplaced and dangling modifiers.**

CHAPTER 6 REVIEW: PROOFREADING THE ESSAY FOR CONVENTIONS

A.   This exercise will help you with the proofreading plan that you have learned and practiced in the chapter. Read the essay first for content. Then, read with an eye for internal punctuation, correct grammar usage, spelling, and sentence formation.

When you find an error, use the proofreading marks which you have seen in the chapter. You may refer to page 103 if you wish. Neatly strike through the error, and clearly write the correct form above the error. If there are any problems with the content, note that separately at the end of the essay.

A local bridal and tuxedo shop is offering a lifetime coupon for a free wedding to the winner of their latest contest. The participants in the contest must write an essay describing the best place to get married. People used to get married only in religious buildings or court houses, but today, people get married in places such as on an airplane, on the beach, or even under the water. What do you think is the best place to get married?

Odd Places To Get Married

Traditionaly churchs and chapels were the main places for young couples to get wed. In the past twenty years or so people have gone away from the traditional wedding's. To be married where you have meet is not that unusual or bizarre. Many couples have been getting more adventureous in their wedding locations; couples marry where they are happiest too. All of these choices are just that: choices. Weddings need to be meaningfull to the people involved. Four popular places where they get married are underwater, on the beach, on a airplane, and sometimes in their schools.

Getting married underwater involves many factors and variables.   First, a scuba-diver lisence needs to be obtained for the bride and groom. So the new couple will need a blood test, and also a swimming test. Second, a good scuba-diving location needs to be found, for example, Key West and the red sea and the Barrier reef is considered the best diving in the world. Third, a pastor or priest with scuba-diving experience need to be found. Those could be a difficult search. Underwater weddings cost the mostest money because of the extra variables. But if that kind of wedding is meaningful to the new couple, I'd say that they should go for it.

Getting married on the beach is a odd, but romantic place to take wedding vows Standing in the sand with the waves roaring, and the sun setting can be romantic. Except for the danger of a jellyfish or stingray alert. Starting the honeymoon after a sting from one of those sea cretures could be unpleasant even with a romantic full moon and the smell of suntan oil. One advantage of beach weddings is that the wedding and honeymoon can be in the same city. Virgin Islands, Cayman Islands and Jamaica are good examples of places people pick for their meaningful, for them beach weddings.

Airplane weddings have become a odd place for people too get married. Airplane weddings are small due to space. Some people like to parachute out of the plane after taking their wedding vows. Airplane weddings can be very expensive and difficult to plan. Because of having to rent a plane and the skydiving equipment and having to have good whether. There would also need to be a separate place for the the reception or party afterwards. The things that must be considered are: food (airplane food?), flowers (thrown to the winds?), and which hospital is closest (in case the wedding is no longer the main event 'cus of injury). But flying free while being married can be very meaningfull to some couples.

This last example of an odd wedding makes a school wedding seem very respectable. To be married where you have met is very romantic and sweet. If two people can learn to love each other they also need to learn how to live together as a married couple what better place symbolizes that intention than a school. Even if space may be cramped in the hallway, there is always a gym or cafeteria for lying out food and presents. Also most of the guests would be old friends and very familiar with the location; so no maps needed to be printed. All these people could help decorate with posters and streamers, and help mix the party punch. This is a win-win situation. The school is appreciated for it's community service, the new couple has a cheap but happy memory.

Getting married should be fun and a unforgettable memory. Underwater weddings and airplane weddings are more costly than beach and school weddings. People for some time have been looking for odd; yet meaningfull places to get married. The most popular odd places to take wedding vows have been underwater on the beach on airplanes, and in a place of youth, memory and magic; the old school house. Support the two people who want to get married at our school. The media attention will benefit the school and our place in the community. So write letters and call talk shows for the sake of true love and for fame.

B. For the Review in Chapter 5: Revising the Essay for Sentence Fluency, you revised several different essays which you wrote for the Chapter 4 Review. Return to those essays now. Proofread them based on the skills that you have practiced in this chapter. You may want to use the checklist below to help you.

- [ ] I made my corrections neatly and clearly.

- [ ] I checked for errors in capitalization.

- [ ] I corrected errors in internal punctuation including, commas, colons, semi-colons, apostrophes, and quotation marks.

- [ ] I corrected any errors in grammar and usage, including nouns, pronouns, adjectives, adverbs, negative words, verbs, and subject-verb agreement.

- [ ] I made sure all words are spelled correctly.

- [ ] I looked for errors in sentence formation, including end punctuation, fragments, run-ons, and misplaced modifiers.

C. In Chapter 5, Practice 7: Revising (page 97), you revised several different essays. Based on what you have learned about proofreading, return to these essays and correct any errors you find. Use the checklist above to help you.

ADDITIONAL ACTIVITIES: PROOFREADING THE ESSAY FOR CONVENTIONS

1. Select 3–4 essays from your portfolio. Practice proofreading these essays. Based on what you learned in this chapter, correct any errors.

2. Choose one essay from your portfolio, and exchange it with another student. Proofread each other's essay. Explain the errors you find in each other's essay. Then make the corrections, and rewrite your essays.

3. After you make your corrections and rewrite your essay, give it to your instructor to look for any errors you may have missed. Make special note of the errors you overlooked, so you don't overlook them on an essay you will be graded on.

4. Read several articles in your local newspaper. Look for proofreading errors that the newspaper editors may have missed. Even professional writers make mistakes!

5. With one other student, choose two Web sites from the list in Appendix B. You and your partner will each visit one of the Web sites. Try to find instruction and activities that will help you with proofreading. Report back to your partner, and compare the strengths and weaknesses of each Web site.

6. Look over all the essays in your portfolio, and make a list of your most common errors. Practice the skills you need to overcome these errors.

7. From all of the essays in your portfolio and the practice exercises in this book, make a list of the words that you have difficulty spelling. Share your list with the class, and make one big list of commonly misspelled words. Study these words in preparation for a spelling bee. Then have a spelling bee in which the winner gets a prize. For added interest, use the format of a popular game show such as "Who Wants to be a Millionaire?"

Persuasive Writing **7**

In Chapters 3–6 of this book, you read about planning, drafting, revising, and proofreading an essay. The type of essay you learned to write in these chapters was a persuasive essay. In **persuasive writing**, you try to convince readers to agree with your point of view. You can write a letter to persuade an employer to hire you. You can also send an e-mail to convince someone to go to the prom with you. Or, you may write a letter to the editor of a newspaper to express your opinion on a current issue.

     In this chapter, you'll learn more features of persuasive writing. These features are listed below.

- **Purpose and Audience**
- **Using Persuasive Language**
- **Building an Argument**

- **Ethical Arguments**
- **Appealing to Emotion**

Have a ♥
☺ Consider Ethics
☺ We need to join together for the good of all!

PURPOSE AND AUDIENCE

Being aware of **purpose** and **audience** is particularly important with persuasive writing.

Purpose

With persuasive writing, your purpose is fairly clear: you want to convince readers to agree with you. However, the amount of convincing you need to do may depend on your topic. For example, convincing your dad to lend you 100 dollars will be more difficult than convincing him to lend you 10 dollars.

Audience

Knowing your audience is especially helpful in persuasive writing. Then, you know what points of agreement or disagreement you may have with your readers. You also know which reasons your readers may accept and which reasons they may not. Your audience could be friends, parents, teachers, local citizens, or an employer to name a few. Before you write, carefully consider who your audience is and what you know about your audience.

Practice 1: Purpose and Audience

In the following practice exercise, decide on the audience and purpose for each topic. Keep in mind that you are trying to persuade your audience to agree with you. Then, compare your choices with those of other students.

1. Topic ___Recycling___   Audience _____

   Purpose _____

   _____

2. Topic ___Entertainer of the Year___   Audience _____

   Purpose _____

   _____

3. Topic ___Dangers of Drinking and Driving___   Audience _____

   Purpose _____

   _____

4. Topic ___Making Friends on the Internet___   Audience _____

   Purpose _____

   _____

5. Topic ___Doing a Walk-a-thon for the Homeless___   Audience _____

   Purpose _____

   _____

USING PERSUASIVE LANGUAGE

When you are trying to persuade, you need to present information in a particular way in order to make readers agree with your position. You must emphasize points of interest to the readers and describe them in language that is attractive to your audience. For example, let's say you worked in a hardware store last year, and you are applying for a new job. When the manager asks what you did at your last job, you could answer with either of the explanations below.

Example 1: *I worked for a while doing odd jobs.*

Example 2: *I mopped floors in the hardware store, and then I took orders at the counter. After proving my abilities in these tasks, I was promoted to sales associate. I am very detail-oriented.*

Both explanations provide the same truthful information. However, the second makes you sound like a responsible and hard-working employee, while the first isn't very impressive. If you want to impress your future employer and convince the manager to hire you, the second explanation would be a better choice. The writer uses vivid description, concrete words, and figurative language.

Special Note: Paying attention to your audience does not mean telling people what you think they want to hear or giving false information. Make up your own mind, stay firm, and tell the truth. However, you want your audience to be able to understand and appreciate what you are saying. So, use language that will persuade your particular audience.

> **Use words, phrases, and reasons that your audience will understand and appreciate.**

Tips for Using Persuasive Language

1. **Use vivid description:** Notice how the writer in Example 2 uses phrases like "mopped floors" and "took orders at the counter." Persuasive language should include strong descriptive details. In Example 1, the phrase "I worked for a while" is vague and too general to convey a clear message.

2. **Use concrete language:** In Example 2, the phrase "promoted to sales associate" contains concrete and specific words. In Example 1, the phrase "odd jobs" does not provide a concrete picture of the work this person has done.

3. **Use figurative language:** Figurative language does for words what spice does for food. It livens up your argument. The phrase "my grasp of details is as strong as a river's current" conveys a vivid image that reflects positively on the job applicant.

Practice 2: Persuasive Language

For each of the following situations, write two or three sentences that will influence or persuade the intended reader. The example provided is NOT persuasive.

1. Convince your mother to let your friend sleep over.
   Example: Mom, can Chris please stay tonight?

2. Motivate your team to win.
   Example: It's half-time, and we're down by five points. We can win.

3. You took care of your sick brother last night, so you couldn't finish your homework. Persuade your teacher to give you an extension.
   Example: Is it o.k. if I turn in my homework tomorrow?

4. While mowing your neighbors' lawn, you ran over their flower bed. Convince them to give you another chance.
   Example: I think your flowers will grow back before I mow the lawn next time.

Practice 3: Persuasive Language

A. Look through newspapers and magazines. Find three examples of persuasive language and determine the author's purpose. Then, find three examples in which the language is not persuasive, and rewrite them in order to persuade the reader to take a stand on one side of the issue. *Hint:* Advertisements and newspaper editorials often contain persuasive language.

B. Imagine that you are the salesperson in the picture to the left. Write 4–6 sentences to persuade the man behind the desk that a laptop computer will make his work easier and more productive.

C. Imagine that you are running for president of your class. Write 4–6 sentences that would persuade your classmates to vote for you.

BUILDING AN ARGUMENT

Your ability to persuade depends not just on *how* you say something, but also on *what* you have to say. You must be able to build a strong **argument**. In everyday speaking, an "argument" is a disagreement between family members, friends, or enemies who exchange heated words. However, in the context of persuasive writing, an argument is a carefully reasoned way of presenting a point of view. The three steps to building an argument are to **make a claim**, to **support the claim**, and to **answer objections**. This process may be compared to building a pyramid.

Make a Claim

The first step in building a good argument is to **make a claim**. A **claim** is the position you take on a particular issue. It can't be just a statement of fact. A **fact** stands alone, cannot be argued, and requires no support. A claim, however, argues for one side of a controversy. Someone may disagree with your claim, so you must support it, just like the pyramid builder needs to support the top of the pyramid. The claim is the "point" you are trying to make, so keep it focused, like the pointed top of a pyramid.

Read the following six statements, and decide which are claims that provide a good starting point for an argument.

1. According to a 1999 Harris poll for the National Consumers League, a majority of Americans believe that water is our second-most-threatened resource, after air.

   – Sarah Milstein

2. Through personal choices, economic reform, and improved schools, we, the citizens of this great democracy, must stop the irreversible destruction of our most precious resources: air, water, and children.

3. We ought to be increasing programs that help the hungry children in our country rather than giving more money to an already well-financed program like the military.

4. Though the Cold War is over, the unpredictable nature of our present national enemies demands that we maintain a strong military through increased funding.

5. The best, indeed the only, method of promoting individual and public health is to teach people the laws of nature and thus teach them how to preserve their health.

   – Dr. Herbert Shelton

6. Over the past three decades, there has been increasing public interest in personal self-help books, including the maintenance of health through self-regulated programs of exercise and diet.

Statements 1 and 6 present information in a factual, non-persuasive way. The information presented could be used to support a claim, but neither statement encourages one belief over another. Statements 2, 3, 4, and 5 urge the reader to take a certain action or have a certain belief. In other words, they make a claim. These statements use words like *must*, *should*, *ought*, *demand*, *only*, and *best*. These key words often indicate that the author is taking a position and encouraging the reader to do the same. You may also notice that the persuasive statements sometimes use the subject *we* in an attempt to involve the reader in the position or idea.

Statement 2 requires a special note. It makes a claim that requires support, but the claim is not focused. Air, water, and children are, indeed, precious resources. However, protecting the environment and improving schools are two topics that would be better addressed by two separate arguments. Try to pick *one* side of *one* issue and take a stand. Make sure your "pyramid" has a focused point.

Practice 4: Making A Claim

For each topic, write a statement of fact and a claim statement. Make it clear that they are different types of statements.

1. Topic: placing parental advisory stickers on music CDs

    Fact: *There is a great deal of controversy over placing parental advisory stickers on music Cds.*

    Claim: *Record companies should not place Parental Advisory stickers on music CDs.*

2. Topic: a year-round school calendar

    Fact: _____

    _____

    Claim: _____

    _____

3. Topic: high salaries of professional athletes

    Fact: _____

    _____

    Claim: _____

    _____

4. Topic: using cell phones while driving

    Fact: _____

    _____

    Claim: _____

    _____

5. Topic: protecting wildlife from construction of new houses on forest land

Fact: _____

_____

Claim: _____

_____

Support the Claim

The entire structure of a pyramid comes to a focused point at the top. Each and every block of the pyramid supports this point. In a similar way, you want each and every sentence of your argument to support your claim. You also want to support your argument with "solid blocks," so it will stand. A **strong argument** is supported by good logic, solid evidence, and appropriate reasons or examples. A **weak argument** suffers from poor logic, weak evidence, and **fallacies** (faulty reasons or examples). Like a pyramid, a strong argument will stand the test of time.

Read the following two passages about weight loss, and decide whether the arguments are strong or weak.

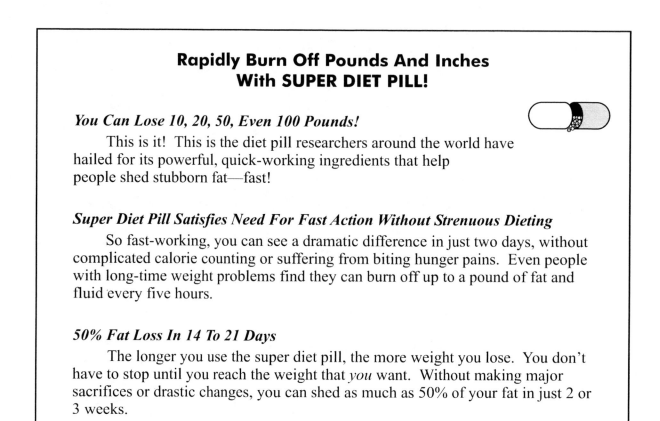

Rapidly Burn Off Pounds And Inches With SUPER DIET PILL!

You Can Lose 10, 20, 50, Even 100 Pounds!

This is it! This is the diet pill researchers around the world have hailed for its powerful, quick-working ingredients that help people shed stubborn fat—fast!

Super Diet Pill Satisfies Need For Fast Action Without Strenuous Dieting

So fast-working, you can see a dramatic difference in just two days, without complicated calorie counting or suffering from biting hunger pains. Even people with long-time weight problems find they can burn off up to a pound of fat and fluid every five hours.

50% Fat Loss In 14 To 21 Days

The longer you use the super diet pill, the more weight you lose. You don't have to stop until you reach the weight that *you* want. Without making major sacrifices or drastic changes, you can shed as much as 50% of your fat in just 2 or 3 weeks.

Increased Metabolism Means Weight Loss

One-half of the women and one-fourth of the men in the United States are trying to lose weight and become fit. The sad truth is that most of us will regain our original weight in a year or less. What's the real secret for losing weight and keeping it off?

The answer is developing and maintaining a healthy metabolism. Metabolism refers to how the body burns energy. A person with a high metabolism burns more calories than a person with a low metabolism. Consequently, the person who burns more calories has an easier time losing weight. Here are some tips for improving your metabolism and melting away that extra fat:

1) **Drink plenty of water.** Filling up on water decreases the appetite. Three quarts of water each day are ideal.

2) **Don't skip meals, especially breakfast.** Eat small meals every two to three hours. In this way, carbohydrates and protein will not be converted into fat.

3) **Eat fat-burning foods.** Raw vegetables, whole grains, fruits, and legumes are your best choices. Consume fruits between meals for extra energy. This healthy snack won't be converted to fat.

4) **Exercise regularly.** Aerobic exercises like swimming, running, and walking are best. Also try lifting weights–a good muscle builder and fat burner. Exercise before you eat. It will decrease your appetite and increase your metabolism.

Each passage strongly suggests a way to lose weight and provides reasons to support its method of weight reduction. Which one is based on valid reasons, and which one is based on fallacies?

There are two big clues that the diet pill advertisement is based on **fallacies,** false statements: 1) It sounds too good to be true; and 2) It's trying to sell you something. A good rule of thumb is that if it sounds too good to be true, *it is*, and if someone is trying to sell you something, *beware*. Beyond these initial clues, an examination of the evidence shows that the diet pill ad offers very limited information about the diet pill. Little proof is presented to support its dramatic claims. The ad never mentions the names of the diet pill researchers, the people who lost weight, nor where or when the testing was done.

The description of metabolism, however, bases its argument on biological principles that are common knowledge to most people who have taken a biology class. From this basis, it provides logical explanations of how to increase your body's metabolism. The author is not selling anything and is not offering an easy "quick fix." A decision to follow the suggestions for changes in diet would be based on much better information than a choice to try the diet pill.

Three Ways to Build a Strong Argument

1. **Show cause-effect connections between your position and the reasons you use to support it.** Use clear logic and valid facts. Avoid fallacies and use commonly-known, easily proven facts.

2. **Illustrate your point of view with a personal story.** Although each person's experience is different, your reader can understand or empathize with events from your life that illustrate your point of view.

3. **Contrast your choice or position with another.** One way to show the strength of your choice is to show the weakness of another choice.

Practice 5: Analyzing an Argument

Read the following argument for CFLs (compact fluorescent lamps). What is the claim? Is the argument strong or weak? Cite examples from the passage to support your viewpoint.

Light Up Your Life!

The best improvement to our house this year has been the addition of compact fluorescent lamps (CFLs). This, no doubt, sounds like an incredibly boring change. However, if you consider the environmental and economic impact of these little gadgets, it can be quite "enlightening." For example, nearly 99% of the energy used by a regular incandescent bulb is turned into heat. I don't know about you, but I don't think light bulbs are a very efficient way to heat a house. I want light bulbs to give off light. That's what fluorescent lamps use 90% of their energy to do. Another great thing about compact fluorescent lamps is that you hardly ever change them. Unlike traditional light bulbs that last a month or two, CFLs last from 5 to 7 years. Yes, that's years, not months! Of course, these long-lasting bulbs are more expensive to buy than the old bulbs. However, when you add up the money that you save in using less electricity, a CFL pays for itself three times over the course of 5 years. So as you can see, a simple change in your life can have a big impact.

_____

_____

_____

_____

_____

"Increased Metabolism Means Weight Loss" (page 139) is a good example of how to use clear logic and commonly-known facts to build a strong argument. The first story below, "Fire Escape," shows how personal experience can be used to prove a point. The second passage, "Where Are All the Animals?" makes good use of statistics from two different respectable sources. Quoting different sources broadens the base of the argument, making the "pyramid" stronger.

Fire Escape

It may not be fun or even convenient, but every family should develop a fire escape plan and practice it regularly. I never believed this until our fire drills saved our family.

I was so mad when my mom came home from work and announced that we all had to develop and practice a fire escape plan. We had to go outside as quickly as possible from whatever room we were in when Mom rang the bell.

My job was to grab my little brother Josh. We had to meet under the maple tree outside our house. Since there were eleven of us, Mom assigned us numbers in case she would forget our names. I hated practicing these fire drills because we had to do these drills in school, too.

One day after two years of these monthly drills, my sister, Carolyn, was playing with logs in the fireplace. Sparks jumped out of the fire and started burning up the living room carpet. Eagerly, the flames licked the furniture and the wallpaper. Smoke filled all of the rooms, setting off our twelve smoke detectors. It was our familiarity with the escape plan that saved our lives, valuables, and even our pets, Fluffy and Foofoo. Unlike our neighbors who had lost all of their valuables in a fire, we were able to save many important pictures and jewelry that had been in our family for decades. After this bad experience, I was very glad we had practiced our fire escape plan.

Where Are All the Animals?

Many people believe that Mother Nature can just take care of herself, but in reality, many life forms on Earth are in trouble. Worldwide, approximately 34% of fish, 25% of mammals, 11% of birds, 20% of reptiles, and 25% of amphibians are on the World Conservation Union (IUCN) Red List of species threatened with extinction. "Currently, we are driving species extinction up to 1000 times faster than the natural rate, which is one in a million per year," says Stuart Pimm, Ph.D., Professor of Conservation Biology at Columbia University in New York. These alarming statistics show how important it is for concerned citizens to support legislation such as the United States Endangered Species Act.

Practice 6: Supporting A Claim

Choose three topics from Practice 4: Making a Claim, and choose an audience for each topic. Then, write two ideas you would use to support the claim statement you wrote for Practice 4: Making a Claim.

1. Topic: _parental advisory on CDs_   Audience: _parents_

    Support: a. _Record companies and parents probably have different standards._

    b. _After listening to the music, parents can discuss it with children._

2. Topic: _____   Audience: _____

    Support: a. _____

    ·b. _____

3. Topic: _____   Audience: _____

    Support: a. _____

    b. _____

4. Topic: _____   Audience: _____

    Support: a. _____

    b. _____

Answer Objections

Knowing your audience not only helps you choose an appropriate language and tone, but it also helps you anticipate objections to your position that your audience may have. Answering these possible objections is like building a wall around your pyramid to protect it from anyone who may want to tear it down.

Let's say that you wanted to go out dancing on Saturday night until 1:00 a.m. Your parents want you home by midnight. You would have to answer their objection to staying out until 1:00 a.m. Since your audience is your parents, you would have to decide how you could convince them to let you dance for one more hour. Think of three ways you would respond to their objection. Would you use impassioned pleas, logical reasoning, or an objective third person's opinion? What type of language and tone works best with your audience? This is a good question to ask yourself before you begin any persuasive writing.

Read the following passage regarding capital punishment, and decide which objections the author is trying to answer.

No More Executions

I want to applaud the governor of Illinois for his recent decision to stop all executions in his state until further review of the capital punishment system. Contrary to popular belief, capital punishment is not a deterrent to crime. In fact, statistics show that states without capital punishment had a lower rate of violent crime in 1999: 3.6 murders per 100,000 persons. States with capital punishment had a higher rate of violent crime in 1999: 5.5 murders per 100,000 persons. Some people claim that the appeals process takes too long, and that's why the death penalty is not a deterrent. However, the Death Penalty Information Center reports that 21 condemned inmates have been released from death row since 1993. This includes seven from the state of Illinois. We cannot risk the execution of innocent people by speeding up the appeals process. The lengthy appeals process also makes capital punishment very expensive. Anyone who has been in a court case knows how much lawyers cost. Those who do not want tax money wasted on criminals should oppose capital punishment because it is actually more expensive to execute someone than to imprison him or her for life. Overall, the system is terribly flawed. The other 38 states with capital punishment laws should join Illinois in placing a moratorium on all executions.

The author of this passage opposes capital punishment and wants to convince others to oppose it as well. In doing so, the writer addresses three popular reasons that others use for supporting the death penalty:

1. capital punishment deters crime;

2. capital punishment would be a deterrent if the appeals process were shorter; and

3. execution is less expensive than life imprisonment.

The author answers these objections to her argument with statistics, authoritative information, and common sense.

> **The three steps to building an argument are to make a claim, to support the claim, and to answer objections.**

Practice 7: Answering Objections

Return to Practice 6: Supporting a Claim. For each topic you chose, list possible objections to your claim.

1. *1) The stickers prevent parents and children from listening to obviously objectionable music. 2) Parents should listen to all the music of their children and decide which music is acceptable.*

2. _____

3. _____

4. _____

Practice 8: Writing Persuasive Paragraphs

Write a persuasive paragraph for each of the three topics you have been working with in Practices 4 and 6. Here's an example:

> *Parents should not rely on record companies to decide what music their children should or should not buy. Each parent has different standards for what kind of music is appropriate for his or her children. Some people say that parental advisory stickers will "weed-out" the really rude music. However, couldn't this also lull parents into a false sense of security, tempting them to rely only on the record companies? When parents listen to what their children are hearing, they can then discuss the music with their children. If parents don't think they have time for this, then they should re-examine their priorities. Parents have the responsibility for raising their own children. They can't let the record companies do it.*

ETHICAL ARGUMENTS

Ethical arguments deal with issues regarding what is right or wrong. Some people consider ethical positions to be matters of opinion rather than true arguments. However, in the last section, you read an example of an ethical argument against the death penalty. The author supported her argument with statistics, authoritative information, and common sense. It was more than a matter of opinion that the death penalty is ineffective.

It is true that an ethical argument is based on certain **assumptions** (ideas, facts, or principles that the author believes are true). However, every argument is based on certain assumptions. Every argument makes a claim, and a claim is a position that the author believes is right. It must be explained and supported with evidence. It is not a self-evident truth or fact. Therefore, you can use the same skills you practiced in the last section to build a strong ethical argument

Read the following two arguments regarding abortion, and write down what you think are the assumptions of the authors. Then, compare your responses with the answers that follow each argument.

Stop Child Abuse

The cruelty of abortion must be stopped. As American citizens, we have many laws against child abuse. In fact, state governments have the legal power to take children away from their parents if a social worker shows that they are being mistreated. Yet, in this same country, the same governments have passed laws that allow parents to kill their children before they are born. The law does not protect children from abuse in their first home: the mother's womb. There is terrible inconsistency in how our laws treat children before and after they leave the womb. What if a mother, father, or doctor smothered a child the day after he or she was born? The adults involved would be arrested, sent to jail, and perhaps face execution. What about before the child is born? Then, it's called "abortion" and everything is legal. Please write to your representatives and demand that they pass laws to protect innocent children.

Author's Claim _____

Author's Assumptions _____

_____

All arguments are trying to prove a point, and it makes no difference if the point rests on an ethical assumption or not. It still needs to be argued. Just because a position is ethical doesn't mean it falls under the category of opinion or emotion.

Ethical assumptions: all people have a right to health care, abortion is a justification for killing, all men are created equal, and human life begins at conception.

Protect Women's Rights

The United States government has an obligation to protect a woman's right to make choices about her own body. What could be a deeper violation of democratic ideals than for the government to control a woman's reproductive decisions? In no other area of law is there a question about a person's right to make decisions about his or her own body. Lack of control over one's own body is a throwback to the days of slavery. Today, medical procedures are decided between the patient and the doctor. The government has no place in these decisions. This is true of decisions for men, and it should be the same for women. Our country claims to provide "liberty and justice for all." Women have as much of a right to liberty and justice as men. The Supreme Court has ruled that women have the right to make their own reproductive choices. Please make sure that your representatives know that you want to keep it that way.

Author's Claim _____

Author's Assumptions _____

_____

You may have written that the author of "Stop Child Abuse" approves of government interference in the lives of its citizens, while the author of "Protect Women's Rights" opposes government interference. This is what appears to be the difference on the surface. However, there is an assumption that lies under these two opposing views. The first author assumes that a developing human fetus is a child even before it is born. The author of the second passage assumes that the developing fetus is part of the woman's body. These two authors will continue to talk past each other until they address their underlying assumptions which are basic to both of their arguments.

Practice 9: Ethical Arguments

Take a position on two ethical problems. Write a paragraph in which you defend your opinion. Then, list your underlying assumptions. The topics below are suggestions.

animal experimentation
euthanasia
sending economic aid to devastated countries

cheating on tests in school
genetically modified food
sex before marriage

SAMPLE TOPIC AND ASSUMPTIONS

End Animal Torture

Even though medical experimentation on animals may sometimes produce health benefits for humans, it also brings into question our own humanity. The word "humane" means to be concerned about the welfare of other humans, but doesn't this also extend to animals?

Build strong ethical arguments in the same way you would other arguments.

APPEALING TO EMOTIONS

The arguments discussed so far have appealed to readers' logical reasoning and their ethics. However, **appealing to the emotions** of your readers can be a powerful force for persuasion.

When you buy new sports shoes, do your parents point out that some generic brands are half the cost of a brand name and that they are just as good? They are **appealing to your rational side** which is concerned with quality and price. However, when you go to school, your friends may laugh at a generic brand of shoes while a name brand may impress them. Your friends will **appeal to your emotions** which are concerned with whether you are "cool" or not. Advertising often appeals to emotion more than to logical reasons, as in the following phrases:

Mega-white toothpaste will give you that knock-out smile.

Twinkling facial cream gets rid of those unsightly wrinkles and makes you look young all over again.

U.S. Motor Company's new Safari sports vehicle gives you the excitement you deserve.

The new Super Wave speakers from Ultrasound let you enjoy theater-like sound without leaving the comfort of your own home.

These advertising claims boast of higher quality, a better value, or an unconditional guarantee. They simply claim that their product will make you feel better. Appeals to emotion may not be based on good reasons, but they can be very convincing.

Emotions are very strong, and, at times they are stronger than reason. So an appeal to emotion may win out over an appeal to reason. For example, Adolf Hitler stirred up Germans' feelings of fear and insecurity during the 1930s. He used these strong emotions to convince his audience that Jewish people and other minorities should be killed. This is one example of how emotions can be a powerful persuasive force.

There are many times, however, when an appeal to emotion is practical, effective, and innocent. Consider the following example.

Sophomores, get ready to show your school spirit at Friday's pep rally. Our school is preparing for the biggest sports event of the year: the homecoming game. In past years, sophomores have not played much of a role, but this year is different. This year, the team's star player is a sophomore! That's right. Without us, the team would not be in contention for the district championship. Let's show the other classes that we deserve respect. Bring your voices, bring your whistles and noise-makers, and make sure you wear the school colors. So, when it's time to show your school spirit, scream as if your life depended on it.

The author of this passage is appealing to the pride of the sophomore class. The author gives an example of why the sophomores should be proud already and encourages them to gain even greater respect in the school by showing great school spirit during the pep rally.

Practice 10: Emotional or Rational Arguments I

Write "E" next to the claims that appeal to emotion and "R" next to the claims that appeal to reason.

_____ 1. The school policy clearly states that students may carry only clear plastic or mesh backpacks.

_____ 2. The backpack rule is a stupid and useless invasion of our privacy.

_____ 3. Standardized tests are a valuable tool to assess student progress in learning.

_____ 4. After your first time riding the cyclone, the thrill will keep you coming back again and again.

_____ 5. Don't get left behind; stay in touch; sign up for a Communicom cell phone today!

_____ 6. The Computech 6500 is rated the fastest, most reliable computer by the three leading computer magazines.

Practice 11: Emotional or Rational Arguments II

For each of the following claims, consider the audience and write whether you would use an emotional or rational appeal. Then, write two sentences you would use to support the claim.

1. Audience: children in kindergarten
    Claim: candy is bad for their teeth

2. Audience: city council members
    Claim: skateboards should be allowed on sidewalks downtown

3. Audience: other students
    Claim: the school mascot should be changed

4. Audience: principal
    Claim   the class trip should be to the Grand Canyon

5. Audience: parents
    Claim: you can see your favorite musical group in concert

6. Audience: pet owners
    Claim: certain breeds of dogs should be banned from cities

7. Audience: high school students
    Claim: earning a high school diploma is important

8. Audience: shoppers
    Claim: shopping on the Internet is better than a trip to the mall

CHAPTER 7 REVIEW: PERSUASIVE WRITING

Read the following two reports. Then, answer the questions below, using complete sentences.

Report 1

The county government meeting broke up after a long debate. Bill Smith's supporters claim that he is the duly elected representative of the people and should be allowed to take his seat on the council. His opponents disputed this, saying that his previous protests of council activities disqualify him from holding public office.

Report 2

We elected Bill Smith, and he's our man. His enemies are just jealous. They think they can throw some mud around and make it stick to Bill. No way! He's squeaky clean. There ain't nothin' they can do to make him look bad. He stood up for us before, makin' sure the council listened to us. Now those jokers say that's a bad thing. Stick by Bill. He stuck by us!

1. What is the author's purpose in each report?

2. Compare and contrast the persuasive language of these two reports. Which report appeals more to emotions? Explain your answer.

Read the following excerpt, and complete the writing exercise that follows.

I stand as firm as the rock of Gibraltar on the right that women have to shape the thoughts, socially and politically, of the world. They can make our country better and purer, just as they appreciate their own rights. I am in favor of women's rights—in their rights to rise up in the majesty of the nature their Creator gave them and emancipate themselves from the foolish fashions and sentiments of the age. When they do rise, they will be more respected by all mankind than all the rulers of the earth from Adam down to the present day.

– Clarissa's speech in *Shams* by John S. Draper

3. Write one paragraph in which you evaluate the language and tone of this excerpt. What are some strengths of the author's choices in language and tone, and what are some weaknesses? How do these affect the persuasiveness of the writing?

Read the following excerpt, and complete the writing exercise on the next page.

There is still a great deal of controversy about the future of the space program. While some people believe it is a waste of much needed funds, others point to the great scientific and technological advances that have resulted from the exploration of space. Supporters of the program most frequently cite the wide uses of microprocessors as one of the major contributions to space-related research. Opponents believe the billions of dollars dedicated to the space program would be better spent on the needs of education, health care, and job training for the poor and disadvantaged.

4. Pick one side of the controversy described in the last passage about the space program, and write a paragraph to persuade other students of your point of view. Share your paragraph with your classmates. Ask for feedback that would strengthen your argument, and incorporate it into your paragraph. Then, write a letter to the President of the United States expressing your opinion. Show the letter to your teacher. Then, mail the letter to President (Full Name), The White House, 1600 Pennsylvania Avenue, Washington, D.C. 20500.

Read the following two letters which nominate Mr. Jimenez for Teacher of the Year. Then, complete the writing exercise that follows.

Dear Fellow Students,

I am nominating Mr. Jimenez for Teacher of the Year, and you should, too. Whether you've been in this school for 1 or 4 years, you know he's got a reputation for being tough. But, he's also known for spending hours after school with kids who need help. (And most of us need help to pass his class.)

You also know how much work he put into the school fair last fall. What a blast that was! Remember how shocked we all were to find out <u>he</u> was the clown?! This is only one way he has shown his love for this school and its students.

Think of how great it would be to hear the announcement that the Teacher of the Year is from Eastside. People across the state would see what a great school we are. So, when the nominating paper comes around, sign it, and show Mr. Jimenez your support.

Thanks,
Bill Johnson

Dear Members of the School Board,

I am writing to nominate Mr. Victor P. Jimenez for Teacher of the Year. As the chair of the Biology Department at Eastside High School, he has challenged his students with a rigorous curriculum and demanding standards of excellence. At the same time, he has shown true devotion as an educator by helping students meet those standards through after school tutoring.

Mr. Jimenez is not only dedicated to academic excellence but also to the development of the school community. Just one example of this is the after school hours he spent in organizing our school's fall fair. During this successful event, Mr. Jimenez showed his sense of humor and surprised us all by dressing up like a clown.

The Teacher of the Year award will honor not only Mr. Jimenez and Eastside High School, but it will honor the State School Board by showing the high educational standards set by this state. Mr. Jimenez provides an example of academic rigor coupled with school spirit that has been an inspiration to our school. He well deserves the title of "Teacher of the Year."

Sincerely,
William H. Johnson

---

5. The same student wrote the above letters about the same topic for the same purpose. However, each letter is addressed to a different audience. Write a paragraph which describes how these two letters differ because of audience. Be sure to discuss language and tone as well as how the letters appeal to emotion and reasoning.

Read the following two letters about trash pick-up, and answer the questions that follow.

To the editor:

This is America! Some people want to decide for me who's going to take my trash away. They say there are too many trash trucks in this neighborhood. Well, my son owns a trash company that services this neighborhood, and he says there're only a few other companies that he competes with, and he should know.

Each resident in this city has the right and the responsibility to choose the trash company that he or she wants. Whichever company provides the best service for the needs of its customers should get the most business. Only in a communist state could it be legal for groups of citizens to band together and limit free choices of consumers and businesses alike. Where would such limitation end? Maybe the different churches shouldn't have their services on the same day because it causes too many cars to drive through the neighborhood.

I whole-heartedly oppose any attempt by the neighborhood association to regulate which company can pick up my family's trash and on what day they can do it. I've been living in this neighborhood for 45 years, and I've never heard of such a ridiculous idea. And, if the neighborhood association tries to pull off such an unfounded scheme, they will find themselves in court!

Your fellow citizen,

Joan Zemsy

Joan Zemsy

To the editor:

Lately, our neighborhood has seemed like a cross between Grand Central Station and the city dump. In the process of gathering information to present to the neighborhood association, I sat by my window and counted the number of garbage trucks that passed in one week: Eleven! An incredible number? I surveyed twenty residents in our neighborhood and found that, in fact, twelve different trash companies are contracted.

I am certainly in support of free enterprise; I believe that freedom of commerce is one of the things that makes America great. However, I also believe in peace and quiet, proper sanitation, and the safety of my children.

I guess I'm lucky that only eleven trucks pass by my house instead of the twelve that could possibly rumble past my door, shaking my windows and rattling my teeth. A trash truck is a huge vehicle which makes a lot of noise when the massive hydraulic compactor goes into action. Once per week this inconvenience may be tolerable, but not two or three times per day.

These trucks also spit out a lot of foul smells and black smoke into the neighborhood. And what about the safety of our children? Should they have to dodge piles of garbage that line our sidewalks every day of the week? And when they ride their bikes to a friend's house, should they fear that from around each corner could come a thundering garbage truck?

Simple common sense demands that all residents of our neighborhood band together to hire one trash company to come once per week to take away our trash.

Sincerely,

James Waterford

James Waterford

---

6. How do the language and appeals differ in the two letters? What are the ethical assumptions behind each argument?

7. Which letter is more persuasive? Why? Explain your answer.

ADDITIONAL ACTIVITIES: PERSUASIVE WRITING

1. In Practice 8 of this chapter, you wrote three different paragraphs on three different topics. Now, write three more paragraphs on the same topics, but each for a different audience. You will want to vary your language and tone, answer different possible objections, and use different support. Return to Practice Exercises 4, 6, 7, and 8 to help you develop your paragraphs.

    The paragraph below is an example of writing to other students about Parental Advisory stickers. Compare this paragraph with the one on page 144.

    Record companies should not place Parental Advisory stickers on music CDs. The record industry wants us to believe it's helping unknowing consumers. As teenagers, we know what is on a CD before we buy it. We hear songs on the radio, talk to friends, watch MTV, and decide what music we want to purchase. If a CD has controversial lyrics we know it, and we know what our parents will not allow. All the music industry is doing is creating controversy and hype over bad music. Some people say the stickers help parents. Well, all parents are different, and they need to listen to the music themselves. Parental Advisory stickers create more sales because of publicity. However, they are not much help to parents and should be removed.

2. Develop three persuasive letters on the same topic but for three different audiences, such as high school students, teachers, your principal, parents, members of the local school board, readers of the local newspaper, or the programming director of a television station. Here are some possible topics with which you can agree or disagree.

    raising the driving age to 18   **offensive bumper stickers**
    voting on the Internet   **sex before marriage**
    using cell phones while driving   **praying in school**
    no homework policy for high school students **prejudice against non-English**
    limited height for high rise buildings   **speakers**
    strict airport security

3. Make a list of 3–4 movies or videos you have seen recently. Choose one of them, and write a composition in which you persuade your readers why they should or should not see the movie.

4. A new student is attending the first day of class in your school. In a 4–5 paragraph essay, advise him or her on how to survive/succeed in your school.

5. Several girls in your high school want to play on the football team. In a 4–5 paragraph composition, convince the coach, the principal, or the school board why these girls should or should not play on the football team.

6. While you were washing your hands in the rest room of the locker room, you saw your best friend sneak into the locker room and steal money from the pants pockets of students who were out in gym class. In a 4–5 paragraph essay, persuade your friend to confess the crime and accept the consequences.

Expository Writing 8

The purpose of **expository writing** is to explain a topic. Essays of this type can include such topics as "Learning on the Internet," "How to Sink a Free Throw Every Time," "Why Skateboarding is Popular," and "What to Look For in a Good Movie." From these examples, you can see that expository writing provides information. It helps us learn more about the world around us.

The word "expository" is related to the word "expose" which means to show and the word "explain" which means to make clear. In expository writing, you can explain how something works or why something happened. You may want to present general information by answering questions like "who, what, when, where, why, and how" about a subject. These key questions are sometimes called the **five Ws and H**. Pointing out similarities and differences between two subjects or ideas is also expository.

You can find expository writing in newspapers, magazines, and on the Internet. Cookbooks, instructional manuals, and schoolbooks include expository writing. Menus, food labels, prescriptions for medicines, billboards, and museum brochures contain expository writing too.

You will need to learn how to write various types of expository essays. You may also be asked to write expository essays as part of your activities in middle or high school English classes.

In this chapter, you will learn and practice writing the following types of expository essays. They are listed below:

1) **A Basic Expository Essay**
2) **Process Essay**
3) **Cause-Effect Essay**
4) **Comparison/Contrast Essay**

BASIC EXPOSITORY ESSAY

In Chapter 3 of this book, you learned about the basic structure of an essay. This structure consists of three main parts: an introduction, a body, and a conclusion. A **basic expository essay** also contains these three parts. Its purpose is to inform or to explain a particular topic.

Let's say that a student named Emmi has a writing assignment. She must write an essay about a particular animal. Since she is being asked to explain or inform her audience about this animal, she would be writing a basic expository essay.

Based on Chapter 3, the **first step for writing** her essay would be to **brainstorm** about the topic. Emmi's brainstorming list looks like this:

Animals I Could Write About

dog	squirrel
cat	parrot
hamster	lizard
rabbit	monkey

The **second step for her essay** is to **choose the animal** that she will discuss. Emmi chose her dog, a purebred Labrador retriever. Once she chose to write about her dog, Emmi moved to **step three, developing the thesis or controlling statement** for her essay. Here is what she wrote for her thesis: **The Labrador retriever is an interesting breed of dog. Learning about this dog can help anyone who wants a Lab for a pet.**

Emmi's Outline

Creating a rough outline, Emmi used the **five Ws and H** to develop the body of her basic expository essay. Here is what she wrote for the outline:

The Labrador Retriever

Who?	Labrador retriever, a type of dog
What?	Size, weight, colors, personality, life span
When?	Feeding times, play time
Where?	Origins
Why?	Benefits of owning a Lab
How?	Treating diseases, puppy care

Emmi's Rough Draft

Now that Emmi has decided on a specific topic, a thesis, and a rough outline, she is ready to write a rough draft of her basic expository essay. As she writes, she will incorporate information from her own experiences with her pet Lab. Read her draft for content, organization, and English language conventions:

The Labrador Retriever

There are many kinds of dogs. Some are big. Some small. They come in many colors too. The Labrador retriever I know best because I own one. The Labrador retriever is an interesting breed of dog. Learning about this dog can help anyone who wants a Lab for a pet.

My veterinarian, Dorothy Howe, says these dogs came from Newfoundland in Canada. The Labrador retriever stands about 2 feet tall. It weighs 60 pounds sometimes 75. Puppies weigh less of course. Howe says a dog should match your personality. So observe a dog before picking one out. So both of you get along. You can also expect Labs to live 8–12 years or longer. depending on keeping up with shots and illnesses.

Care of the Labrador retriever involves regualr feeding. Usually 2 cups of food each day with plenty of fresh water. A high qwuality dog food should be bought. Snacks are ok, but not too many. Labs will overeat if allowed. So don't overfeed them. labs also love to play fetch. So keep a frisbee or rubber bone handy. A Lab are also a very strong. They'll pull you, train it to walk with you and not chase other dogs.

I also know that these dogs can get diseases like dihrea, blindess, worms, especially heartworm, distempr, and hip disease so they deed regulr checkups. A Lab can also get skin infecsin. So be careful. Puppies can die quick if its too cold. So keep it warm. Pups are nice too because they play a lot. He knows you right from birth.

Lab retrievers are an animal that eevery one likes. They're playful, loyal, and good hunting dogs too. I look into my dog's eyes and see smart and lovable eyes. That's what I know about Labs.

Practice 1: Evaluating a Draft of a Basic Expository Essay

Reread Emmi's rough draft on the Labrador retriever. Then, answer the following questions.

1. What makes Emmi's essay expository? Cite examples from her rough draft.

2. On your own or in a group, evaluate the content and organization of Emmi's essay on the Labrador retriever. List the strengths of this essay. Suggest ways that Emmi could improve the content and organization of her essay.

3. Review Emmi's essay for sentence variety. Does she vary the types of sentences she uses in her essay? Or are the sentences similar? Would you change her sentences? How?

4. Read Emmi's essay for correct use of English language conventions. What changes would you make in grammar, spelling, and punctuation?

Emmi's Revision

After feedback from other students and her teacher, Emmi wrote the following revision of her basic expository essay on the Labrador retriever:

The Labrador Retriever

Dogs come in many sizes, shapes, and colors. Some dogs are large while others are small. I own a Labrador retriever which is an interesting breed of dog. Learning about this dog can help anyone who wants a Lab for a pet.

My veterinarian, Dorothy Howe, says Labrador retrievers originally came from Canada. These dogs stand about 2 feet tall and weigh between 60 and 75 pounds. They come in either black, yellow, or chocolate, and they are sometimes used for bird hunting. Howe says the personality of a Lab should match that of the dog's owner, so, before choosing a Lab, a person should observe its personality and behavior. Labrador retrievers can live 8–12 years or longer depending on the owner's attention to their health.

Care of the Labrador retriever involves regular feeding, usually two cups of food each day with plenty of fresh water. Dog experts recommend a high quality dog food with a few nutritious snacks now and then. Labs should never be allowed to overeat. Labrador retrievers love to play fetch, so always keep a frisbee or rubber bone handy. Labs are also very strong dogs who will drag you along on their leash unless they are trained to walk with you. They also must learn not to chase other dogs or cars.

I learned that Labrador retrievers can get diarrhea, worms, especially heartworm, and distemper. They also can become blind, get hip disease or a skin infection. They need checkups and shots on a regular basis. As puppies, Labs can die quickly if they become too cold. Both puppies and adult Labs are fun-loving, affectionate, and protective of their owners.

Most people enjoy Labrador retrievers. They're playful, loyal, and good hunting dogs too. When I look into my Lab's eyes, I see a smart and lovable dog. That's what makes him interesting to me.

Practice 2: Evaluating a Revision of a Basic Expository Essay

Reread Emmi's revision of her expository essay on the Labrador retriever. Then, answer the following questions.

1. Compare Emmi's revision of her essay with her rough draft. What improvements did she make in her revision?

2. Based on your answers to Practice 1, did Emmi make changes in content, sentences, and English language conventions? Explain.

> When writing a basic expository essay, you can use the five Ws and H to guide you in explaining a particular topic.

Practice 3: Writing Basic Expository Essays

To build your writing proficiency, write 2–3 basic expository essays. Organize each essay into 4–5 paragraphs. Use Emmi's revised essay on the Labrador retriever as a model. Follow the writing steps of choosing your topic, brainstorming, developing your thesis, creating a rough outline, writing a rough draft, making corrections, and revising your essay. Decide on your own topics, or select some of the following topics:

an animal	a sport
an athlete	an entertainer
a book	a movie
a restaurant	a car
a hobby	a store
a place	a fad
a food	a planet

If you wish, use the following questions based on the five Ws and H as a guide for writing your basic expository essay.

> What is the title of your essay?
> State your thesis.
> What will you explain about your topic?
> When or where did you learn about your topic?
> Why are you writing about this particular topic?
> How will you explain your topic?
> Express your concluding statement.

After you complete each essay, share it with your teacher or with other students for feedback. Then, revise each essay as needed.

A PROCESS ESSAY

Have you ever followed a recipe while preparing a meal or a dessert? Or perhaps you have taken lessons to learn the steps for a new dance. You may even have taught someone else a game or how to administer first aid. For each of these activities, you followed a process, a step-by-step procedure. These steps also occur in a time sequence.

The purpose of a **process essay** is to explain how to do something or how to make something. A process essay can also include an explanation of how something works such as how the heart pumps blood through the body or how a tiny computer chip processes many bits of information.

Like the basic expository essay, a process essay consists of an introduction, body, and conclusion. It includes a thesis in the introduction and two to three body paragraphs. Sentence variety is also important.

In addition, a process essay contains the following key features:

- **focused step-by-step instruction**
- **a clear and logical sequence**
- **frequent transitional words that lead the reader from one step to the next step**

Now, let's begin by looking at a simple paragraph example that explains how to cut grocery bills.

You can follow several easy steps to cut the cost of groceries. **First**, purchase generic or store brands of groceries instead of the popular brands advertised on television or magazines. Cereal, peanut butter, and canned vegetables with store-brand labels are usually of the same quality as widely advertised national brands. **Next,** clip money-saving coupons from newspapers and magazines to save on your grocery bill. **Thirdly,** buy groceries in bulk sizes to cut per-item expenses. **Furthermore,** shop for fresh fruits and vegetables when they are in season to reduce your grocery bill. **Finally,** bring a shopping list with you to the supermarket and stick to it. In this way, you will avoid buying something on impulse which can raise your grocery bill.

Notice how, even in this simple example, this student presents each step clearly and logically. The **topic sentence**, the first sentence of the paragraph, alerts the reader that steps for cutting the grocery bill will be the focus of the paragraph. In addition, the student uses several **transitional words** to guide the reader easily from one step in the process to the next step. Words like **first**, **next**, **third**, **furthermore**, and **finally** help the reader see the progression of steps.

In Chapter 4 of this book, you learned that **transitional words** help the reader understand the relationship between the writer's ideas. The list below presents transitional words that you can use to explain a process.

first, second, third, etc	furthermore
next	finally
also	later
in addition	after that
then	besides

Explaining a process involves clear steps in a logical sequence with transitional words for each step.

Practice 4: Analyzing a Process

Complete the following activities to improve your understanding of the process essay.

1. Introduce the topic that matches the sentences below. Then, put these steps in a logical sequence with transitional words.

    Do the same for the other slice using jelly.
    Open the jar of peanut butter.
    Put two slices of bread on a plate.
    Take a bite and enjoy.
    Put the slices together so the peanut butter and jelly are completely touching.
    With a knife, spread the peanut butter on one side of one slice of bread.

2. In the following exercise, use each outline to practice writing steps in a process. Limit your explanation to one paragraph. As a guide, the transitional words are provided for you. Use the suggested topics shown below, or choose your own topics.

    how to wash your hands properly   how to program a VCR to record
    how to make a milkshake or a smoothie   how to play a game
    how to wash a car   how a hair dryer works
    how to fly a kite   how to do a dance (choose one)
    how to catch a fish   how to choose the right skateboard
    how to get an autograph of a musician   how to live a healthier lifestyle

A. Title of Paragraph

   _____

   Topic Sentence

   _____,

   _____

   First

   _____

   _____

   Next

   _____

   _____

   Third

   _____

   _____

Then

_____

_____

Finally

_____

_____

B. Title of Paragraph

_____

Topic Sentence

_____

_____

First

_____

_____

Next

_____

_____

Third

_____

_____

Then

_____

_____

Finally

_____

_____

3. Read the process essay below on sinking a free throw. Then, answer the questions that follow.

How to Sink a Free Throw Every Time

The sure-fire way to sink a free throw every time is to practice, practice, practice. A basketball free throw is just what it sounds like: an opportunity to toss the ball through the hoop while you are free from other players trying to distract you. You just stand at the free throw line (fifteen feet from the basket), with no other players defending you, and take a shot. It should be easy but many players miss because they don't practice the essential elements of free-throw shooting.

The first thing you want to do is to relax. Free throws are the easiest shots in the game, so just take it easy and let your practice pay off. When you practice your shot, set your feet shoulder width apart with your shooting foot slightly forward of the other foot. In other words, if you shoot with your right hand, put your right foot slightly forward. Then, you should look at the hoop to let your eyes register the distance. This lets your brain know where you want the ball to go.

After you bounce the ball a few times to relax your shooting muscles, hold the ball gently but with confidence. Make sure your shooting hand is directly under the ball and your elbow is pointing down at your knee. Then, look again at the hoop, take a deep relaxing breath, bend your knees, and take your shot. After you release the ball, remember to follow through with your fingers pointing toward the hoop, and watch the ball "swish" through the net.

Finally, repeat these steps, establish a routine that works for you, and practice it regularly. Stand in the same place on the free throw line. Bounce the ball the same number of times. Take your breath at the same time. Keep your routine the same. In this way, every time you step up to the free throw line, you don't have to think. Your body goes on automatic pilot, and you sink the free throw every time!

What is the topic for the paragraph above?

Topic _____

List all the steps. Then, put them in order by writing the numbers next to each step.

_____ _____

_____ _____

_____ _____

_____ _____

_____ _____

_____ _____

_____ _____

_____ _____

Write any key terms that the author uses and explains.

_____

_____

What transitional words does the author use?

_____

_____

Now that you have analyzed the essay on sinking a free throw, you can use a similar process for creating your own steps that explain a process. Choose a topic, and then list the steps.

Topic _____

List all the steps. Then, put them in order by writing the numbers next to each step.

_____ _____

_____ _____

_____ _____

_____ _____

_____ _____

_____ _____

_____ _____

Write any key terms that you need to explain.

_____

_____

What transitional words can you use?

_____

_____

Practice 5: Writing Process Essays

For practice, write 2–3 process essays. Organize each essay into 4–5 paragraphs. For a model, use the essay "How to Sink a Free Throw Every Time." Choose your topic, brainstorm, develop a thesis, create a rough outline, write a rough draft, make corrections, and then revise each essay. Decide on your own topics, or choose some of the following topics:

how parents and teenagers can communicate better
how to solve school conflicts based on race or culture
how to celebrate a birthday
how teachers and students can communicate better
how to make someone laugh
how to conduct a lab experiment in science class

how to care for a pet
how to prevent tardiness
how to pack for a rafting trip
how to waste time
how to reduce stress
how to fix a flat tire

If you wish, use the following outline as a guide for developing your process essay. Combine one or more steps into paragraphs as needed.

Title of Essay
Thesis
First Step
Second Step

Next Step
Fourth Step, etc.
Final Step
Concluding Statement

After you finish each process essay, seek feedback from your teacher or from other students. Revise it as needed.

A CAUSE-EFFECT ESSAY

Using **cause and effect** is another way to explain a topic. Both cause and effect involve ways of showing relationships between one event or idea and another event or idea. Let's say that one morning you notice that a classmate is extremely cheerful, singing and telling jokes on the way to school. You are curious about this unusual behavior. You wonder why this person is acting so cheerfully. As a result of this experience, you soon find that you are feeling happy too. Later that morning, you learn that your classmate entered a contest and won a free computer. In this example, you can see how cause and effect work. You were curious about why your classmate was acting so cheerfully. You were trying to determine the cause of her happiness. Later, you found out the cause—winning a free computer. The effect or result of this good news was that you felt happy too.

The cause is the reason for an event, and the effect is the result of the event.

The purpose for writing a cause-effect essay is to explain relationships between issues, ideas, or events. These cause-effect relationships impact us, our friends, our community, and our world. For example, forgetting to put out the trash on time (cause) can affect you and others. The importance of graduating from high school requires that you understand the reasons and advantages (causes) of completing high school and the negative effects (results) of dropping out of high school. To reduce drug addiction, researchers must study the causes and effects of this social problem. To stop world terrorism, countries must investigate why terrorism occurs (causes) and its impact (effects) on humanity.

In the following diagram, notice how one cause can lead to an effect, which itself becomes the cause for another effect, and so on.

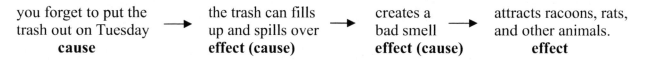

cause ⟶ effect (cause) ⟶ effect (cause) ⟶ effect

Now, study the following diagram that Kurt created to show the causes and effects of his not putting out the trash on time. Notice how the main event (forgetting to put out the trash) has both causes and effects. As you read Kurt's diagram, think of other reasons (causes) and results (effects) of his action. See an example of this below.

| you forget to put the trash out on Tuesday | ⟶ | the trash can fills up and spills over | ⟶ | creates a bad smell | ⟶ | attracts racoons, rats, and other animals. |
| **cause** | | **effect (cause)** | | **effect (cause)** | | **effect** |

As an aid for his brainstorming about causes and effects, Kurt created the following **Cause-Effect Map** on forgetting to put out the trash on time.

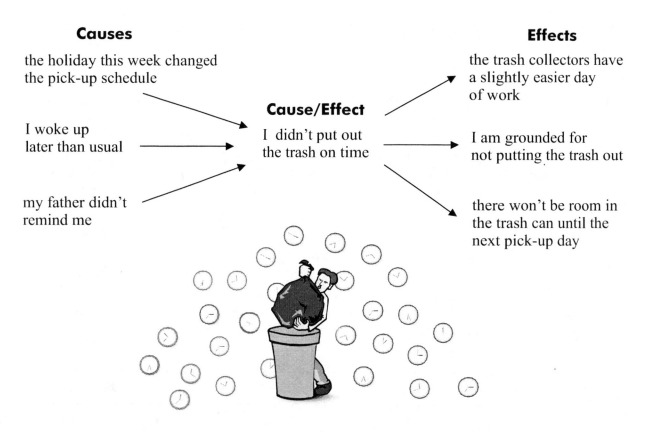

Causes

the holiday this week changed the pick-up schedule

I woke up later than usual

my father didn't remind me

Cause/Effect

I didn't put out the trash on time

Effects

the trash collectors have a slightly easier day of work

I am grounded for not putting the trash out

there won't be room in the trash can until the next pick-up day

Practice 6: Brainstorming Causes and Effects

A. Using Kurt's cause-effect map as a model, brainstorm about causes and effects for three or more of the topics below. Or choose some of your own topics. Next, discuss your diagrams with a partner or with a group of other students. See if they can add any more causes or effects to your diagram. Then, share your findings with the class or your teacher.

exercise	dirty laundry
surfing	poverty
earthquakes	volunteering
overspending	stress
family harmony	family conflict
new hairstyles	tattoos
messy room	good grades
success	gossip

In the beginning of this chapter, you learned that expository essays present or explain information about a particular topic. When you write a cause-effect essay, you can explain just causes, just effects, or a combination of both causes and effects. The audience and purpose of your essay determine what your focus will be. For example, if your purpose is to explain the dangers of smoking, and your audience is composed of teenagers, you will probably focus on the unhealthy effects of smoking. If your purpose is to explain the reasons why teenagers smoke, and your audience is a group of parents, you might stress the causes of smoking. If your purpose is to explain the reasons and dangers of smoking, and your audience is made up of both teenagers and adults, you can discuss both causes and effects of smoking.

In the following sample essay, notice how the writer focuses on the reasons (causes) for tardiness. After you read this essay about causes, complete the activity that follows it. This essay also contains some key words that signal that the author intends to explain the causes of being late. Underline these words as you read this essay.

Why Are Some People Late?

There are many different reasons why people are late getting somewhere. The first thing that makes people late is incorrectly estimating how long it takes to do something. For example, if you think it will only take you 15 minutes to ride your bike to school, and it really takes you 30 minutes, then you will be late to school. Another thing that prevents people from being on time is getting distracted from the task at hand. If you stop  to talk to someone while you are riding your bike to school, you may lose track of time and end up being late for school. Getting distracted happens much more easily if you don't have a watch on. Not having a watch or a clock nearby prevents people from knowing what time it is, and can lead to tardiness.

The last thing that can make people late is something called "unforeseen circumstances." An example of "unforseen circumstances" is a flat tire. If you get a flat tire on your way to school, you probably won't have a repair kit with you which means you will have to walk to school. Walking takes a lot longer than riding a bike, so guess what? You're going to be late.

As you can see, even if you do everything right to be on time, including planning enough time for travel, not getting distracted, and keeping an eye on your watch, your plans for being on time can still be undermined by the dreaded "unforseen circumstances." Even if you make every attempt to be on time, there are events that you just can't plan on. Everyone is late once in a while, so estimate time correctly, don't get distracted, and keep an eye on the clock. With this plan, your chances for being on time will improve.

B. **The paragraph describes four general causes for one specific effect. Write these on the lines below.**

Effect _____

Cause _____

Cause _____

Cause _____

Cause _____

Which words in this essay show that the writer is focusing on the reasons (causes) for being late? Here are some words you should have found: **why, reasons, then**. The writer uses these key words to focus on the causes of tardiness. Look below for a list of key words that writers use when they are explaining causes or effects in an expository essay.

Causes	
reason	basis
why	due to
because	therefore, thus
source	

Effects	
result	outcome
consequence	affect
therefore, thus	impact
product	

Practice 7: Writing Cause-Effect Essays

For practice, write 2–3 cause-effect essays. Each essay can focus on causes or on effects. Organize each essay into 4–5 paragraphs.

For a model essay that presents causes, review the essay "Why Are Some People Late?" For a model essay that explains effects, read the essay on the next page entitled "Consequences of Pursuing a Rich Lifestyle." Use the topics you developed in Practice 6, or create some new ones of interest to you.

Brainstorm, develop a thesis, create a rough outline, write a rough draft, make corrections, and then revise each essay. Whenever possible, use key words to signal the purpose of your discussion. If you wish, use the following outlines as a guide for writing your cause or your effect essay.

Essay About Causes	**Essay About Effects**
Title	Title
Thesis	Thesis
First Cause	First Effect
Second Cause	Second Effect
Third Cause	Third effect
Concluding Statement	Concluding Statement

After you complete each cause or effect essay, seek feedback from your teacher or from other students. Revise each essay as needed.

Sample Student "Effects" Essay

Consequences of Pursuing a Rich Lifestyle

A big majority of people in the world dream of being rich, but only a few of them will realize their dream. The reason why most people struggle financially is because they want to look rich, even if they are not. This behavior can be very dangerous; indeed, people are willing to do anything to achieve their goal. We will see later in this essay what the consequences of pursuing a rich lifestyle really are.

One of the most common consequences of pursuing a rich lifestyle is the financial struggle. I remember one of my father's friends who used to change his car every three months. Even though he didn't have enough money to finance this kind of expense, he continued doing so until he ended up selling his house to pay off the debts he had. Even after that, he got so used to spending incredible amounts of money that he couldn't handle the fact that he had no money left. The shock was so big for him that he got a cancer and died two years later, leaving huge debts for his son.

The second consequence of pursuing a rich lifestyle, that I have seen as being worse than the first one, is related to stealing. I had a friend in Morocco whose parents "lived well," were not rich, but had enough money to send their son to a good school, and enough extra to go on holiday to Paris every summer. My friend used to come with us to a nightclub every Saturday. He was used to stealing money from his parents just to feel rich and buy us some dinners. Even today, he still steals money from his father to go out on Saturday nights. That is, in my opinion, the worse thing that a child can do to his parent. And once again, he did that only because he wanted to feel rich.

The last consequence of pursuing a rich lifestyle, that I have noticed, is that some people lose their personality. Indeed, they are so possessed by money that they will do anything just to have some of it. A friend of mine told me one day about a guy who used to study in France. This guy used to work every day and every night at two different places, so that he could save some money in order to go to clubs when he returned to Morocco and buy fancy clothes that cost more than a hundred dollars. These kinds of guys are not themselves anymore because they don't live for themselves. They live for people; they live to prove to other people that they can afford some "stupid" expenses like the one I talked about.

Therefore, I will conclude by saying that people react differently to different situations and behaviors, but pursuing a rich lifestyle can affect people in a negative way. The main problem still is that these people don't have a strong personality to affirm themselves as they are. They try to act rich, and the consequences are that they hurt themselves and others.

A COMPARISON-CONTRAST ESSAY

The words comparison-contrast sound complicated, but you compare and contrast things more often than you think. For example, when stopping for fast food, you may compare taste, quantity, or price before deciding on which menu item you will buy. Comparing style, comfort, and mileage can help you select one car over another car. You probably choose the friends you hang out with based on how similar all of you are in the hobbies you share, the music you enjoy, or the places you like to go.

The purpose of a **comparison-contrast** essay is to explain the similarities and differences between two things or ideas. Therefore, it is another type of expository essay because you are trying to inform or explain a topic to your audience. You are presenting a new view of things, people, or ideas by **comparing** (showing how they are alike) and **contrasting** (showing how they are different) from each other. This type of expository writing can also provide more understanding or new insights about a topic.

While you can just compare or contrast two things, it is more common to link the two together in an essay. In addition, when you compare or contrast two things, they must have something in common. A cat and a bowl of spaghetti share little in common other than that the cat might decide to eat the spaghetti when you aren't looking. However, a cat and a rabbit do share some common characteristics. They are both animals, they have fur, and they are kept as pets. Therefore, finding something in common (compare) or not in common (contrast) is an important starting point for comparing and/or contrasting two persons, things, or ideas.

> **When you compare and contrast, you show similarities and differences between two persons, things, places, or ideas.**

Brainstorming to Compare and Contrast

Let's say that your assignment was to compare and contrast cats and rabbits. A good way to begin would be to try **brainstorming** about your topic. One way to brainstorm would be to create three columns. In the first column, you would list what cats and rabbits share in common. In the second column, you would list what is different about cats, and in the third column, you would list what is different about rabbits. Here is an example:

Cats and Rabbits

Share in Common	Cats Only	Rabbits Only
animals	cat family	rodent family
fur	coarse fur	soft fur
ears	short, pointed ears	long, narrow ears
eyes	small, narrow eyes	large, round eyes
tail	long, narrow tail	round, stubby tail
movement	running, leaping	crawling, hopping
eating	eats other animals	eats plants
kept for pets	family pets	pets and food
hunt for food	climb trees	can't climb trees

Another way to brainstorm about cats and rabbits would be to use a **Venn diagram**. A Venn diagram can help you organize ideas that are similar and different. You simply draw two ovals that overlap. In each oval, you list the details that are different for each subject you are comparing. Where the ovals overlap, include the details that both subjects share in common. To understand this type of brainstorming, study the following Venn diagram that again compares and contrasts cats and rabbits:

A Cats
cat family
coarse fur
short, pointed ears
small, narrow eyes
long, narrow tail
running, leaping
eats other animals
family pets
climb trees

C Both
animals, fur
ears, eyes
tail, movement
pets, eating
hunt for food

B Rabbits
rodent family
soft fur
long, narrow ears
large, round eyes
round, stubby tail
crawling, hopping
eats plants
pets and food
can't climb trees

You can also create an **H-map** to brainstorm about the similarities and differences about two topics. An H-Map is a simple diagram shaped like the letter H. In the bridge of the H, you list the similarities. In each column of the H, you list the differences. Make sure you label each column with the key concept you are comparing and contrasting.

Below is a completed H-map. It shows the similarities and differences between the United States and the USSR (United Soviet Socialist Republics) during World War II and the Cold War.

Differences
US

Similarities

Differences
USSR

- attacked by Japan
- democracy
- free enterprise
- contributed much hardware and technical superiority
- relatively few soldiers killed: 290,000
- in Cold War, pushed for free elections and open markets in many countries

- didn't want to enter WWII
- forced into fighting by sneak attacks
- allies against the Axis powers
- used political and economic means to exert influence in other countries during Cold War
- competed in nuclear arms race

- attacked by Germany
- strict one-party communist rule
- government controlled economy
- few technical contributions to war
- contributed millions of soldiers' lives: 20 million lives lost
- wanted friendly Communist governments installed in former territories

Practice 8: Brainstorming about Similarities and Differences

Brainstorm about similarities and differences for three or more of the following topics, or think of some of your own topics. Brainstorm about these topics using any or all of the following approaches that you learned about: three columns, Venn diagram, or H-map. Share your brainstorming with a partner or group. See if they can add any similarities or differences to your topics. Then, share your work with the class or with your teacher.

a city and a small town	an apple and an orange
an apartment and a house	a car and a motorcycle
you and a cousin	you and a friend
a car and an airplane	football and soccer
a shake and an ice cream cone	a book and a movie
two types of cars	two theme parks
two holidays	two summer jobs
two types of music	two schools
two movies	two entertainers

WRITING A COMPARISON-CONTRAST ESSAY

Like other types of expository essays, a comparison-contrast essay consists of four to five paragraphs written according to the following steps:

Brainstorming about Your Topic and Thesis

Writing a Rough Draft Consisting of the Following:

> **Introductory Paragraph with a Thesis and 2–3 Points to Compare and/or Contrast**
> **Two to Three Body Paragraphs Explaining the Points of Comparison and/or Contrast**
> **A Concluding Paragraph that Summarizes the Thesis and the Key Points of the Essay**

Reviewing and Revising Your Rough Draft for:

> **Content and Organization**
> **Sentence Variety**
> **Grammar, Punctuation, and Spelling**

Writing A Final Draft

To better understand what a comparison-contrast essay is, read the following sample essay in which the author explains how he and his brother are both similar and different:

Two Family Members

My brother Thomas and I are very similar but very different in many ways. Thomas and I grew up together in the same household and shared the same bedroom. Eventually, Thomas got a bedroom of his own after my older brother moved out. But, through the years, he and I have grown very close and have begun sharing goals and hobbies. Also, Thomas and I have developed our own personalities and habits.

I feel Thomas and I are very similar. For example, Thomas and I really enjoy playing sports; both of us played high school football and basketball. He and I have spent many evenings playing basketball together at the gym. In off seasons, Thomas and I have spent a lot of time working out in the weight room. He and I also like staying up late at night and looking at car magazines, and we often talk about having fast cars. On the weekend, we enjoy going to the mall and purchasing nice clothes. Also we both enjoy spending time with our dog. For example, we both like to take the dog for walks or wash him. Every Sunday, Thomas and I go to church. We both feel church is very important. I feel the biggest goal in our life is to succeed in school, and we both work very hard in school.

I feel Thomas and I also have some differences. First of all, Thomas is just starting high school, and I am a junior. I have better communication skill than Thomas. For example, Thomas is quiet around people, and I like to talk to people. Thomas is going to be the richest man in the world. He saves more money than any man I know. However, I can not save money. I spend more money than I make. Also, I would have to say that Thomas is a pig. His room is messy while I could not have a messy room. My room has to be clean. Thomas's personality is different from my personality because he is laid back, and I am very active and outgoing.

Since Thomas and I grew up sharing a room, he and I have grown very close. I feel we have more similarities than differences. For example, he and I will always work hard and enjoy sports. I will never forget all the good times spent with my brother.

Analysis of "Two Family Members"

Notice how the author establishes a clear introduction and a thesis: ". . . he and I have grown very close and have begun sharing common goals and hobbies. Also, Thomas and I have developed our own personalities and habits." From this thesis, we learn that the author is going to compare their "common goals and hobbies" and contrast their "personalities."

In the second paragraph, the author writes about Thomas and his own common interests in sports, cars, clothes, the dog, church, and school. In the third paragraph, the author writes about the differences between him and Thomas in their personality and habits. Thomas is shy while the author is outgoing. The author also keeps a neat, clean room while Thomas's room is messy.

In the final paragraph, the author restates his thesis while expressing that he and his brother are more alike than they are different. In addition, the author has revised and edited his essay, paying attention to correct use of English language conventions in grammar, punctuation, and spelling. He also includes a variety of sentences in his essay.

Use of Transitional Words

In "Two Family Members," you should be aware of the **transitional words** used. These transitional words are often used to compare and contrast ideas. They help to signal the similarities and differences between the author and his brother. These words also help the audience read the essay more easily.

How many transitional words did you find in this essay? Here are several that the author included in "Two Family Members": **similar**, **different**, **same**, **also**, **both**, **than**, **however**, and **while**. When you write a comparison and/or contrast essay, learn to use some of the following transitional words:

COMPARISON	CONTRAST
similar	different
and	but
both	while
alike	unlike
in the same way	however
in addition	in contrast
the same	instead of
also	whereas

Practice 9: Understanding a Comparison or Contrast Essay

For practice in understanding comparison and/or contrast essays, read the essay entitled "My Sister and Me." Then on your own paper, answer the questions that follow.

My Sister and Me

My parents' friends think that it is strange that two children can come from the same parents and be so different. We had the same family, shared the same hobbies, and even shared the same room. When we were little, we looked identical, but as we grow older we don't even look the same. Our personalities are like summer and winter. Even though we are different, we are still sisters and love each other no matter what we look like or how we think.

My sister is five years older than I am. She has always been my big sister. We both have dark hair and brown eyes, but she is almost six feet tall and I am barely 5'5". She stands a whole head and a half taller than I do. That never made much difference except that she could reach things on the top shelf for me. Since she was older, she usually got to do things before I was allowed. She went to high school before I did, but that was nice since she told me what to expect. She got to take horseback riding lessons before I could. That made me jealous, but my time came.

My Big Sister   Me

Even more than our physical features, our personalities are different. I was always good in school, while my sister was always good with horses. I would bring home straight A's on my report card from school, unlike my sister who would bring home championship ribbons from horse shows. I am outgoing and social whereas my sister is an introvert. She would much rather spend time with the horses instead of be with another person.

In summary, even though my sister and I are very different, we are from the same family. Rather than be jealous of each other, we try to share our strengths. She is tall, so she helps me get things I can't reach. I am good in school, so I help her write her papers. She is good with horses, so she gives me riding lessons. Math comes naturally to me, so I help her figure out how much she can save in a store sales event. I guess what's most important is that we will always be there for each other.

1. What is the thesis of this essay? Is the author's focus on comparing or contrasting herself and her sister?

2. List 3–4 examples of comparison or contrast in this essay.

3. Does the concluding paragraph summarize the key points of the essay?

4. List four transitional words that the author uses to connect her ideas together.

5. Has the author paid attention to English language conventions (grammar punctuation, spelling) and sentence variety? Cite examples.

6. Rate this essay on a scale of 1 to 6, with six being the highest and one being the lowest. Use the material in this chapter to develop reasons for the rating you choose to give the essay.

Practice 10: Writing Comparison-Contrast Essays

For practice, write 2–3 comparison and/or contrast essays. Each essay can focus on similarities, differences, or both. For models, review the essays "Two Family Members" and "My Sister and Me." Use the topics you brainstormed about in Practice 8, or you may also create new topics to write about.

Brainstorm, develop a thesis, create a rough outline, write a rough draft, make corrections, and then revise each essay. Use some transitional words to connect your ideas together. If you wish, review the outline in this section of the chapter on Writing a Comparison-Contrast Essay. Use it as a guide for writing your comparison and/or contrast essay.

After you complete each comparison and/or contrast essay, seek feedback from your teacher or from fellow students. Revise each essay as needed.

CHAPTER 8 REVIEW: EXPOSITORY WRITING

To improve your understanding of expository writing, complete the following activities.

1. Find 3–4 examples of expository essays in newspapers, magazines, textbooks, or on the Internet. Try to find essays that are between 400–1000 words. Decide whether each of these essays is primarily a basic expository essay, a process essay, a cause-effect essay, or a comparison-contrast essay. Form a group and make copies of these essays for each member of the group. The group will exchange these essays among the members, and each will respond to the following questions.

    A. Which essay did you enjoy the most? Why?

    B. Which essay did you enjoy the least? Why?

    C. How would you classify each expository essay? Is it a basic expository essay, a process essay, a cause-effect essay, or a comparison-contrast essay? Offer 3–4 examples from the essay to support your answer.

    D. Evaluate each essay by responding to the following questions:

        1) Is the thesis clear and concise?

        2) Does the author support the thesis well? Cite 3–4 examples or reasons from the body paragraphs of the essay.

        3) What transitional words does the author use to connect the ideas together? List 3–4 examples.

        4) Is the essay organized around an introduction, body, and conclusion? Point out examples of each of these parts in the essays.

        5) Are there any pictures, charts, or diagrams in the essays? Do they help or hinder the understanding of key ideas and facts? Explain.

        6) Is the diction (use of words) vivid, concrete, and clear?

        7) Does the author include a variety of sentence lengths to maintain interest in the essays?

        8) Who is the primary audience for the essay? Is there evidence in the essay to support your answer?

        9) Does the author use the English language conventions such as correct grammar, punctuation, and spelling? What might account for any errors you find?

If possible, ask your teacher to model this assignment for you with a sample essay before you begin this assignment in your groups.

2.   Write a process essay consisting of directions to a particular place. Include specific turns, landmarks, and a map for a visual aid. Share your essay with the class, with a small group, or with your teacher. If the place is within walking distance, have members of your group follow your directions to see if they can find the place.

3.   To improve sequencing and processing skills, divide the class into small groups. In two to three pen strokes, each member of the group takes turns drawing a simple design on the same sheet of paper. The designs must be connected so there is only one complete design at the end.

Working from the design, each group writes instructions to another group about how to draw the design. Each group then passes its paragraph of instructions to the next group without seeing the original design.

Reading only the paragraph of instructions, each group then tries to create the design. Groups cannot speak to each other. Students can only talk within their group. After each group completes its design based on another group's written instructions, they can see the original design.

Each group then discusses the following questions:

- How close was the design to the written instructions?

- Decide how accurate the design was compared to the original design.

- If the design was not completely accurate, discuss how the instructions could be improved. Rewrite the instructions so they are more accurate.

- Has someone ever given you wrong instructions or directions? Discuss how this experience affected you.

- Why is it important to provide accurate instructions or directions?

- Suggest ways to improve the writing of instructions or directions.

4.   A foreign student wrote a process essay on this topic: How would you survive a visit to the United States? Read and evaluate this essay on the next page. Rate the essay on a scale of one to six, with one being the lowest rating and six being the highest. Use the material in this chapter to develop reasons for the rating that you choose for this essay.

Suggest ways that the student could improve this essay. Then revise the essay, and share the new version with your class or with your teacher.

How to Survive a Visit to the USA

The first thing that any one that is coming to visite the United State is the launglish. The second thing that the person that is coming here should know that some of the new laws and diffrent rules. As of the last thing Every one should know is how is life here diffrent.

As of the launglish It is the main thing that all people should know. The reason is that it would be hard to comunicat. In the United States the main spoken launglish is English. It would be hard for a Person who lives here to understand What is the Spaken launglish to them.

The person that would come here would have to know some of the rules here in the States. The country that they live in might have diffrent laws and rules to obey every day. The reason could be because if that person want to drive. Or do any thing that would have diffrent laws.

Life is diffrent then any other country so that could make a big diffrance to a lot of people. As of clothing. Also that might be help full because that person that is visiting might fell like living here. So, for that reason they should know.

For a person to visite the United States, for my opinion to them, they should know some one here to help them know the launglish if they speak the same one. The laws that are diffrent. They also need to know if they want to live here how life is diffrent.

5. Lorrie wrote a cause-effect essay for her English class. Her topic was the following: If you could change some things in your life, what would they be? Why would you change them?

    Read and evaluate this essay on the next page. Rate the essay on a scale of one to six, with one being the lowest rating and six being the highest. Use the material in this chapter to develop reasons for the rating that you choose. If corrections are needed, revise the essay. Then, share the revision with your teacher or with the class.

Oh, Grow Up!

I wish I were older so that I could drive and have money for things I want. But since I can't change time, I'll have to figure out how to get the government to change the driving age and the working age.

I want to change the driving age so that I can go places. I live far away from any kind of civilization. Any time I want to go to the mall with my friends, I have to ask my older brother or my parents. My parents are always busy working on something. My brother doesn't want to be seen anywhere with his little sister. He says it would kill his social life. If I could drive myself, I wouldn't have to bother any of them when I wanted to go somewhere. I could go where I want and do what I want. I could even get a job to buy a car and pay for the gas.

If the working age were changed, then I could work to earn money for the things I want. I could buy my own clothes and wouldn't have to wear the things my mom buys for me. I could even buy some things for my family. My dad needs a new briefcase. My mom could use a new cell phone. My brother could use a new attitude, but I can't buy that. He'll have to settle for a new CD burner.

If I were to try to change the ages for driving and working, I would start a campaign. First, I would talk to my friends and tell them my ideas. Then, I would ask them to tell their friends and have their friends tell their friends. Finally, I would get everyone to write letters to their congressman to lower the driving and working ages because kids shouldn't have to wait.

6.   Chad's assignment was to write a comparison and/or contrast essay about himself and another member of his family. He decided to write about himself and his father. Read and evaluate Chad's essay which appears on the next page. Rate the essay on a scale of one to six, with one being the lowest rating and six being the highest. Use the material in this chapter to develop reasons for the rating that you choose.

If any changes are needed, make them. Then share your results with the class or with your teacher.

Like Father—Like Son

My father and I are very close. He has always been the one to teach me the importance of life, and what it has to offer. My dad knows a great deal about life, and for that reason he is the best teacher a son could ever have. My father and I are much alike, but our most comparable attributes are those of being friendly, and being honest.

My father and I share many of the same characteristics, but the most notable one is that of being friendly. Dad has always been the one who starts a conversation. I have tried to followed in his footsteps, and often find myself making the first attempt to start a conversation with all those around me. Telling light jokes is a trait my father has mastered. I find myself coming to school and telling the same jokes, and being the same "class Clown" that my father is. He has always taught me to treat everyone the same, this teaching has become a motto for me. I find myself helping those who are less fortunate. Helping others is a trait my father is famous for, and I hope I can carry on this tradition. Being friendly is a notable characteristic that my father and I both share, and so is that of being honest.

Being honest is a very important attribute in life, and it is one that my father and I both have. My father has spent many hours trying to teach our family about the importance of being honest. Ever since I was a small child my father has taught me to tell the truth. Telling the truth has now become a habit to me. My father would not lie to anyone. He is the most honest man I know. His honesty has effected me greatly. I now find it hard not to tell the truth. I dislike it very much when people lie to me, and I feel that this is a peeve that my father and I both share. I recall when I was a child I accidently broke a lamp. I lied to my father, and did not tell him the real reason why I had done it. He knew that I was lying, and took the opportunity to teach me. From that day on I knew not to tell lies. I am glad that my father has taught me to be honest. I know that being honest is a great attribute that my father and I both posses.

In summary, I know that my father and I are comparable in many ways, but the most notable characteristics are those of being friendly, and being honest. I know that by his example he has taught me a great deal. I hope that one day I can be even more like my father. I pray that one day I can be as good to my future children as he has been to our family.

Narrative Writing   **9**

Since the beginning of civilization, people have enjoyed hearing and telling stories. Some of these stories convey the experiences of ordinary individuals living their lives each day. Other stories recreate the struggles and the triumphs of influential persons and the actions of the deities of a particular culture or society.

Sometimes storytellers use costumes, dances, chants, music, and gestures to recreate an important event or experience in the life of a family member or a great hero. Celebrations of special holidays in a particular culture often include this kind of storytelling.

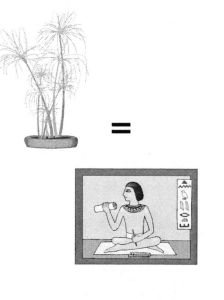

As human beings told their stories over and over again, they would pass down the significant experiences of their personal lives or the history, customs, and traditions of their ancestors. As time went on, various cultures began developing a written language which could be recorded on stone, *papyrus* (writing material made from a grass-like plant that grows in water), cloth, or paper. With these innovations, cultures were better able to preserve their stories and pass them on to their descendants.

WRITING A NARRATIVE

Just as storytellers told their listeners about personal or historical events in their culture, so you, too, will tell your readers about an actual or imagined event in a written narrative.

In this chapter, you will learn how to write a narrative. Writing this narrative involves learning the key steps for this type of writing. Applying and practicing what you learn in this chapter will help you improve your ability to write a successful narrative.

KEY STEPS FOR WRITING A NARRATIVE

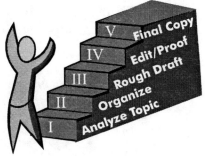

When writing a narrative, follow these simple steps:

STEP I   **Analyze the Writing Topic.**

STEP II   **Organize Your Narrative.**

STEP III   **Write a Rough Draft of Your Narrative.**

STEP IV   **Edit and Proofread the Draft of Your Narrative.**

STEP V   **Write a Final Copy of the Narrative.**

By studying these steps, you can gain a better understanding of how to write a narrative. They can also guide you in the writing process. In this way, you should be more prepared for your writing tests, and you should feel more confident about your ability to write a narrative.

In the next sections of this chapter, you will learn more about the steps for writing a narrative. Study these steps carefully, and practice the activities as you complete each section.

STEP I: Analyze the Writing Topic I

Analyzing the writing topic is the first step in learning how to write a narrative. The **writing topic** helps you think about what you will write. It establishes a focus for your writing. You should read and reread the writing topic carefully. In this way, you will respond only to the stated topic without straying from it.

Now read the following writing topic that would require a narrative response:

Topic For A Writing Sample

> Tell a story about a first time experience such as driving a car, riding a horse, a skateboard, a roller coaster, etc. Develop your story with specific details about the experience.

Identify Your Audience

Once you understand your writing topic, you should **identify your audience**. You will want to use words that most readers would understand, so you should avoid slang or foul language as well as words that are too simple or too difficult.

To illustrate the importance of audience, look at the three sentences below. All of them are about the same topic, but only one of them would appeal to educated adults. Which one is it?

A

When we were persons between the ages of 13 and 19, we would avail ourselves of the contingency of the piscatorial sport at an acquaintance's water-filled cavity in the ground.

B

When we wuz dudes, we'd chill out at our bro's crib and ketch some fish in his mud hole.

C

When we were teenagers, we would go fishing in our neighbor's pond.

If you chose sentence C, you are correct. This sentence captures the reader's interest, and the words are easily understood. Sentence B contains slang and improper English, and the words in sentence A are long-winded and too difficult to understand.

Develop Ideas For The Topic

Notice that this writing topic requires you to **think about a first time experience**.
A good way to prepare for this writing topic is to **brainstorm** (See Chapter 3) about some of your first-time experiences.

Here is how a student named Ben brainstormed for this writing topic:

First Time Experiences I Could Write About

When I played first basketball game   My first date

Time I had to go to the hospital   My wild horseback ride

First fast food job   My first driving lesson

As you can see, Ben has started to brainstorm about some of his first time experiences. Eventually, he decided to write about one of these experiences for his narrative essay. He felt he could write a good narrative about his wild horseback ride.

Practice 1: Brainstorming About First Time Experiences

On your own or in a group, think about some of your favorite first time experiences. If you cannot recall any first time experiences, think about such things as foods, clothes, trips, sports, school, jobs, books, movies, or other topics that will trigger ideas. On a separate sheet of paper, make a list similar to Ben's. List first time experiences you could share with others. Discuss your lists with your group or with your teacher. Identify your audience. Then, choose the best topic for your narrative essay.

Establish a Point of View

When you write a narrative, you should choose a **point of view** or perspective from which the story is told. A point of view is the position or outlook from which a character tells the story. Establishing a clear and consistent point of view in your narrative helps your readers to follow the events and characters in your story more easily.

The typical points of view to select would be either a **first-person point of view** or a **third-person point of view**. When you tell a story about a personal experience, you would write from a first person point of view using words such as *I, me,* and *my*. When you write about events as an observer rather than a participant, then you would use words such as *he, she, her, him, his, they, their,* etc.

Now, let's look at two passages on the same subject. The first passage conveys a first-person point of view, and the second passage is told from the third-person point of view. As you read, notice the differences between these two points of view.

First-Person Point of View

School was over, and my dream vacation was about to begin. I took off my shoes, so I could run in the soft, wet sand. An endless stretch of beach welcomed me into a world of rolling waves, soaring sea gulls, and serene solitude. The soft salt spray tickled my face as I turned on my favorite hip hop station. I ran into the breakers ahead of me. Then I felt something large, rough, and scaly rubbing my ankles.

Third-Person Point of View

School was over, and his dream vacation was about to begin. He took off his shoes, so he could run in the soft, wet sand. An endless stretch of beach welcomed him into a world of rolling waves, soaring sea gulls, and serene solitude. The soft salt spray tickled his face as he turned on his favorite hip hop station. He ran into the breakers ahead of him. Then he felt something large, rough, and scaly rubbing his ankles.

As you can see, the words *I* and *my* are used to represent the first-person point of view in the first passage. The writer tells the story as a participant in the actions. It is a natural way to tell a personal experience. It gives a story a feeling of immediacy, and the readers can put themselves in the place of the narrator, seeing through the narrator's eyes.

In the second passage, however, the writer does not take part in the story. Instead, the writer becomes an observer describing the thoughts and actions of another character. This can give credibility to a story and a more complete picture of the characters since the inner thoughts of many characters can be described, not just the narrator's.

Ben needed to decide on a point of view for his narrative about the wild horse ride. Since he personally experienced the wild horse ride, Ben chose the first-person point of view for his narrative. He felt that since he was writing from personal experience, the story would have a greater impact on the reader with the use of the *I* point of view.

Practice 2: Establishing a Point of View

Like Ben, you should now have chosen a topic for your narrative essay. The next step is to decide on a point of view. Choose either a first-person point of view or a third-person point of view. Provide one or two reasons for your choice. Then, discuss your choice with your group or with your teacher.

STEP II: Organize Your Narrative

Ben was not sure about how he should proceed with the next step, "Organizing Your Narrative." However, he took careful notes in Mrs. Connor's English class and learned how to organize a narrative. She said that a story should begin by establishing a **setting**. A setting is the time, place, and general background for a narrative. Ben chose his setting to be near Yellowstone Park in the summer of his fifteenth birthday. He would describe the mountains, valleys, the lodge, and the stables where he picked his horse to ride on the trail.

Mrs. Connor also explained that a narrative needs one or more **characters** (persons in the story). Ben decided that he and his family would be the characters. In addition, a story must contain a **plot**, a series of related events including **conflict** (struggle between different forces in a story) and leading to a **climax** (turning point in a story). A writer should also use **suspense**, so readers look forward to the next event in the narrative. Therefore, a narrative essay should have a setting, one or more characters, a clear plot with a beginning, a middle, an end, and suspense.

Mrs. Connor, then, stressed that most narratives follow a **chronological order** which is one event following another event in the order of time. The reader can then experience each event as it happens in a logical time sequence. She recommended that her students create a **plot diagram** before they write their narrative essay. In this way, students would have a basic outline to follow as they list the main events in their story. Here is Ben's plot diagram for his wild horseback ride. Notice how he labeled the events that show setting, suspense, conflict, and climax.

Plot Diagram for Wild Horseback Ride in Chronological Order

Day of Horseback Ride at Yellowstone Park (Setting) ¹	Woke up and Ate Breakfast at Lodge (Setting) ²	Ride to Stables Saw a Bald Eagle (Setting) ³
Family and I Picked Out our Horses ⁴	Started Riding up the Ridge to Higher Trails (Setting) ⁵	Goal was to Reach Top of Mountain (Setting) ⁶
My Horse Got Hungry and Left the Trail (Suspense + Conflict) ⁷	Horse Neighs Loudly We See Mountain Lion (Suspense + Conflict) ⁸	Lion Tries to Attack Horse Rears Up (Climax + Suspense) ⁹
Horse Races Down Mountain with Me Hanging On (Suspense) ¹⁰	Safe Return to Stables Family Follows Later ¹¹	Helicopter Ride I Refuse to Ride a Horse Again ¹²

After Ben showed Mrs. Connor his plot diagram, she praised him for following a chronological order and including setting, characters, conflict, suspense, and a climax.

Mrs. Connor also suggested another strategy Ben could use to organize his narrative. She called it **pentading**. Basically, pentading is creating an outline for a narrative using the 5 W's (*who, where, when, what happened,* and *why*). She stated that the 5 W's would still include the main parts of a story such as setting, character, plot, and chronological order. Here is how Ben used pentading to organize his narrative essay:

My Wild Horseback Ride

Who? Ben, Jes, Mom, and Dad (Characters)

Where? Near Yellowstone Park (Setting)

When? Summer, I was 15 (Setting)

What Happened? Woke up, ate breakfast at lodge, drove to stables, saw an eagle, picked out horses, rode the ridge, climbed the tougher trails, my horse leaves the trail, my encounter with a mountain lion, my horse rears up and races down the mountain, safe return to stables, helicopter ride, I won't ride a horse again (Plot)

Why? To reach the top of the mountain to see the view (Purpose)

Mrs. Connor mentioned that students could decide whether they wanted to use a plot diagram or pentading to organize their narrative. Now that Ben has practiced these two strategies, he is ready to write his rough draft.

Practice 3: Organizing Your Narrative

Review Ben's plot diagram and pentading for his narrative essay. Using his examples as guides, create either a plot diagram or a pentading list about the topic you chose for your narrative essay. Then, seek feedback by sharing the results with your class or with your teacher.

Step III: Write a Rough Draft of Your Narrative  III

In class, Mrs. Connor told her students that they should write a **4–5 paragraph narrative essay**. In the first paragraph, the writer introduces the story by describing the setting and by stating the purpose of the narrative. In paragraphs 2–4, the writer tells the main parts of the story. In the last paragraph, the writer ends the narrative. This ending is sometimes called the **resolution** because it wraps up the loose ends of the story, so the writer can conclude the plot.

Based on Mrs. Connor's guidelines, Ben writes a brief outline of his essay. He also decides to change the title for his narrative.

My First (and Last) Horseback Ride

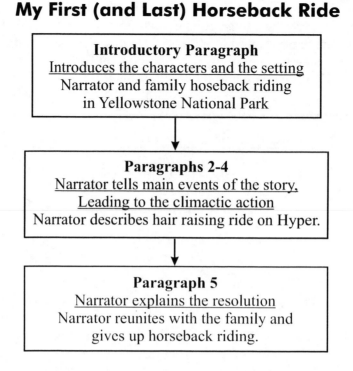

Introductory Paragraph
Introduces the characters and the setting
Narrator and family hoseback riding
in Yellowstone National Park

↓

Paragraphs 2-4
Narrator tells main events of the story,
Leading to the climactic action
Narrator describes hair raising ride on Hyper.

↓

Paragraph 5
Narrator explains the resolution
Narrator reunites with the family and
gives up horseback riding.

Mrs. Connor further explained that the rough draft will contain errors and will probably need some changes, but the reader should be able to read the entire narrative from beginning to end. In addition, the rough draft contains sentences and paragraphs, and therefore, is a big step forward toward the completion of a narrative essay.

Later that evening, Ben starts to write a rough draft of his narrative essay. He gives the narrative a title and follows a 4–5 paragraph format. Using his plot diagram and pentading as guides, he chooses a first-person narrative point of view. In addition, he adds more details to the plot and tries to connect the events together in chronological order. Now read and evaluate Ben's rough draft of his narrative essay.

My First (and Last) Horseback Ride

The sunrise over the skies of Yellowstone National Park. The mountains in the morning. Barely 15 years old I was on a two week vacation out West with my family. We were spending our last day horseback riding in the mountains and valleys. The night before I dreamed, my horse was riding along the ridges and mountain tops. That took us into the clouds and back to earth again. Little did I realize. What an day was I about to have.

Early that morning my older brother Jes and I got out of bed, dressed, and ate breakfast in the lodges dining room. we had to drive to the stables, so Mom and Dad hurried along for the short drive their. we arrived at the horse stables, I noticed a bald eagle flaping overhead, his screaches sounded an alarm throughout the valley. we reeched the stables, we picked out our horses. I chose a horse that I nicknamed Hyper. Jes rode a stalion named Snowball, Mom and Dad settled for two horses called Dolly and Sam.

We were starting to climb the path along the ridge above the stables. Ahead of us was another ridge that led us on to the trails above. we would be able to reach the top of the mountain we could view the entire valley and the surrounding mountains. we climbed higher, I was feeling dizzy. Hyper ahead, suddenly turning and galuping far off the trail to reach the wild grasses that grew along a gully.

With my family out of sight, Hyper started naying, I could sense something was wrong. and it was. Ahead of us on a rock ledge was a loud mountain lion with a menasng look in his eyes. Suddenly, Hyper got up on her hind legs I hung on her back with all my might. Eying those dangerus hoofs, the mountain lion sqweealed but backed away from an attack. At that moment, Hyper quickly twisted and headed down the mountain. Scared and angry. I continued to hang on the falling rocks and clouds of dust from our quick dip. Hyper was amazing as she bounced over rocks, leept over gullies, tore through the plants. I could tell that her idea was to get back to those stables. and then, we were almost there.

Practice 4: Evaluating Ben's Rough Draft for Content and Organization

Reread the rough draft of Ben's narrative essay, *My First (and Last) Horseback Ride.* **Then critique the content and organization of his essay by analyzing its strengths and areas for improvement. As a guide, respond to the following questions.**

1. What is the purpose of Ben's narrative? Where in the narrative does Ben state his purpose?

2. Does Ben describe the setting well? Cite some examples.

3. List the key events in the narrative. Is the story chronological?

4. Briefly describe each character in the narrative, including the main animal characters.

5. Identify the main conflict(s) in the narrative.

6. List two examples of suspense in the story.

7. State the climax of the narrative.

8. Is there a clear resolution when the story ends? Explain.

Analysis of Content and Organization of Ben's Rough Draft

Ben states the purpose of *My First (and Last) Horseback Ride* in the first paragraph of his rough draft: "Little did I realize. What an day I was about to have." As Mrs. Connor advised, he states the purpose of his story in the introduction. However, she has told him to strengthen how he stated his purpose.

In several places in the narrative, Ben describes the story's setting: the mountains and valleys around Yellowstone Park, the ridges and trails on the mountain, and his age at the time of his vacation. However, his description of the setting needs to include more specific words.

The narrative follows chronological order although, based on Ben's pentading, there seem to be some gaps in the action at the end. Otherwise, Ben tries to follow his plot diagram and includes those key events in his narrative. Ben adopts the first-person point of view for his main character while the minor characters are his brother, Jes, his mother, and his father. Ben's horse, Hyper, becomes a character because of her independence and courage. The mountain lion's menacing character contrasts vividly with the horse's bravery.

Ben does a good job of creating conflicts between the human characters, the rugged mountain terrain, the horse, and the mountain lion. The writer includes suspense several times in the narrative, particularly when Hyper leaves the trail and when Ben and Hyper confront the mountain lion. The climax of the narrative occurs when Hyper threatens the mountain lion by rearing up on her hind legs, and the mountain lion backs away. This action allows horse and rider just enough time to escape the danger.

In Ben's rough draft, Mrs. Connor indicated that the resolution of the narrative is not clear. In his rush to finish his rough draft, Ben forgot to include the final events of the story. When Ben and his teacher reviewed his plot diagram and pentading, they found the events that Ben had omitted. Mrs. Connor suggested that he create a **dialogue** (conversation between characters) in the last paragraph. Readers like to hear people talking, and dialogue can be an engaging way to wrap up a narrative.

Practice 5: Evaluating Your Rough Draft for Content and Organization

Based on what you have learned about a rough draft from this section, write a rough draft of your narrative essay. Use your plot diagram or pentading from Practice 3 to guide your writing. Then, critique the content and organization of your essay by analyzing its strengths and areas for improvement. Use Ben's questions from Practice 4 to help you evaluate your work. Also seek feedback from your teacher or peer group.

STEP IV: Edit and Proofread Your Narrative's Draft

The next step in writing a narrative essay is to edit and proofread the rough draft. After completing a rough draft of his narrative essay, Ben started to reread what he had written. His English teacher, Mrs. Connor, also offered feedback on Ben's use of language, sentence variety, and writing conventions (spelling, punctuation, and grammar and usage). She recommended that he review previous chapters on drafting, revising, and proofreading an essay.

Practice 6: Editing and Proofreading Ben's Rough Draft

Reread the rough draft of Ben's narrative essay, "My First (and Last) Horseback Ride." Based on editing and proofreading strategies he learned in previous chapters, what corrections should Ben make in his rough draft? As a guide, respond to the following questions about *language* and *writing conventions*. Discuss the findings with the class or with your teacher.

1. Are there clear transitional words in Ben's narrative that show the relationship between the various events in the story? List them.

2. Could Ben strengthen his choice of words to improve the narrative? How?

3. Does the narrative include a variety of sentences? Explain.

4. What changes in spelling, punctuation, and grammar should Ben make in his narrative essay?

Analysis of Language and Writing Conventions

After reading Ben's rough draft for language and writing conventions, Mrs. Connor recommended that Ben review earlier chapters in this book on drafting, revising, and proofreading the essay. For example, to strengthen the chronological order in his narrative, he needs to add transitional words as he writes the story. These words clarify the time relationships between the events. They also help the narrative to flow smoothly. Here are some transitional words Ben could use to improve his narrative essay:

after	before	as	then
second	third	finally	at that moment
during	meanwhile	eventually	when
next	now	soon	
while	early	in a short time	
last	later	first	

189

Working with Mrs. Connor, Ben found out that he needs to strengthen his choice of words. Specific and concrete words are more effective than general or vague words. For example, Ben changed the phrase, "*I chose a horse*" to "*I chose a lively brown mare.*" Instead of the more general phrase "*loud mountain lion,*" he used the more vivid expression "*snarling mountain lion.*" Ben should start adding more vivid and specific adjectives, adverbs, nouns, and verbs wherever possible.

Mrs. Connor also pointed out that Ben's sentences needed more variety. His rough draft contains mostly simple sentences, so she suggested that he review the section on "Developing Sentence Variety" in Chapter 5 of this book (page 95-96). Ben began to combine his simple sentences. He also worked on starting his sentences with something other than a subject.

For example, in his rough draft, Ben wrote the following three simple sentences in a row: "*we arrived at the horse stables, I noticed a bald eagle flaping overhead, his screaches sounded an alarm throughout the valley.*" To vary his sentences and words in this example, Ben combined these three simple sentences, intro-  ducing them with a dependent clause. Notice how Ben's revision of these sen- tences creates a smoother flow of ideas and spurs the reader's interest in the events to come: "*Before we arrived at the horse stables, I noticed a majestic bald eagle overhead, his screaches sounding an alarm throughout the valley.*" As he rewrote the final draft of his story, Ben continued combining his sentences and varying the pace of his narrative.

After reviewing errors in writing conventions with Mrs. Connor and with his peer partners, Ben also found that he needed to improve his capitalization, spelling, punctuation, and grammar in the narrative. For example, in the second paragraph, he misspelled "*flaping, screaches, and reeched.*" In addition, each paragraph contains punctuation errors that result in either fragments and/or run on sentences, missing commas, or other types of punctuation errors.

For example, in the third paragraph, Ben saw these two run on sentences: "*we would be able to reach the top of the mountain we could view the entire valley and the surrounding mountains.*" He corrected them by adding and capitalizing the transitional word <u>eventually</u> followed by a comma and then adding the conjunction <u>where</u>: "*Eventually, we would be able to reach the top of the mountain where we could view the entire valley and the surrounding mountains.*"

Finally, Ben's errors in grammar are minimal. He consistently maintains the past tense throughout the narrative, and his subject-verb agreements are generally correct. He also uses the nouns, pronouns, adjectives, and adverbs correctly. However, in the first paragraph, he noticed an error in his use of indefinite articles. He changed "*What <u>an</u> day*" to "*What <u>a</u> day.*"

Practice 7: Editing and Proofreading Your Rough Draft

Reread the rough draft of your narrative essay. Based on editing and proofreading strategies you learned from Ben's experiences, what corrections should you make in your rough draft? As a guide, respond to the questions about language and writing conventions from Practice 6. Discuss your findings with your peer group or with your teacher.

STEP V: Write a Final Copy of the Narrative

This is the fifth and last step of the writing process. After
thoroughly revising his essay, Ben has written the final draft of his
narrative. He added a fifth paragraph that concludes the story
with some dialogue and a fuller resolution of the plot. Now his narrative contains
a setting, plot, characters, and suspense, with a clear beginning, middle, and end.

Ben has also included appropriate transitional words, so the reader can follow the events in
the narrative more easily. By using more vivid and concrete words and expressions, he has
strengthened the narrative. In addition, he has worked on varying his sentences, and he has
corrected most of his errors in capitalization, spelling, punctuation, and grammar.

Now, read and evaluate Ben's final copy of his narrative.

My First (and Last) Horseback Ride

The sun rose brightly over the clear blue skies of Yellowstone National Park. The
surrounding mountains reflected the glow of a new morning. Barely 15 years old, I was
on a two week vacation out West with my family. We were spending our last day
horseback riding in the mountains and valleys near this magnificent park. The night
before I dreamed that my horse was almost flying along the ridges and mountain tops in
huge leaps that took us into the clouds and back to earth again. Little did I realize what
an incredible day I was about to experience.

Early that morning my older brother Jes and I jumped out of bed, dressed, and ate
breakfast in the huge lodge's dining room. First, we had to drive to the stables, so Mom
and Dad hurried us along for the short drive there. Before we arrived at the horse stables,
I noticed a majestic bald eagle gliding overhead, his screeches sounding an alarm
throughout the valley. After we reached the stables, we picked out our horses. I chose a
lively brown mare that I nicknamed Hyper. Jes rode a big white stallion named Snowball,
and Mom and Dad settled for two gentle older horses called Dolly and Sam.

In a matter of minutes, we were starting to climb the well-worn
path along the ridge above the stables. Ahead of us was another
higher ridge that led us on to the steeper, more challenging trails
above. Eventually, we would be able to reach the top of the mountain
where we could view the entire valley and the surrounding mountains.
As we climbed higher, I felt light-headed and dizzy. Meanwhile,
Hyper forged ahead, suddenly turning and galloping far off the trail to reach the wild
grasses that grew along a gully.

With my family out of sight, Hyper started neighing loudly. I could sense something
was wrong, and it was. Ahead of us on a rock ledge was a snarling mountain lion with a
menacing look in his eyes. Suddenly, Hyper reared on her hind legs as I hung on her back
with all my might. Eyeing those dangerous hooves, the mountain lion howled and
screamed but backed away from an attack. At that moment, Hyper quickly pivoted and
headed straight down the mountain. Scared and angry, I continued to hang on despite the
falling rocks and clouds of dust caused by our quick descent. Hyper was amazing as she

bounded over rocks, leapt over gullies, and tore through the underbrush. I could tell that her intent was to get back to those stables, and in a short time, we were there. Then, I thought about my dream the night before and how different my ride turned out to be.

About an hour later, Mom, Dad, and Jes returned to the stables. "I guess you took the short cut," said Jes. Shaking my head, I told them about the mountain lion.

"We're glad you're safe," Mom said, relieved.

"Well, we went looking for you, Ben, and never got to the top of the mountain," remarked Dad. "Would you like to try again?"

"No, thanks, Dad," I stated firmly. "How about a helicopter ride instead?"

So on that last day, we finally saw the top of that mountain and many other mountains besides and valleys too. And, from now on, I'll stick to horseback riding in my dreams.

Practice 8: Comparing the Rough Draft and Final Copy of Ben's Narrative

In a group or on your own, reread the rough draft and the final copy of Ben's narrative, "My First and (Last) Horseback Ride." Using the following questions (which continue on the next page) as a guide, compare the two versions. Record your responses, and then discuss them with your class or with your teacher.

A.   Explain the **resolution** in the final draft of Ben's story. Compared to the rough draft, does it improve the narrative? Why or why not?

B.   **Foreshadowing** is clues or hints of events to come. Although it is not essential to a story, foreshadowing can add suspense and interest to a narrative. Cite an example of foreshadowing in Ben's final copy. Does it improve the narrative? Explain.

C.   Compare Ben's dream about riding a horse in the beginning of the story with his actual horseback riding experience in the story. How is his dream different from the real experience? Then look up the word **irony** in a dictionary or literature book. Does Ben's final copy of his narrative contain irony? Explain.

D.   Find four examples of **transitional words** in Ben's final copy. How do they improve the narrative?

E.   Circle four examples of **vivid, concrete words** in Ben's final copy. How do they improve the rough draft? Explain.

F. Compare Ben's sentences in his rough draft and in his final copy. Cite 2–3 examples of improvements in **sentence variety** in his final copy.

G. In Ben's rough draft, find 4–5 examples of each of these errors: **punctuation**, **spelling**, and **capitalization**. How did Ben correct them in the final copy of his story?

H. A **flashback** is a scene or event that happened earlier in the story or in a character's life. In some stories, a character may experience a flashback. A flashback can be in the form of a story retold, a dream shared, or a promise remembered, etc. Point out an example of flashback in Ben's final copy. What is the purpose of the flashback in Ben's story?

Practice 9: Writing the Final Copy of Your Narrative

Based on the corrections in your rough draft, write a final copy of your narrative. Then, share your final copy with your teacher or peer group. Have them rate your rough draft compared with your final copy. Evaluate your strengths and challenges in narrative writing.

Practice 10: Model Stories or Narratives

The final copy of "My First and (Last) Horseback Ride" is an example of a well-written story. To find other model narratives, ask your teacher for examples. You can also work with a partner or group and search through newspapers, magazines, textbooks, or the Internet. Locate stories between 400–1000 words in which the author uses first-person or third-person point of view. Make copies of these narratives and share them with your partner or group. Then evaluate them for content, organization, language, and writing conventions. Choose the best ones, and keep them as models for your own narrative writing. Make copies of these to discuss what makes them model narratives.

CHAPTER 9 REVIEW: NARRATIVE WRITING

To improve your proficiency in writing a story or narrative, complete the following activities.

1. Using the five steps for writing a narrative from this chapter, write two or three more stories. Organize each story into several paragraphs. For models, review Ben's final story about his horseback ride. Or reread the model narratives you found in Practice 10. After you complete each narrative, share it with your teacher or with your class for feedback.

Choose some narrative topics from Appendix A, or select some of the following topics:

*   Tell a story about a time you were really afraid. What made your experience so frightening? How did you feel when it was over? Develop your story with details.

*   Write an imaginary story about meeting an alien from another planet for the first time. Tell the reader about the experience. Develop your story with details.

*   Write about a dream you have had. If you cannot recall a dream, make up a dream. Tell what happened in the dream. Develop your narrative with details.

*   Tell a story about a friend or family member who made everyone laugh. Write a narrative about the experience. Develop your story with details.

*   Write about an experience you had that taught you a valuable lesson about life. Tell about the main events of that experience. Develop your story with details.

*   Tell about an experience that made you happy, sad, or upset. Write a story about that experience. Develop your story with details.

*   Skim through a photo album, a magazine, or a book, and find an interesting picture. Write a story about the person(s) in the picture. Include details in your story.

2. A student wrote a story on the following topic: **_Write a story about an unusual vacation experience. Tell what happened. Develop your story with details._**

On your own or in a group, review the story and decide whether it needs to be revised or not. List the reasons for your decision. If the story needs revision, suggest ways that the student could improve the narrative.

My Trip

I went to the Virgin Island last year. My sister Shonda and my Mom went also. The water so blue, cabs were everwhere. we took a cab first to our hotel. The winding road up the mountan. Then we ate seafodd and watch the sun set on the beech. What a site.

Next day we take a cab to downtown, but cab very high price. We see many ship people leaving ship to shop every where. Donkees on streets make me laugh with thare funny hats and faces. Downtown is full of many color, sizes, and shape. So many people, so much to buy. But we get tird and spent a lot of money.

Next day we rent a car. That was wild. Shonda said I shoud drive. Then I see you drive on left side of street. Not the right side. Mom and Shonda screemd at me a lot. Your gonna kill us, they say. I didn't know. I turn left and go to rite side of street but I must go to left side of street. Many drivers beap at me and yell I was nervus.

Then we went under the sea to watch fish, sharks, and tirtels. Then a lady snuk in ore car at the groceri store, she ate ore leftover food. Then she wanted a ride to a hotel cuz she was broke. We took her and left the next day flew back to Cleavland.

3. Alex's assignment was to write a story about someone else. His topic was: **_Tell a story about your favorite or least favorite student at school. Create a real or imagined narrative about this person. Develop your story with details._**

Read and evaluate Alex's story which continues on the next page. On your own or in a group, review the story and decide whether it needs to be revised or not. List the reasons for your decision. If the story needs revision, suggest ways that Alex could improve his narrative. If changes are needed, revise the story. Then, share the revision with your class or with your teacher.

Jason

My least favorite student in school is Jason. He's a show off. One day in math class he started humming real loud, Mr. Logan was writing on the board. and turned around but Jason stopped. Jason hummed again when Mr. Logan's back was turned. Mr. Logan said to the class to stop that. Then Jason stopped, but a few minutes latter, Mr. Logan was writing more math problems on the board. Jason motioned to the class to be quiet. Then he stood up and started doing the moves for that dance the macarena. Some students broke out in a laugh. Then before Mr. Logan turned around, Jason sat down.

Nobody would tell on him

Jason's a show off and and keeps us from learning. Mr. Logan knows about Jason. But he ignores what Jason does. Couldn't he say, stop acting dumb, Jason. Or I'm teaching a lesson, so behave, dude. In the lunch room Jason calls some of us nerds. Some of us want to finish school and go to college. Where will Jason be in a few years? Jason can learn but does he want to.

4. Read and evaluate the following student stories. The topic for these stories was as follows: **We all experience times when nothing seems to go right with our lives. Tell about a time when nothing seemed to go right. Develop your story with details.** On your own or in a group, review each story, and decide whether it needs to be revised or not. Next, list the reasons for your decision. If a story needs revision, suggest ways that these students could improve their narratives. Then, when changes are needed, revise each story on your own or in your group. Finally, share the revision with your class or with your teacher.

Wings & Strings

Fran and her college roommate, Philena, enjoyed listening to bluegrass music. Sounds of guitars and fiddles could be heard coming from their dorm room every night. Fran's father belonged to a band, so she was raised listening to the lively music.

One fall, Fran's parents asked the girls if they wanted to go to the Wings and Strings festival, a bluegrass festival. The festival was held on the grounds of an old airfield, and many vintage airplanes were parked there; that's how the festival got its name. The event was several hours away in Polk City, Florida, so it would be a nice weekend getaway with Fran's family and friends. Several members of her father's band were going to be there. Philena liked Fran's family and wanted to go, but being poor college students, neither of them could afford a hotel room for the weekend. They decided to pitch a tent and make it a camping trip.

After packing up the cars, the vacationers left Miami for Polk City. Four hours later they arrived at the airfield where the festival was taking place. Fran and Philena immediately began to set up their tent. They got everything out of the back of Philena's truck only to find that they had the tent but left the tent poles behind. They couldn't sleep out in the open; they'd freeze. It was November and cold for the warm-blooded teenagers from Miami. Fortunately, they had an air mattress, and the truck had a cap. They could safely sleep in the back of the truck. With that crisis averted, they began to dig around for the pump to the air mattress.

It didn't take them long to discover the poorly-repaired hole in the air pump. After one compression, the adhesive gave way on the duct tape and a gust of air blew back in Philena's face. Being industrious college students accustomed to thinking outside the box, they figured out a way to hold the hole in the pump closed enough to get a little air into the mattress. It would be slow going, but it was better than trying to blow it up the old-fashioned way. Two hours and several hand cramps later, the girls had filled the air mattress to their liking.

Just as they were finishing up, a man, who had been sitting in a camp chair watching the process for most of the time, yelled out to them that he had an electric air pump that would have filled the mattress in ten or fifteen minutes. But, he added that he admired the perseverance they showed. They smiled politely and groaned in frustration. They had missed most of the day's activities but were ready to forget their troubles and dance the night away.

Finally free from their preparations, the girls headed for the stage where they found Fran's parents and friends. Fran's father asked Philena to dance and taught her to Louisiana two-step. By midnight, they were danced out and tired. They headed back to the truck and a hard-earned night's rest on their old adversary, the air mattress.

Gettin' Thru the Blues

I always wore that blue dress when I went out, even if I were just goin' to store to pick up some onions for a stew. My mama always said that you should look your best in public, 'specially when you might run into your future husband. It wasn't really blue, but navy blue, almost black and made of gauzy nylon that lets the cool breeze through. It has short gathered sleeves. Some of the threads that pucker the fabric have pulled loose from me reaching too far in front of myself. That's another thing mama always told me not to do. "Don't go reachin' too far ahead of yourself. You'll only be disappointed when you can't get hold of what you want." That's a piece of advice I never heeded, as you can see by those danglin' threads on my dress. It's a good thing I listened to those first bits of wisdom, 'cause just last month, I was in the store tryin' to get a gumball out of the machine, and I met my husband-to-be. I was wearin' the blue dress, and when I bent forward to collect my gumball, I heard those last few stitches give way. I was so embarrassed and sad. This was my only dress. Now, I couldn't come to town in my overalls. I could just hear mama, "Just wouldn't be right for a young lady, traipsin' around town in work clothes." I just may never get to come into town again. With that thought, all the muscles in my face started to tremble, and I started to cry. Just then, I felt a large hand on my shoulder and saw the other one holding a handkerchief in front of me. He asked me not to cry, sayin' if I kept up with the tears, he'd have a cry right along with me. And it doesn't look good when a man cries standin' next to a gumball machine. Well, that made me laugh so hard I almost finished off the dress right there. He introduced himself as Harry. When I went to shake his hand, I noticed the gumball I'd been clutchin' melted and left my palm a bright blue. I felt like such a child, but he just handed me the handkerchief again and got me a new gumball a yellow one. The next week, a delivery boy from the store came to our door with a package all wrapped up in paper. There was a note attached that said, "So you can continue your visits." Inside there was a navy blue dress, just like the one I'd torn.

Scoring the AIMS Essay 10

Since you are a student writing the essay, not a trained scorer grading the essay, why should you practice scoring essays? There are two reasons: (1) Scoring will help you improve your writing; and (2) You will learn about holistic scoring, a scoring method commonly used to assess writing proficiency.

An important part of the writing process is reviewing. A good writer steps back from his or her work, takes time away, and returns to the work with a fresh outlook. Then, the writer can see more clearly which ideas are unrelated and which need more development. Errors in grammar and punctuation stand out more, and the writer can hear whether the ideas, organization, and words are appropriate and consistent throughout the essay.

When teachers and students learn about holistic scoring, they will be better able to evaluate their writing. To determine a score for an essay, you must distance yourself from the work and use an objective scale to evaluate the work. This process will help you develop better skills in reviewing your own written work, thus making you a better writer.

As you or your teacher score your own paper and the papers of your student peers, you will be using the same **criteria** (standards) as when you are writing an essay. For scoring practice, this chapter is set up so that you may focus on one trait at a time to score. (Example: The first two essays will be scored for their ideas and content only.) In this process, you will become more familiar with the writing skills that the trained scorers will evaluate. Then, you will be better able to include those skills in your own writing, so you can write a better essay for the written test.

This chapter provides you with a scoring overview, as well as detailed scoring information about six analytical **traits**. The traits provide the guidelines for scoring your AIMS essay. They include the following areas:

- **Ideas/Content**
- **Organization**
- **Voice**
- **Word Choice**
- **Sentence Fluency**
- **Writing Conventions**

This chapter also contains some sample essays for you to practice scoring. The best practice, however, is for you, your teacher, and your peers to review your own essays and work together to score them. Then revise your writing as needed to improve your scores.

SCORING OVERVIEW

This chapter will evaluate the six traits using a six-point scale for **holistic grading** of your essays. (Holistic grading means the essay will be scored as a whole and not simply by counting the number of errors.)

Recommendations:

To make sure your paper can be graded properly, do the following:

Write on the assigned topic. Make sure you clearly understand the topic, purpose, and audience for your assignment. Keep a clear focus, and do not stray from it.

Write in English. This test is intended to evaluate your skill in writing Standard American English.

Write legibly. You want the graders to be able to read your essay easily. You may have great ideas, but if the graders can't read them, you will not get credit for them.

Write a well-developed composition. Make sure you allow time to organize and present your ideas for the essay. You will have two to three hours to complete the essay.

Write in prose. This isn't a test in poetry. Extended use of musical lyrics will not be graded.

Write respectfully. Essays that use offensive language or discuss offensive content may not be graded. If you can't express your ideas without vulgarity, then don't express them.

Write your pre-writing and your essays either on your own paper, or on paper given to you by your teacher, or in the appropriate, labeled spaces provided in an answer document. Pre-writing can be a simple cluster diagram or a quick listing of the major points you want to make about the topic. From this you can develop a central idea and tone. Be prepared to change the tone of your writing as you move from one prompt to the next.

Write your own essay. You may not copy a published source or another student's writing.

By following these recommendations, you make sure only that your paper will be graded. For your paper to receive a passing grade or an excellent grade, you must demonstrate skill in the **six traits** (areas of writing skill) outlined in the next section which professional graders generally use to evaluate writing proficiency.

Traits

As you read in the introduction to the diagnostic writing exam at the beginning of this book, the scorers will assess your essays according to the six traits and their corresponding components.

1. **Ideas/Content:** The writer develops a clear, focused main idea or ideas related to the prompt. In addition, he or she demonstrates completeness in his or her writing through the use of elaboration, anecdotes, images, or carefully selected details that build understanding or hold a reader's attention. This trait includes the following components:

   - Response to assigned task
   - Clearly established main idea(s)
   - Sufficiently relevant supporting ideas
   - Well-suited to audience and purpose

2. **Organization:** The writer uses his or her organizational method to provide logical links in each detail or new development in the essay, leading the reader to a turning point, key revelation, or well developed conclusion. The writer also provides smooth transitions between details or events in the essay. This trait includes the following components:

- Clearly discernible order of presentation
- Logical transitions that tie the ideas together
- Natural flow of ideas
- Clear description of topic found in both the opening and closing.

3. **Voice:** The writer uses his or her ability to connect to the purpose and audience by using the following components:

- Tone consistent with type and purpose of the essay
- Sense of audience, appropriately formal or informal

4. **Word Choice:** The writer uses specific words and phrases to convey the message in an interesting, precise, and natural way using the following components:

- Word choice is appropriate to audience
- Word choices energize writing
- Varied vocabulary, specific words, and figurative language when appropriate

5. **Sentence Fluency:** The writer uses varied sentence types to help convey the message in an interesting way using the following components:

- Sentence structure enhances meaning
- Sentences flow smoothly
- Variation in sentence structure, length and beginnings adds interest to the text

6. **Writing Conventions:** The writer forms sentences and paragraphs correctly. This trait includes the following components:

- Appropriate usage (clear pronoun references, subject-verb agreement, etc.)
- Appropriate mechanics (proper spelling, capitalization, punctuation, etc.)
- Appropriate end punctuation
- Complete sentences or functional fragments
- Legible and well-edited text

Holistic Grading Based on the six-point scale on the next page, the readers will assign a score for each trait.

When scoring essays, readers will consider each essay as a whole. For example, an essay may show a good command of mechanics and usage overall, even though there are a few errors here and there. In this case, you can consider the errors as oversights due to the time limits of the test. However, if a paper consistently has repeated errors in it, then the writer has demonstrated a lack of skill in this particular area. A short essay may have few errors, but it may not give enough evidence that the writer has good writing skills. On the other hand, a longer essay may have a number of errors, but overall, the paper also shows that these were exceptions to the generally good performance of the writer.

A Six-Point Scale for Holistic Scoring

Score	Explanation
6	A **six** paper exceeds the standard. It does ALL OR MOST of the following: Focuses and develops ideas in a sustained and compelling manner, showing creativity and insight. / Clarifies and defends or persuades with precise and relevant evidence; clearly defines and frames issues. / Effectively organizes ideas in a clear, logical, detailed, and coherent manner using appropriate structures to enhance the central idea or theme. / Demonstrates involvement with the text and speaks purposefully to the audience in an appropriate, individualistic, and engaging manner. / Uses multiple sentence structures and word choices effectively and with a sense of control for stylistic effect. / Commits few, if any, errors in standard English rules for grammar/usage and mechanics.
5	A **five** paper is distinctly above average. It does ALL OR MOST of the following: Focuses and develops ideas in an effective and detailed manner. / Defends and/or persuades with important and relevant evidence; defines and frames issues. / Organizes ideas clearly and coherently using structures appropriate to purposes. / Communicates a sense of loyalty to the topic and to the audience's involvement. / Uses varied sentence structure and word choice effectively. / Commits few errors in standard English grammar/usage and mechanics.
4	A **four** paper is adequate. It exhibits ALL OR MOST of the following: Adequately focuses and develops ideas with detail. /.Defends and/or persuades with support and clarity, using relevant evidence. / Organizes ideas in a satisfactory manner with adequate coherence and logic. / Uses a voice that is appropriate to audience and purpose. / Uses a variety of sentence structures and word choice, but occasionally displays some wordiness or ineffective diction; sentences may be predictable. / Commits some errors in standard English grammar/usage and mechanics that do not impede meaning; indicates basic understanding of conventions.
3	A **three** paper is inadequate. It is clearly flawed in SOME OR ALL of the following: Focuses, but may not display mature or well-developed content. / Attempts defense or persuasive stance but position is unclear and/or evidence is brief, tangential or based solely on personal opinion. / Displays minimal organization; contains irrelevancies, digresses, rambles, or lacks logic. / Lacks sincerity of purpose in the writer's attempt to involve the audience appropriately. / Uses sentence structure and word choice that are somewhat limited, simplistic, mundane, or otherwise inappropriate. / Contains flaws in Standard English rules of grammar/usage and mechanics that don't confuse meaning; indicates some consistent misunderstanding of the conventions.
2	A **two** paper is very weak, revealing serious, persistent problems in communications. It compounds the weaknesses of the 3 paper in SOME OR ALL of the following: Lacks focus and development; may list items with little or no supporting detail. / Defense or persuasive stance is unclear or absent; evidence is vague or missing. / Contains serious flaws in structure, organization and coherence. / Attempts, but fails to involve the audience appropriately. / Uses sentence structure and word choice that are highly limited, simplistic, or otherwise inappropriate. / Displays consistent violations in Standard English rules of grammar/usage and mechanics that impede understanding.
1	A **one** paper is extremely weak and falls far below the standard. It has few good qualities. It mentions the topic, but generally fails to communicate with the reader. It does SOME OR ALL of the following: Simply repeats the topic or fails to provide adequate development. / Fails to establish a position and/or develop persuasive view; evidence is not apparent. / Shows almost no structure, organization or coherence. / Doesn't address the audience appropriately. / Uses limited and/or immature sentence structure and word choice. / Overwhelms the reader with serious violations in Standard English rules of grammar/usage and mechanics.

IDEAS/CONTENT

Your teacher will assess your essays on how clear, focused, and interesting they are. He or she will also be looking for them to hold the reader's attention. Relevant anecdotes and details should enrich the central themes or story lines. The best ideas are fresh and original. Ideas are the heart of the message, the main thesis, impression, or story line of the piece, together with the documented support, elaboration, anecdotes, images, or carefully selected details that build understanding or hold a reader's attention.

Assigned Task

Each writing prompt asks you to create a particular type of written work on a given topic. This is your **assigned task**.

Clearly Established Main Idea

The writing has balance; main ideas stand out. Your paper must be clearly organized around a **thesis** or **main idea**. The main idea is a brief summary of your focus and purpose for the essay. Though the main idea may be implied, stating the idea directly is helpful to the reader. A direct statement of the main idea can also help you maintain your focus while you write. Your response is expected to have ideas that are creative and insightful pertaining to the prompt.

Relevant Supporting Ideas

Supporting, relevant, telling details give the readers important information that they could not personally bring to the text. The writer needs to be writing from experience and showing insight: a good sense of how events unfold, how people respond to life and to each other. The writer should use facts and appeal to emotion to support the central idea. This support may include assumptions, reasoning, emotion, irony, humor, examples, testimony, or data. Make sure that your **supporting ideas are related to your argument**. Because the test does not allow time for research, you will not be graded on whether these ideas are factually correct or incorrect. However, they should make sense and sound reasonable as well as being enlightening and entertaining.

Sense of Completeness

The readers must have a **sense of completeness** about the paper as a whole. You must be sure that there are no gaps in the information you present. In addition, the concluding paragraph must lead the grader to a sense of ending and a summary of the whole essay. This displays the control the writer maintains to the end of the essay.

Practice 1: Scoring Ideas/Content

Read the following essays. Using only the guidelines for *ideas/content*, assign each essay a score based on a six-point scale (page 201). Then, explain why you gave each essay that score.

Students wrote the two essays below, based on the following topic:

> **Write a story about an adventure, either in work or elsewhere in life, that you have experienced. The story can be real or imaginary.**

1.   I was working at a local ski resort over the winter holidays looking for a little extra cash. My job was to test the slopes every morning and check for problems such as obstructions in the slope and to make sure all of the lights were working. You see, at this resort, people can ski at night because the trail is lit up like a Christmas tree.

   On the early morning of December 23, I trudged out to take a run down the expert slope. I turned on the outdoor lights and watched as my breath spread out like a thick, smoky fog. I worked up the skis and got ready for a slow, methodic descent. It's my job to pick up any rocks, sticks, or trash left in the pathways. Once that is done, the resort can open the slope. Out of the corner of my eye, I saw a furtive movement to my left.

   I had to investigate, so I yelled, "Hey you, you're not supposed to be on the slopes yet."

   Every so often, some idiot decides to run the slope while it is closed, usually getting hurt in the process. When I saw the vague shape move faster away from me, I knew I had to pursue.

   As I raced down the slope on my skis, the shape grew larger and took on more definition. As I moved closer to the person, I became more frightened. The shape looked huge, white, and very furry, and it was no longer moving away.

   "Hey, a, a, you need to get off the slope!" I stammered. The creature was hunched over and looked as if it was saying something. It turned and glared at me with these red, piercing eyes. I decided it was best to ski quickly down the mountain—away from the creature.

   As I continued skiing, I heard the creature scream, "My mountain!" He heaved a snowball at me the size of a boulder which came down to the right of me.

   I notified the authorities from an emergency call box at the bottom of the mountain, but the creature could not be found. In fact, I never saw the creature again. I was just happy I lived to tell the tale.

2.   I remember an adventure that started when I wasn't even looking for one. I was walking down the street in my hometown of Phoenix, Arizona on a Saturday morning. I was headed to the library to check out some materials for a school project on the lost city of Atlantis. I walked past our local pizzerias and couldn't resist. I had to go in and snarf up some food.

   I went inside the place and ordered me a calzone and a Pepsi. There were just a couple of people in the place—an old man reading the paper and a mom there with her daughter. My big surprise came when the food was brought to the table by what must have been the most beautiful girl I had ever seen. She looked like some sort of supermodel.

   I asked her, "So, I haven't seen you before, are you from around here?"

   "Yeah, as a matter of fact, I am," she said "I go to school right here. You know, Central High School? I'm on the basketball team."

   "That's great!" I said, kind of nervous, "That's kind of funny, I'm on the swim team. How come I've never seen you?"

   With our mutual interest in athletics established, we started going out and now we're going to the prom together.

ORGANIZATION

Organization is the internal structure of the piece. It is both skeleton and glue. Strong organization begins with a purposeful, engaging lead and wraps up with a thought-provoking close. In between, the writer takes care to link each detail or new development to a larger picture, building to a turning point or key revelation and always including strong transitions that form a kind of safety net for the reader, who never feels lost.

Your essay should include a clearly structured introduction, body, and conclusion. Within this structure, one idea should flow logically to the next, and each detail should support the main idea of the paragraph and the overall essay. Do not simply state your key ideas but **develop** them with appropriate explanation and detail.

Sequencing

Your paper should follow a definite **sequence** or pattern of organization. There are many ways to arrange ideas in an essay. Whatever type of sequence is used, there should be an inviting introduction and a well-thought out conclusion. Types of sequences are found in Chapter 1 of this book, discussing four methods, including spatial order, time order, order of importance, and contrasting ideas. You may use any one of these for each essay, but the order you choose should be clear to your readers.

Logical Transitions and Progression of Ideas

Your paper should have smooth transitions both between paragraphs and within paragraphs. If the scorer doesn't know how you got from one idea to another, you are missing a transition. You want to lead the reader through the essay with **one idea naturally flowing to the next**. Your ideas should progress through the paper, moving the reader smoothly through the essay.

Practice 2: Scoring Organization

Read the following two essays. Using only the guidelines for *organization*, assign each essay a score based on a six-point scale (page 201). Then explain why you gave each essay that score.

Students wrote the following two essays based on the following writing prompt.

> **What characteristics must a student possess to be successful in college?**

1. When students decide to go to college, they have many responsibilities to obtain their college degree. After they have been accepted into college, they must remember some points on how to be successful. Students could be successful because they have good attendance, and they have good study habits.

    First of all, students must have a good attendance record. They have to be in their classes each class period, so that they would not miss important information. You must maintain passing grades. These grades have to be at least an A, B, or a C to pass any college class. You must attend learning labs. You have to participate in these labs to help you understand your class better. These labs also help students to comprehend their class information.

Last of all, students must have good study habits. They have to learn to dedicate themselves to their course of study. They must manage their time. Students have to be involved in their class. They must attend lectures. All of these things help students to complete their course of study. When students have graduated from college, they could give themselves credit for all the hard work. They know how to be successful in college. So what, college was difficult. Students would have learned that college was worthwhile.

2.   Today, with the seemingly infinite number of students attending college, it is important to receive a quality education in order to be successful. In receiving a quality education, a student must possess certain characteristics. The characteristics that students must possess are good study habits, good note taking skills, and good listening skills.

First, students must have good study habits in order to be successful in college. To insure good study habits a student should make a study schedule in order to allow him or her to have time to study everyday. This way students will not have to cram the night before an exam. When a student is studying, he or she should be in a studying frame of mind. The student should think about what he or she is doing, so that they can get the most out of there time. He or she should try to keep focused and have a good attitude. Also, the students should pick a study place like their room, if it is quiet. If the students room is not quiet, then they should pick a place that is. One that has no distractions. Usually the library and lunch room are not good places to study because there are to many distractions. For example, the students eating lunch and the clouds outside. The students can not keep focused, therefore they do not learn the material as well.

Second, students should have good note taking skills. The students should review there material before they start so that they can get an idea of what they will be taking notes on. Also students should take notes on what they are studying and what the teacher is going over. When the teacher is lecturing the students should try to abbreviate and not write sentences so that they can get as many notes down as possible. The students can always go back and fill in the sentences later if they like writing in sentences. If the students are still having trouble, then they should ask another student if they could look at their notes.

Finally, the students should have good listening skills. If the students do not have good listening skills, then their note taking skills will probably be poor too. The students should try to be attentive and assertive. Also, the students should try not listen to what their classmates are saying next to them and should not talk in class. The students can not learn if they are talking. Another suggestion to better help the students listening skill is for them to eat a good healthy breakfast. This will give the students energy and help them stay awake. The students can not learn if they are asleep.

In conclusion, one can see that there are many important skills and habits a student needs in being successful in college. The students not only need to be successful, but also do their best. No matter how hard college gets, the students should not give up because the reward of a degree will be wonderful.

VOICE

Voice is the presence of the writer on the page. When the writer's passion for the topic and concern for the audience are strong, the text virtually comes alive with energy, and the readers feel a strong connection to both writing and writer. The language needs to be natural but stirring.

Tone and Language

Tone is the attitude you express toward the topic and the audience. Make sure the tone of your paper is appropriate for your audience and purpose. Different examples of tone include *sarcastic*, *humorous*, *candid*, *ironic*, *respectful*, etc. Keep your tone consistent so the readers will not be confused about your meaning. To accomplish this, you need to also use appropriate language for your audience. Choose effective words that convey your ideas and feelings through your writing. For example, if you were writing a letter of concern to the principal about a new dress code ruling, you wouldn't write, "Hey man, like, I think it stinks that we can't use green hair color! It's a free country, you know." A more appropriate written response would be, "Mr. Caliente, I'm really worried that this new dress code ruling will infringe on the rights of students to express themselves. I would urge you to bring this matter up in a school discussion."

Sense of Audience

The writing prompt will indicate that you should address **a particular audience**. It may be other students, parents, a legislator, or some other person(s). Each audience is concerned with certain issues. The support for your position should take that into account. Also, your word choice and tone should be appropriate for the specified audience. For example, if you are writing to the zoning board to approve an under 21 club in your city, you will want to point out how a club would keep teens out of trouble and not focus just on entertainment. You will also want to use a respectful and formal tone.

Sense of Writer

The writer must have a strong presence on the pages of the essay. The two elements—the vivid voice of the writer, addressing a specific audience—allow for a feeling of interaction between the writer and the reader. The writer needs to have a clear sense of purpose when writing, so the reader is clear on the point the writer is making.

Practice 3: Scoring Voice

Read the following two essays. Using only the guidelines for *voice*, assign each essay a score based on the six-point scale (page 201). Then, explain why you gave each essay that score.

Students wrote the two essays below in response to the following prompt:

> **Provide a detailed description of any room in your home or apartment.**

1.   Walking into my brother's room is such a traumatic experience. First thing you notice is the smell: pungent odors of dirty socks and shirts assault me immediately. Then there's the smell of the hamster cage, which he cleans once every two months. Yuck! If you've never smelled the room before, it will bring you to your knees! By this point, I usually attach a clothespin to my nose and prepare to wade further in.

There is no clear path in the room: clothes, textbooks, comics, half-finished homework papers and old food bits are strewn all over the floor.

What is even scarier is the feel of the room. You can't sit down too long in one place before you feel the tingly sensation of ants and roaches crawling over your body. Once, I felt the creamy feel of an old banana's insides touch my warm fingers when I extended my arm back on his bed. I found it inside his pillowcase.

If you have allergies, watch out! Light and fluffy dust bunnies fly easily through the room and multiply faster than real bunnies. We're talking sneeze city.

At night, you can hear the scurrying of small rodents, the chattering teeth of small mice looking for a quick meal, hamsters nestling in their feces-rich cage, and the raspy mating calls of crickets. It's amazing my brother can sleep in this mess!

2.   Describing my kitchen is fairly easy to do, our kitchen has three windows and two doors. One door faces outside to the deck, the other door connects to the living room. The kitchen has pots and pans, forks, spoons, and knives. There are several appliances in the kitchen such a microwave oven, a blender, a stove, and an electric oven. All appliances work fine and are all black. The floor is made of linoleum vinyl squares. There is wallpaper on three of the walls. The fourth wall has the three windows, so we decided to paint it yellow instead. There is a ceiling fan to take away any food odor in the middle of the room. There are a large number of electrical outlets, fifteen, in fact. The kitchen has approximately six cabinets and twelve drawers of various sizes. The wooden cabinets and shelves are stained a reddish color, and the hinges are painted with a gold trim. Several hanging plants are suspended from the ceiling. We have two puppies who stay in the kitchen. The kitchen sink is made of stainless steel and also comes with a black sprayer. All in all, the kitchen is very well planned and beautiful.

WORD CHOICE

Word Choice, as it pertains to writing, means that you choose effective words to convey your ideas and feelings through writing. You are able to find the right words to correctly express yourself, and you use words that are appropriate to your tone and audience. For example, if you were writing a letter of apology to the principal for shoving another student into a locker, you wouldn't say, "Hey man, like I shoved that dude! Get my drift?" A more appropriate response would be, "Mr. Henderson, I'm really sorry I shoved Billy Ray into the locker."

Effective Word Choice

Your **word choice** needs to be appropriate for your audience, topic, and tone. You also want to use specific words. For example, you should replace a general word like *talk* with more specific words such as *whisper*, *shout*, *blab*, or *babble*. Each of these words describe a particular manner of talking. In addition, be sure you use appropriate adjectives and adverbs to accentuate your argument. Effective word choice is discussed in Chapter 4 of this book on pages 59-63.

Energized Writing

The writing uses fresh and effective words and phrases. Vocabulary is striking and varied. The writer conveys his or her passion for the subject and involves the reader in the discussion.

Uses Figurative Language

The writer uses images and words that convey experiences to the reader in a vivid way. Example: instead of saying, "The day was long and boring," the writer could say, "The day seemed to creep on for weeks instead of hours." Many other types of figurative language are available to the writer as well. The writer can also use such figures of speech as metaphors, similes, hyperbole, and personification.

Practice 4: Word Choice

Read the following two essays. Using only the guidelines for *word choice*, assign each essay a score based on the six-point scale (page 201). Then, explain why you gave each essay that score.

Students wrote the two compositions below in response to the following prompt:

> **Describe one person you have met or known. Include details such as this person's appearance and mannerisms.**

1.   When I first met my grandfather, I remember his wide smile and how he made me feel special. His eyes sparkled with a youthful intensity that seemed to clash with the white hair and beard he had. His skin was wrinkly, and his ears had long, whitish hair growing on them about the length of match sticks.

      His hands were large and calloused from all the hard work he was accustomed to doing. His shoulders and neck were massive. He definitely looked as if he had been the football captain when he was a teenager. His voice was low and gravelly, but every word he spoke was kind. He reminded me of a cross between Santa Claus and a gentle giant. There was a sense of enthusiasm for meeting people that they immediately understood from the large bear hugs he gave everyone who entered the home.

      His shirts were usually cotton or wool plaid. His shirts smelled of a combination of sawdust and the musty cologne he wore. His hands were usually hidden by the old leathery work gloves he wore. He mostly wore blue jeans for pants and enjoyed riding loud and fast motorcycles when he was not making some new piece of furniture in his shop for us, his grandchildren.

      You knew when he was coming or leaving a room. His large boots plodded in and out with the confidence of a man who has a purpose to every daily movement. His shoes were worn thin, but he wore them as if they were part of his feet. Mostly, I remember the way he made me feel every time I came over—safe and loved.

2.   My friend, Brittany, is one of the most interesting persons I have ever met. Her long, flowing skirt swishes through the halls at school. People always stop and stare at her, but she does not care. She wears these multicolored clothes. Between the skirt and the loose fitting, ruffled blouses she wears, she looks like a gypsy.

      She wears her hair long and curly, and it falls down her shoulders really thick like dark vines, and her earrings are very large, usually with vibrant images of delicious-looking fruit on them. Her makeup is very striking. Swirls of purple eye shadow and pink blush cover the upper part of the face, followed by a deep crimson lipstick and lip liner. When she walks, she seems to careen effortlessly across the floor. Her pointed shoes sparkle in the sunshine of the skylight hall. People usually hear the rustle of her skirt before they see her. Everyone always turns around to notice what new accessory she's purchased for her outfits.

      She wears a perfume on her hands which reminds me of almonds, and her skin is the color of cinnamon. She said she was born here, but her exotic appearance reminds me of another time and another place. Some people make fun of her, saying the fabric she wears in one outfit could easily make three dresses, but she does not care. The comments don't seem to bother her, and her appearance is memorable enough to make the cut for this essay.

SENTENCE FLUENCY

The rubric advises readers to look for **sentence variety**, that is, variety in the use and arrangement of words, phrases, clauses, and sentences. You practiced this skill in the section on sentence variety in Chapter 5 (pages 95-96). In writing a persuasive essay, you want to attract and maintain the reader's attention. One good way to do this is to avoid repetitive language.

Varied Sentence Structure

A series of similar sentences may be clear and correct but lacking in style. Each sentence in an essay is connected to those around it. By varying the structure of your sentences, you create interest and emphasize certain points. Return to pages 95–96 in Chapter 5 for a discussion of **sentence variety**.

Sentence Structure

The writer needs to create sentences that convey complete ideas and yet do not become so complex that the reader becomes confused and loses the meaning of the discussion. The writer should avoid fragments and run-ons whenever possible. If the writer uses dialog, the conversation should be punctuated correctly.

Practice 5: Sentence Fluency

Read the following two essays. Using only the guidelines for sentence fluency, assign each essay a score based on the six-point scale (page 201). Then, explain why you gave each essay that score.

Students wrote the following two essays in response to the question, "Should teens wait for sex until marriage?" On your own or as a class, compare the two essays in regard to *sentence fluency*. Which essay is more effective? Why? Be able to give reasons for your evaluation.

1.   Why wait for sex? Why wait for something you can have right now? T.V., radio, movies all tell us that we don't have to wait. Put it on your credit card! No money down! Buy now pay later! It's better to wait until you have money to pay for something, and it's better to wait for sex until you are married.

          Many people believe that it's a good thing for condoms to be freely available in school. Unfortunately, or tragically, this gives the impression that condoms are 100% effective when they really are not. If I were buying a plane ticket, and the salesperson said that their planes usually get there 90% of the time, let me tell you, I would <u>not</u> buy that ticket. The same is true with condoms. I know people that have used condoms and still contracted sexually transmitted diseases, including AIDS, or gotten pregnant. The only sure way to not get pregnant or get a disease is to not have sex.

          Imagine getting pregnant while you are in high school, or even college. Look at your life now, and imagine what it would be like if you were taking care of a baby. Not much fun, huh? Well, that's another problem with having sex before you are married. If you are not ready for the commitment of marriage, then you are not ready for the commitment of sex because with sex comes the possibility of a child, and a child is a commitment!

The soaps on T.V. show everybody sleeping with everybody else. They're happy for a while. Then they get upset for awhile. Then they sleep with somebody else. But you know what? That's not reality. Some of my friends have caught sexually transmitted diseases, even AIDS. Others have slept with a few people and regret that they don't have that one special thing to give to whoever they decide to marry. It's been really hard for them to be that close to someone and then to break things off. Marriage is supposed to be for keeps, and so is sex.

Why wait for sex? How about condoms don't always work, you're not ready to take care of a kid, and sex is something special for the person you marry. Those sound like pretty good reasons to me. What do you think?

2.   Abstinance from sex before you are married is a good idea. There are many reasons why you should not have sex. Before you are married.

First, before you are married you are probably too young to take care of a child. In case one comes from having sex. You are probably in school, or don't have a very good job. If the girl got pregnant, you would not want to take care of the baby. Because you had two many other things to do.

Second, it takes at least two people to take care of children. It's really hard to be a single parent. I know because my mom is one. She has a really hard time. Taking care of my little brother and I. It would be a lot easier on her. If my dad were still around to help take care of us.

Third, some people say birth control is a good idea, but it doesn't work all the time. I know. Because a friend of mine was using birth control and she got pregnant. A lot of people use condoms but the only work about 80% or something like that.

So, you can see that there a lot of good reasons for abstinance. From sex before you are married.

WRITING CONVENTIONS

Almost anything a copy editor would attend to falls under the heading of **conventions**. This includes punctuation, spelling, grammar and usage, capitalization, and paragraphing–the spit-and-polish phase of preparing a document for publication.

For more practice in these areas of writing, *Basics Made Easy Grammar and Usage Review* (American Book Company) is very helpful.

Appropriate Usage

Usage refers to how you "use" the English language. The scorers will grade your essay based upon the rules and practices of Standard American English. The graders will be looking for clear and correct pronoun references, correct agreement of subjects and verbs, and the appropriate form of adjectives and adverbs. Slang and jargon are inappropriate for a writing test and will reduce your score unless they are used in a quote from someone. You are also expected to use English words appropriately, including commonly confused words such as *accept/except*, *to/two/too*, *sit/set*, and *lie/lay*. (See American Book Company's *Basics Made Easy Grammar and Usage Review* for a more in-depth study of usage.)

Punctuation

Writers are expected to have a strong grasp of **punctuation**. Noting that this is a testing situation, a few errors will be tolerated as long as the essay can be read smoothly without confusion in the logic because of errors in punctuation.

Spelling needs to be generally correct. As with punctuation, a very few errors will be tolerated due to the timed test situation.

Format refers to the appearance of your paper including standard writing practices of margins, paragraph indentation, spacing between words, and spacing between sentences.

Stylistic effects through manipulating conventions, are permitted.

Editing is the writer's final review of a piece of writing. In this stage of the writing process, the writer corrects errors in capitalization, punctuation, spelling, and grammar. A flaw in proofreading, such as "I am going to go to the store," does not indicate an error in mechanics. Such a flaw does not count as much as an actual error in mechanics, such as "I going to go to store."

Practice 6: Scoring Writing Conventions

Read the two essays on the following page. Using only the guidelines for *writing conventions*, assign each essay a score based on a six-point scale (page 201). Then explain why you gave each paper that score.

In response to the following prompt, two students wrote the essays in Practice 6. Some argue that teens under 18 are too immature to handle the responsibilities of driving. Many teens, however, have come to depend on cars to get them to and from work and school. Using only the guidelines for writing conventions, assign each essay a score based on the six-point scale (page 201). Then explain why you gave each essay that score.

> **Write a paper expressing your opinion about raising the age requirement for obtaining a driver's license. Support your opinion with clear reasoning that will convince your audience to agree with you.**

1. Learning to driver is one of peoples main things to learn now. Driving as good and bad pointes. The good thinges are geting from places'es far off to see folks, to work, or shopping to.

    Some people don't understand that drinking and driving killes other people. Druges also as the same effect on killing people. The law now is .02 is drunk driving. i was told it.

    Learning to drive is every 15 'n ahaff year oldes dream. After some pratace they can go out on dates, be with friendes, or just go riding around town, or back roades.

    Teen agers are 50% of the drunk drivers. The state law needs at least to be 18 year or more before geting permited to get a car.

    The reason why it is important to me now is because, it get me home, to see my folks, help me get my billes paied, and get me to school.

2. There is no reason why a person who is fifteen years old should not be allowed to get a driver's license. There is nothing magic about the number of years in a person's age. The real issue when considering whether a person should drive or not is their level of responsibility.

    Driving a car puts you in a position of great opportunity and risk. Driving too fast, or recklessly, puts not only your life in danger, but endangers the lives of everyone else on the road. A good driver must always be alert to changes in road conditions and the movements of other cars and trucks on the road. Listening to the radio or talking to a another passenger have caused many accidents on the road. But a responsible driver has the wide open road in front of them and endless opportunities.

    For a teenager who has already proven to be a responsible person, the ability to drive provides many benefits. For one, it encourages further development of responsibility. By rewarding a responsible teen with the freedom of driving, society teaches the teen that responsible behavior pays off in the long run. Whereas, if a responsible teen is denied the right to drive, he or she may think, "What's the point of trying to be responsible?" This lesson can carry over into school, work, and personal life. The parents of the teen will also benefit by not having to drive their teen around to work, school, extracurricular activities, etc.

    Some people question whether fifteen-year-olds are old enough to drive. My answer is that some are and some are not. The question is not the numerical age of the person, but how mature they are. If mature and responsible teens are given the opportunity to drive, then everyone benefits. Those who are not responsible should not be allowed to drive. But don't punish everyone just because of a few bad apples.

213

CHAPTER 10 REVIEW: SCORING THE ESSAY

On your own or in a group, read the following essays and assign each one a score based on the six-point scale (page 201). On a separate sheet of paper, provide an explanation for your scoring. Then, edit these passages for errors in ideas/content, organization, voice, word choice, sentence fluency, and writing conventions.

Essays 1 and 2 are student responses to the statement, "Explain a career you would not want to pursue."

1.   This is quite an unusual topic. I've never been asked what I <u>don't</u> want to be. I <u>don't</u> want a job pushing papers. I like to work with my hands, and to be free to move about. I can't be locked into some desk job, scribbling and typing my life away. I don't want any job where I am required to look busy or business-like, or make idle

chatter by the water cooler or coffee machine. Barely can I stand the choking stench of an "office" (A.K.A. Claustrophobic Nightmare). A place of physical and mental decay, where drones trade their souls for a pension and a paycheck.

    Not me, dear heart, not I. I must be where clouds roam like buffaloes of yore and sunlight, like a tidal wave, drenches and covers all that it can. I do not want a stagnant job in a stagnant city. Driving my stagnant car and living my stagnant life. To that I kindly reply "No, Thank You. I'll just sit over here in the corner and paint something . . ."

2.   President of the United States used to be the sole dream of my early childhood. Having been born outside of the United States on a U.S. Naval Base, I was concerned about whether or not I would be permitted to run for the candidacy. After learning that I would be able to run for office, but discovering what politics was all about, my dream was shattered.

    Looking back on the idea of being President of the United States now, appears to me to be ridiculous. Without the power Of the Senate behind the President, the office is empty and useless. If the President were to be given more power in the voting process, I would reconsider my opinion. All decisions that come out of Washington D. C. now, are nothing more than

a shakedown between the Republicans and the Democrats. Besides, the President will always have to worry about pain and death, not only to himself, but to all of the American people as well.

One quote from William Shakespeare would be a great description of childhood, "Ignorance is bliss". In childhood one does not have to worry about whether or not his dream is plausible or what all that dream would include. Overall, I have decided that the office of President of the United States will be better suited to someone who enjoys the game of politics, and not by myself who would actually like to enjoy life without the pressure of relection.

Essays 3 and 4 are student responses to the following prompt.

> **Explain how individual actions can affect the environment. Use clear examples and convincing arguments to persuade other students.**

3.   There was once an adult and a child walking along the beach. Every time the boy saw a starfish washed up along the beach, he would pick it up and fling it back into the water. The man turned to him and said, "There must be thousands of starfish washed up  on this beach. What difference does it make to throw a few back in?" The boy looked at the starfish in his hand, then turned to the man and said, "It makes a difference to this one." In the same way, efforts spent to conserve and restore the environment matter. Anyone can make a difference.

The easiest way anyone can help is through recycling glass, plastic, aluminum, and paper recycling. Recycling just one can conserves enough energy to run a television for two hours. At a nearby high school, one student wanted to share her commitment to the environment. Now, the entire school recycles paper and aluminum. If she had not been devoted to this cause, many trees would have been cut down. One person saved all of them.

Some people argue that they do not need to change their lifestyle for a couple of trees. Yet, if they save the trees' lives, they will save their own as well. The entire planet is like a global village. An event happening in one region affects all of the others. When too many trees are cut and not replaced, levels of carbon dioxide increase and global warming occurs.

Another way to make a difference in the environment is through energy conservation. Gas consumption can be reduced through the use of mass transit and carpooling. Simply turning off the lights when you leave the room can also help. When these fossil fuels are used, it can literally take millions of years to replace them.

Protecting the environment does not simply rescue a tiger or save a tree from extinction. Environmental quality affects everyone. If someone does not want to conserve in order to retain their own quality of life, that person should do so for the sake of their children.

4.   Everyone can make a difference. I, also, felt the task of making the environment cleaner and safer was daunting and believed there was nothing I could do. However, that was just an excuse, an easy way out. All things start with one person—you. Others usually follow a leader and convince others to go along with the movement, this phenomenon is called peer pressure.

Most of the time, peer pressure is discussed as a negative term, with destructive effects. Drug abuse, the growing acceptance of pre-marital sex, alcoholism, and even the growth of gangs and teenage suicides. Peer pressure is a forceful tool, we need to grasp it from those using it to undermine society and use it to the advantage of everyone.

You, as one member of a global village, can accomplish many things using peer pressure. To begin with, you can recycle your own garbage such as old newspapers, aluminum cans, and glass bottles. Next, convince your friends to be part of your effort by telling them of all the advantages, and how they can make a difference.

There are many problems which come from lack of care for the environment. Someone at a particular point in time must seize the initiative to fix these problems. If you truly believe in the cause, you will do your part. Get started today.

Sometimes you may get discouraged over the way things are going, or lack of going anywhere. Do not lose heart. Keep in mind, you took the initiative when no one else would. You've planted seeds that change minds in the many people around you. You can't fail. It's not your task to change the whole world. Even small changes in our backyards can go a long way.

Essays 5 and 6 are student responses to the following narrative prompt.

> **Tell a story about the most *challenging* experience you have had. Include details such as who you were with and what occurred.**

5.   I should have known there would be a problem when I saw the oil bubbles rising near the engine of the motor boat. We just thought it would be fun to try out the boat. Freddie the recreational director gave us such a good deal on it. $5.00 per hour plus fuel costs! Me and my best friend, Shelly, each had our older sisters us—just us girls having some summer fun, we thought. We suited up and jumped in the boat. With a little tug, we were off.

My sister, Mary, screamed as we crashed through the waves others had made. Soon, we were in an alcove on a deserted island in the middle of the river. Freddie told us that this was as far as we could go before needing to turn back because we would have used half our fuel.

After walking the island a couple times, Shelly's sister, Amy, glanced at the fuel gauge and almost fainted. She screamed, "It's on empty! It's on empty!" While we had looked around the island, an oil slick as big as a mack truck surrounded our boat. "No!" we all screamed. We rushed back in the boat and decided we would paddle back using our hands if we had to. Suddenly, instead of enjoying where we were, we were consumed with the need to get back to our every day lives. We cupped our hands and paddled to get the boat to its correct location. I shuddered as I felt the slimy mouths of fish attacking my fingers as if they were a mound of worms.

Getting to the island took 1/2 hour, while getting back to the dock took over 6 hours! My arms were killing me, I was sunburned, and my fingers had been nibbled so much they felt like strips of raw hamburger! We marched into Freddie's office and gave him a piece of our mind. He trembled in his old Hawaiian shirt as we told him how his lack of attention to detail caused us unbelievable misery. Hours later, I remembered the saying, "If something's too good to be true, it probably is." I finally understood that.

6.   In computer class, they told us we were going to learn something cutting edge, fun, and very effiecient. "Networking for beginners!" It was called. I was excited as I imagined the possibilities. "20 computers—all using the same printer and Internet connection. I can't wait to learn how! The teacher started by words I was only beginning to grasp. "cat-5," "Fiber optic," "Wireless," and "Ethernet" immediately come to mind. Along with "scuzzy," "ghosting," "DSL," and "T1." Our teacher, Mrs. Hayworth, told us she needed two volunteers to network the computer lab at school for their final grade. My teammate, Julie, and I agreed to network the 20 computers in the lab. Over one weekend, we used cat-5 cable and routed 20 computers to one server. We had cables going all over the place and kept tripping over the wires! Once we had the cables set, we had to individually program every computer to align itself with the server! We did not sleep at all that weekend. I was sick from lack of sleep and could not make it to school Monday. This task was definitely the most difficult thing I had ever done. However, the rewards were unmistakable. The network worked beautifully, we both made A's, and the article in the local newspaper landed me a summer job with a network company. It was a challenging experience but definitely worth the rewards.

Essays 7 and 8 are student responses to the following prompt.

> **Have you ever read a book that made you look at life a little differently, or made you think about the people around you differently? Think about the last book that made a difference in your views and describe how the book made this happen for you. Use as many examples and details as you can from the book.**

7.   Literature can change readers' perspectives on life by drawing them into characters' inner thoughts and the events in their lives. When readers begin to sympathize with a character, they begin to see life through the eyes of that character. One of the books that changed the way I thought about something was *I Know Why the Caged Bird Sings,* Maya Angelou's autobiography about her childhood in the South.

When Maya's parents divorce, she and her brother are sent to live with their grandmother in rural Stamps, Arkansas. The children observe and are subjected to the cruelties of the racism rampant at that time. Maya and her brother are sent to live with their mother in St. Louis when Maya is eight years old. Life in St. Louis is different but not better for the children. Her mother's boyfriend molests and eventually rapes Maya, inflicting physical and emotional damage on the child. Before the boyfriend can be tried in court, he is sentenced to death by a less merciful and more swift lady justice. The young Maya feels personally responsible for the man's death and decides to stop speaking to everyone, except her brother, Bailey.

The children's mother sends them back to their grandmother in Stamps where Maya is introduced to literature through Mrs. Bertha Flowers. The power of literature breaks through Maya's long-held silence. One evening, after spending several hours reading Mrs. Flowers' books, Maya returns to her grandmother's house full of things to say. In her excitement, she casually turns to Bailey and says, "By the way, . . ." Before she can finish her sentence, she is punished for taking the Lord's name in vain. (The Lord is the Way, thus "by the way" is blasphemy.) Maya returns to her silence.

It is this part of the book that most affected my ways of seeing the importance of literature and words. This incident brought to light both the positive and negative power of words on a child's delicate perception of the world. A victim of abuse and racism, Maya needs escape. Literature provides her with the means to escape her world into another where she may have some control. She can enjoy, through the authors' eyes, parts of the world and experiences she may never see. She can learn things she may never learn in school.

Words are multifaceted. One word can carry several meanings. Idiomatic phrases and slang can often be misconstrued by someone who is not familiar with the current language. A popular example is the phrase "get outa here" to mean that something is unbelievable. Someone who is unfamiliar with the phrase might actually leave the room. Maya's grandmother, who is deeply religious, feels that the "way" is God, and to say "by the way" Maya was saying "by God." To her grandmother, this was blasphemy. To Maya, the phrase was a casual way of saying "Oh, I almost forgot . . ." In this way, a simple phrase may take on two different meanings depending on who hears it.

The power of words is the caged bird's song and has become the theme of Maya Angelou's life story. When Maya stops speaking, it is because she believes that her story in court, her words, brought about a man's death. Her speech is brought back through literature and squelched again by her grandmother's religious fervor. *I Know Why the Caged Bird Sings* became a reminder to me to watch what I say because my words can be more powerful than I intend them to be. It also reminds me to be precise and weigh my words carefully so that what others hear is what I intend to say.

8.   *I Know Why the Caged Bird Sings* effected me for three reasons: the book taught me about the South; it gave me a firsthand view of racism; it was a true story.

I grew up in the North, so I didn't know what the South was like for a little girl. I never really saw racism, and this book showed pictures of racism in Maya Angelou's time. It was a true story and described an important part of American History that we are not taught in schools.

What happened to that child growing up was awful. No one should have to go move away from home because they feel unsafe but Maya and her brother had to leave Arkansas because lynchings and other kinds of racism made their home unsafe. I wonder how many other little girls and boys had to leave home because of racism in the South?

I Know Why the Caged Bird Sings taught me about the South, racism, and a part of American History that students should hear more about.

Targeting the AIMS In Writing Practice Test 1

Imagine that you were participating in the AIMS Writing Test today. How would you do? In what areas would you perform best? The practice test that follows can help you answer these questions. It can show you where your strengths and weaknesses lie. With this awareness of your strengths and weaknesses, you will be able to plan your studies accordingly. This test is based on the Arizona AIMS content standards that focus on writing.

For assessment purposes, this practice test will consist of one essay preceded by one writing prompt. Make sure you understand what the prompt is saying and respond correctly.

How to Use Your Time

To use your time wisely, you may want to follow the suggestions below.

Planning/Prewriting
Read each writing prompt carefully, make brainstorming lists of your ideas, and organize those ideas into a clustering diagram or outline.

Drafting
After organizing your ideas, write them in complete sentences and develop them into well-formed paragraphs.

Revising
Now is the time to read over each draft and make improvements. You want to make sure all of your ideas are developed in a logical order and supported by relevant reasons and examples. You also want to eliminate unrelated ideas and unnecessary words. This is a good time to improve your word choice as well. Make sure all of your corrections are neat and legible.

Proofreading
Take advantage of the last few minutes of the testing time to review your essay one more time. This time look for errors in capitalization, punctuation, and grammar. These small corrections can make a big difference.

Review your paper using the **Writer's Checklist** listed at the end of your prompt.

At the end of your essay, you or your teacher should complete the **Writing Evaluation Chart**. It will help you identify your areas of strength and areas for improvement in writing essays. You can also use the **scoring guidelines** in **Chapter 10** to help you evaluate your essays.

TEST 1: WRITING APPLICATION

Below is one **writing prompt** that gives you instructions about writing an essay. Read the prompt carefully so you understand the topic and the purpose of your essay. Then, use the **Writer's Checklist** below to make sure you write an effective and interesting essay.

Use your own paper for your planning, drafting, and final copy. Your instructor will tell you when to begin and when to stop writing. Do your best, and remember, the purpose of this practice is to improve your writing proficiency.

Writing Prompt

Surviving in strange or hostile places is a popular topic on television these days. Many people enjoy the challenge of surviving in these environments.

Imagine that you are stranded on a tropical island for two weeks. Besides three days of food and clothing, you can take only three other personal items.

Write an essay in which you list these items and tell why you would take them. Include details and examples to support your discussion.

WRITER'S CHECKLIST

- ❏ Does my paper have a specific audience and a specific purpose?
- ❏ Does my paper contain a strong controlling idea?
- ❏ Does my paper stay on topic?
- ❏ Does my paper include specific and relevant details, reasons, and examples?
- ❏ Does my paper have an effective beginning, middle, and end?
- ❏ Does my paper progress in a logical order, and do my ideas flow smoothly?
- ❏ Does my paper contain words that make it interesting?
- ❏ Does my paper contain sentences that are clear and varied in structure?
- ❏ Does my paper include effective use of paragraphing?
- ❏ Does my paper include correct grammar/usage, punctuation, capitalization, and spelling?

Targeting the AIMS In Writing Practice Test 2

Imagine that you were participating in the AIMS Writing Test today. How would you do? In what areas would you perform best? The practice test that follows can help you answer these questions. It can show you where your strengths and weaknesses lie. With this awareness of your strengths and weaknesses, you will be able to plan your studies accordingly. This test is based on the Arizona AIMS content standards that focus on writing.

For assessment purposes, this practice test will consist of one essay preceded by one writing prompt. Make sure you understand what the prompt is saying and respond correctly.

How to Use Your Time

To use your time wisely, you may want to follow the suggestions below.

Planning/Prewriting
Read each writing prompt carefully, make brainstorming lists of your ideas, and organize those ideas into a clustering diagram or outline.

Drafting
After organizing your ideas, write them in complete sentences and develop them into well-formed paragraphs.

Revising
Now is the time to read over each draft and make improvements. You want to make sure all of your ideas are developed in a logical order and supported by relevant reasons and examples. You also want to eliminate unrelated ideas and unnecessary words. This is a good time to improve your word choice as well. Make sure all of your corrections are neat and legible.

Proofreading
Take advantage of the last few minutes of the testing time to review your essay one more time. This time look for errors in capitalization, punctuation, and grammar. These small corrections can make a big difference.

Review your paper using the **Writer's Checklist** listed at the end of your prompt.

At the end of your essay, you or your teacher should complete the **Writing Evaluation Chart**. It will help you identify your areas of strength and areas for improvement in writing essays. You can also use the **scoring guidelines** in **Chapter 10** to help you evaluate your essays.

TEST 2: WRITING APPLICATION

Below is one **writing prompt** that gives you instructions about writing an essay. Read the prompt carefully so you understand the topic and the purpose of your essay. Then, use the **Writer's Checklist** below to make sure you write an effective and interesting essay.

Use your own paper for your planning, drafting, and final copy. Your instructor will tell you when to begin and when to stop writing. Do your best, and remember, the purpose of this practice is to help you improve your writing proficiency.

Writing Prompt

Field trips become an important way to experience new ideas, inventions, works of art, and cultures. In a narrative essay, tell about one field trip you were on, what happened, and what you learned.

WRITER'S CHECKLIST

- ❑ Does my paper have a specific audience and a specific purpose?
- ❑ Does my paper contain a strong controlling idea?
- ❑ Does my paper stay on topic?
- ❑ Does my paper include specific and relevant details, reasons, and examples?
- ❑ Does my paper have an effective beginning, middle, and end?
- ❑ Does my paper progress in a logical order, and do my ideas flow smoothly?
- ❑ Does my paper contain words that make it interesting?
- ❑ Does my paper contain sentences that are clear and varied in structure?
- ❑ Does my paper include effective use of paragraphing?
- ❑ Does my paper include correct grammar/usage, punctuation, capitalization, and spelling?

APPENDIX A: ADDITIONAL WRITING PROMPTS

PERSUASIVE ESSAY PROMPTS

1. Recently, the newspaper reported that a student shot and injured several students in your school district. The school board is proposing that students in all schools be required to carry clear plastic book bags and purses for easy inspection. In addition, an armed security guard will be hired to carefully check items with a metal detector as students enter and leave the building. This policy has caused mixed reactions in your community. Express your opinion about this proposal in a letter to the editor of the local newspaper.

2. You are entering a contest in which you must write an essay on the following topic: If you were granted one wish to change the world, what would you change, and how would you change it? The writer with the best entry will win $10,000. Write a convincing essay for the judges. Include reasons and evidence in your proposal.

3. Persuade your classmates that television's impact on people is mostly positive. Cite examples and reasons for your choice.

4. Persuade your classmates that television's impact on people is mostly negative. Cite examples and reasons for your choice.

5. We find out about many issues and topics through newspapers, television, and the Internet. What recent issue or event in the news has affected you the most? Give reasons for your opinion.

6. Are parents or their children more responsible for school success? Explain your viewpoint clearly.

7. Confucius once said: "Choose a job you love, and you will never have to work a day in your life." Agree or disagree with this statement. Provide reasons for your point of view.

8. People sometimes say "Where there's a will, there's a way." What is your opinion about this statement? Explain your response.

9. Some people believe that prayer should be permitted in public schools. Others feel that praying violates the law that separates the church and the state. Write a letter to your congressman explaining whether you agree or disagree with prayer in the public schools. State your position, and support your arguments.

10. Agree or disagree with this statement: "Cars are more dangerous than guns." Support your viewpoint with reasons and examples.

11. Shopping on the Internet increases by 300% each year. Purchasing products is quick, easy, and usually tax-free. Should Internet shoppers be required to pay federal and state taxes like people who shop at malls and stores? Why? Why not?

12. Skim through the editorial section of your local newspaper. Find a controversial issue in the news and take a position on that issue. Write a letter to the editor explaining your viewpoint.

13. In recent years, pit bulls have injured or killed children and adults in the United States. Should owning a pit bull be illegal? Or should a pit bull be considered a legitimate pet like other dogs? Cite evidence for your point of view.

14. Many professional athletes earn millions of dollars each year while teachers, nurses, firefighters, and law enforcement officers earn much less per year. Is it fair that professional athletes earn such high salaries compared to these public servants? Why? Why not?

15. Should the personal life of the President of the United States reflect the high moral standards on which this nation was founded? Or is the personal life of the President of the United States irrelevant to his/her public contribution? Take a position on this issue and argue for your point of view.

16. Some students make fun of other students. They may even pick fights with others, causing injury or disrupting classes. Write your principal a letter in which you propose penalties for students who bully other students.

17. "It's not what you know. It's who you know that counts." Argue for or against this statement. Provide reasons for your point of view.

18. "You will be much happier if you wait for sex until after marriage." Do you think this statement is true? Why? Why not? Support your opinion with specific reasons.

19. After drinking four cans of beer, your best friend wants to drive you and your friends home from a late-night party. Why is this a foolish decision? Develop a convincing argument.

20. As tools for learning, computers are becoming more popular in schools. Do you think computers will replace textbooks as learning tools in high school? Include evidence for your point of view.

21. Some students drop out of school before earning a high school diploma. Should high school dropouts be denied a driver's license unless they graduate from high school or get their GED? Or should all teenagers of legal age be allowed to drive whether they attend school or not? Decide on your viewpoint, and develop a convincing argument.

22. Should separate schools be established for students who frequently disrupt classes? Why? Why not? Provide reasons for your opinion.

23. Citizens and conservationists alike are concerned about the poor air quality in many big cities. Cars, buses, planes, and industry contribute to this pollution. You have been asked to speak at a community forum on this issue. Convince your audience of the best ways to improve air quality in your community. Be specific in developing your argument.

24. Drinking and driving can have dangerous consequences. Should teens who are caught drinking and driving lose their license until they are 21? Or should the courts give them another chance before they lose their license? Include reasons for your opinion.

25. Do you think athletes should be dismissed from a team for breaking the law? Why? Why not? Support your opinion from your observations or experiences.

EXPOSITORY PROMPTS

CAUSE-EFFECT ESSAY PROMPTS

1. You may have lost a family relative at some point in time. Relate the impact this loss had on your life or your family's life.

2. Our clothes and hairstyles send a message to others. Why are clothes and hairstyles important in today's society?

3. Deciding on a career is an important step in life's journey. If you could choose any career and money was no object, what career would you choose and why?

4. Your personality often affects others more than you know. Reflect on your own personality. In what ways does it affect those around you?

5. "I'm bored" is a phrase often heard in today's world. What causes boredom? Provide enough details to explain your answer.

6. Perhaps your parents or the parents of someone you know have been involved in a divorce. Discuss the effects of divorce on a family.

7. We all have our favorite person in the news whether it be a world leader, scientist, athlete, singer, movie star, or local celebrity. Choose your favorite person in the news, and tell why you admire this person.

8. Some people in the news can affect us in a negative way. Choose someone in the news that you do not admire, and explain why you dislike this person.

9. Traveling to different places is getting easier all the time. Among ways we can travel are walking, riding a bike, going by car, train, bus, or airplane, etc. What is your favorite way to travel? Why?

10. Many teenagers and adults still smoke even though it is harmful to their health. Write a letter to someone who smokes, and explain the effects it has on his/her health.

11. For some people, television has turned us into a nation of couch potatoes while others believe television improves our lives. Explain the positive or negative effects of television on your life.

12. Teenagers often strive to be different, yet they sometimes dress exactly alike. Explain why this statement is true.

13. Computers influence our lives at home, in school, and in the world. What effects have computers had on your life?

14. Our parents, relatives, or guardians influence our lives in many ways. Choose someone who has influenced your life deeply, and explain why.

15. Name a sport or hobby that you really enjoy. Tell why you enjoy it.

16. Movies are sometimes rated better than they actually are. Name a recent movie you saw that was disappointing. Discuss why it was disappointing.

17. An old Latin proverb states: "Sooner will men hold fire in their mouths than keep a secret." Think of a secret that you or someone else tried to keep. Explain why the secret was so hard to keep.

18. What is your favorite time of the year? Give reasons for your choice.

19. Kingsley once said: " . . . there is nothing more wonderful than a book." Think of a favorite book or story. Why did you enjoy reading this book or story?

20. Sometimes children or teenagers run away from home. What do you think are the main reasons that they run away?

21. Think of a job that you would absolutely refuse to do. Tell why you could never do that job.

22. Have you or someone you know been rejected because of the way you looked or acted? Explain how this rejection affected you or someone else.

23. If you could live in any country in the world, where would it be? Explain why you would want to live there.

24. Setting goals helps us plan ahead. Name one goal you would like to achieve soon. Explain why this goal is important to you.

25. Congress has passed laws to control the pollution of our air, water, and food. Explain the effects of pollution on our environment.

PROCESS ESSAY PROMPTS

1. Your teacher has paired you with a new student to help orient the person to your class. Explain to the new student how to survive a typical school day.

2. Some people avoid responsibility by wasting time. Explain how you have wasted a whole day and accomplished nothing.

3. Success in school often leads to a better life. Based on your experience and observations thus far, explain how to be a successful student.

4. A six-year old girl has just fallen from a playground swing. She is lying on the sidewalk unconscious, and her leg is bleeding. You are one of the first persons on the scene. What steps would you take to aid in her survival?

5. Life does not have to be boring if we know what to do. Explain how you avoid boredom.

6. When there is money to spend, shopping sprees can be exciting. You have one hour to spend $200 at the mall. What items would you buy, and in what order would you buy them?

7. Weight training is a popular form of exercise today. Teach someone a step by step program that will build muscles and self-confidence too.

8. An old proverb says: "Happiness is a habit to be cultivated." Create a simple recipe for happiness. Explain your recipe step by step.

9. Many people continue debating the issue of crime and violence in our society. Explain the steps you would take to reduce crime and violence.

10. Review the following sets of pictures. Think about what is happening in each picture in each of the sets. Then, number the pictures, so they are in a logical sequence *to you*. Next, choose one set of pictures, and explain, in your perspective, what is happening in each picture in logical order. Develop a process essay from beginning to end.

11. An old saying states: "The only thing worse than hearing the alarm clock in the morning is not hearing it." After you wake up in the morning, explain the routine you follow in preparing for school.

12. The famous scientist, George Washington Carver, once said: "Ninety-nine percent of failures come from people who have the habit of making excuses." Based on what you have seen, people who are failures follow certain patterns. What steps does a person take to become a failure in life?

13. Shy people are more common than we realize. How would you teach a shy person to be more outgoing?

14. Fishing can be fun and rewarding when we land a big one. Advise someone new to fishing how to catch the fish of a lifetime.

15. You enjoy the company of your best friend except for one thing. This friend is always late. Tactfully, tell him how to be on time, all the time.

16. Many people enjoy playing sports. What is your favorite sport? Teach someone to play this sport in a few easy lessons.

17. Your principal has asked you to serve on a committee of students and teachers. Your mission is to tell them how to improve the food in the school cafeteria. Offer your ideas in a short essay.

18. Some people would say more if others talked less. Most people know someone who talks too much. Suggest some specific steps to cure compulsive talking.

19. Everyone has a favorite recipe for a main dish, snack, or a dessert. Using simple steps, teach someone this recipe. Be sure to include all of the ingredients.

20. Staying healthy improves the quality of life. Suggest the best steps to a healthy lifestyle.

21. An old saying states: "Losing weight is the triumph of mind over platter." How do you lose weight? Offer your advice to someone who has tried everything.

22. Some famous words of Victor Borge are: "Laughter is the shortest distance between two people." Residing in a nursing home, an elderly woman with no family nearby refuses to laugh at anything. As a student volunteer there, tell what you would do to make her laugh.

23. Teach someone else how to do something. For example, you might have tried to teach a brother or a sister how to brush their teeth or tie their shoes.

24. Pressure and stress are often part of everyday life. How do you handle stress? Suggest steps you take to reduce stress in your life.

25. At times, gaps in communication between parents and teenagers can occur. How can parents communicate better with teenagers? Or tell how teenagers can communicate better with parents? Offer some practical tips for improving the communication process.

MIXED EXPOSITORY ESSAY PROMPTS

1. Compare and contrast two fast food restaurants that you attend on a regular basis.

2. Present your view of your two best friends. How are they alike and yet different?

230

3. What are the two entertainment places or theme parks that you visit the most? Compare and contrast them.

4. How are you and your Dad similar and different?

5. Compare and contrast two cities or two countries in which you have lived.

6. What high school event or experience has impacted you the most so far in your life? Tell about it.

7. What is the most memorable holiday you have experienced? Was it positive or negative? Tell why it is so memorable for you.

8. By overcoming great obstacles, a young person may acquire greater maturity. What struggles have you experienced lately that have caused you to grow in character? Explain.

9. What lesson(s) did you learn in elementary school that have stayed with you, and benefitted you, through high school?

10. What are the benefits/advantages of your position in your family? (Hint: Are you a first child, last child, only child, or middle child?)

11. We live in a society of rapid and dramatic change. What are the greatest changes you have seen in the city (area) or country where you live?

12. Sometimes people are given a grave diagnosis or have a near death experience that turns their lives upside down. One of the most common responses is "It gave me a new perspective of what is really important in life." What is really important in your life and why?

13. There are people whose abilities and energy take them far past any limitation life tries to place on them. How does this relate to your life? Explain.

14. The Supreme Court has ruled (5/4 vote) that states may give parents money to send their children to religious schools as well as independent non-religious schools and magnet schools. What impact do you think this will have on public education?

15. Harle Wilson Baker once said: "Courage is fear that has said its prayers." What are your sources for courage and hope when you feel discouraged or "down and out"?

16. The Golden Rule states: "Do unto others as you would have others do unto you." Discuss why this statement is true.

17. Listening to good music often lifts our spirits. What kind of music do you enjoy? Explain how it affects you and those around you.

18. In many parts of the world, families are living in poverty. What are the most significant effects of living in poverty?

STORY OR NARRATIVE PROMPTS

1. Booker T. Washington rose up from slavery and illiteracy to become the foremost educator and leader of black Americans at the turn of the century. Are you struggling for an education? If so, tell about that struggle. If not, write about your pursuit of an education and the events involved in that pursuit. Include important details.

2. Young people sometimes feel the need to perform daring stunts just to experience the thrill. What is the most daring stunt you have performed? Narrate that event.

3. Have you ever taken a trip with a family pet? Was it an adventure or a disaster? Relate an experience of traveling with/or going on vacation with your pet.

4. Look at the pictures below. Think about what is happening. Choose one of the pictures, and make a list of the actions in that picture. Put the actions in logical order. Then write a story about that picture. Develop your story with details.

5. Find a favorite picture or photograph. Study it, and make a list of important actions and details. Put them in an order that makes sense. Then write a story about the picture or photograph. Attach a copy of the picture or photograph to your story. Add details.

6. Listen to a favorite song or musical composition. Can you picture a story to go with the music? Make notes about your story. Write your story, and give it a title like "The Story in (Name of Song or Musical Composition.)"

7. Think of a recent conversation you had with a friend or family member. Write down what you remember about the conversation. Then write a dialogue between you and the other person. Include details.

8. An **autobiography** is a story about your life. Make a time line of the key events in your life. Include details about each event. Then write your autobiography from the time you were born to the present. Include significant events only. Use details.

9. What was the most embarrassing moment in your life? Explain what happened.

10. What is the most often told baby story your parents tell about you. Write that story. Develop your story with details.

11. Tell about a situation that occurred when a "good Samaritan" helped you, and no one else would. Develop your story with details.

12. Think about a funny or serious story concerning a pet. Imagine that you are that pet and write the adventure from that point of view.

13. Were you ever the victim of a practical joke? Or have you ever played a practical joke on someone else? Recall what happened, and write a narrative about the experience.

14. Try to recall a situation when a person or group wanted you to do something that you knew was wrong. Tell a story about how you resisted peer pressure.

15. What is the most memorable school field trip you have ever taken? Where did you go? What did you do? Recall the important details of the event.

16. Have you ever helped with the Special Olympics? Is there a memorable experience you can relate? Do so.

17. Volunteering to help with the elderly, the handicapped, the sick, or a humane society always expands your horizons. What interesting story can you relate?

18. Who is the most remarkable teacher you have ever had? Recall an experience in which this teacher made an impression on you. Relate the details of the experience.

19. Recall the time you took your driver's test. Recount the emotions, waiting in line, the strain, and the actual test itself. Tell about the experience with details.

20. Tell about the worst weather you have ever experienced. This weather could have been a thunderstorm, tornado, hurricane, tidal wave, avalanche, monsoon, or a snowstorm. Write a narrative about that experience.

21. What is the most amazing sports event you have experienced? Tell about it.

22. Many people experience prejudice or discrimination for various reasons. For example, you may have been treated rudely because of your age, intelligence, race, sex, religion, appearance, opinion, income, athletic ability, etc. Tell about a time when you or someone you know experienced prejudice or discrimination. How did you respond?

23. "Gossip and lying go together." Tell a story of how gossiping about someone caused great harm.

24. Create a story based on your own idea or one of these story starters:

    While I was walking home one night, I heard heavy footsteps behind me. I was afraid to turn around, but . . .

    My best friend and I love doing things together. Last week we decided to...

    The best job I ever had was . . .

25. Mark Twain once said: "I can live for two months on a compliment." Has anyone ever given you a compliment? What were the circumstances that led to the compliment?

APPENDIX B: WRITING RESOURCES

WEB SITES FOR WRITING AND GRAMMAR

These Web sites include a variety of information with links to still more sites designed as supplemental aids for students. We visited these sites and devised a rating system for them.

Ratings:

Excellent

Good

Fair

Poor

Annenberg / CPB: Learner.org: Theme

A very well-presented site. It contains valuable information about the five major topics for reading and writing analysis: theme, plot, point-of-view, setting, and characters.

Web address   http://www.learner.org/exhibits/literature/read/theme1.html

Rating -

Ask Miss Grammar

For this site, first, you must ignore the silly, stereotypical cartoon lady. Then, and only then, does this Web site have a lot going for it. There is an option to look through "archives," where you select an item you wish to learn more about, bring up facts and games, or you could choose the option to e-mail a specific question to the site. The site states that it cannot answer all e-mails, but it tries to answer many of them.

Web address   http://www.protrainco.com/grammar.htm

Rating -

Awesome Library

This comprehensive web site offers resources and lessons on most school subjects. The section on reading and writing contains numerous links and activities designed to improve the writing of sentences, paragraphs, and essays as well as vocabulary, grammar, and spelling. In addition to English, many explanations and lessons are also available in other languages including Spanish, Portuguese, Chinese, and Arabic.

Web address   http://awesomelibrary.org

Rating -

Classic Reader

Offers almost 3,000 free books, essays, poems, and stories by such authors as Dickens and Twain among many others. Downloads are free but may require registration on the web site.

Web address   www.classicreader.com

Rating -

Dave Sperling's Guide to the Internet's Best Writing Resources

This is a list of web sites that teacher and Internet lover, Dave Sperling, has found useful and engaging for his ESL students. This site is 7 pages packed with web sites and a critique of each one. This one is definitely worth a look.

Web address   http://eslmag.com/mayjun03art.htm

Rating - 🖉🖉🖉🖉🖉🖉

English Club ESL Quizzes

There is not so much instruction on this web site as there is practice. The quizzes are often set up as games so it is a fairly painless practice session. This web site does create a community for English students for all levels of learning.

Web address   http://quizzes.englishclub.com/

Rating - 🖉🖉🖉

English Grammar Quizzes - Easy

This site has a variety of grammar and usage quizzes at several levels for the ESL student. The quizzes provide immediate feedback which could provide a lot of practice for students motivated to learn correct English.

Web address   http://a4esl.org/a/g.html

Rating - 🖉🖉🖉

English Works!

This is the official web site for Gallaudet University's English Tutoring and Writing Center. It provides plentiful information on the writing process, main types of essays, the research paper, and writing and grammar exercises. This site also contains links to other helpful writing and grammar web sites.

Web address   http://dept.gallaudet.edu/englishworks

Rating - 🖉🖉🖉🖉

ESL Home Page

The ESL Home Page is a great starting place for ESOL and ESL students working on the Web. It contains many links to the areas of study that any student requires help in, as well as having a site for jobs and for ESL chat rooms. The best features are the grammar and writing games and activities which can be found here. We were unable to visit every site linked to this home page, so choose your links carefully. Some possibilities are Grammar Slammer, Guide to Grammar and Writing, Dave's ESL Cafe, and Word Dragon.

Web address   http://www.rong-chang.com/

Rating - 🖉🖉🖉🖉🖉

The Grammar Lady

This is a very different sort of site. There are no real grammar and writing guidelines. However, there is a listing of informal grammar tips, a grammar advice column, and a Grammar Hot line (an 800 number). This Web site is designed to handle specific grammar questions, but we do not suggest relying on someone to answer the phone. This is a real one-woman show, and her material is interesting and well written. It would be a good site for those who need a specific answer or who have become interested in more than common grammar concerns.

Web address   http://www.grammarlady.com/index.html

Rating - ✎ ✎ ✎

Guide to Grammar and Writing

This is an exceptional Web site for English grammar and writing. The site is colorful, interesting, and well organized. There are guidelines for writing elements from simple sentences to full essays. The site has activities, examples, and quizzes. The quizzes, however, lack feedback to the student. There are many links to other English grammar and writing Web locations at this site, including a link for an on-line grammar textbook. The site includes an option of sending questions and receiving answers about grammar and writing issues.

Web address   http://ccc.commnet.edu/grammar/

Rating - ✎ ✎ ✎ ✎

Paradigm: Online Writing Assistant

This site features long discussions on how to write essays and some tips on revising and editing work. Clearly written and organized, this is a good source for those who want a review of the composition process.

Web address   http://www.powa.org/

Rating - ✎ ✎ ✎

Project Gutenberg

Project Gutenberg is the Internet's oldest producer of FREE electronic books.
This site is a worthy source of classic materials both fiction and non-fiction. It is not the easiest to navigate, however. It takes a little time and patience to find materials. On the site's Welcome page, there is a dialogue box labeled "**Quick Search.**" This is an index of the complete works that you can find on the site. You may search by author, title, or book. The index is in a "Winzip" file so there may be certain programs which can deal with the index better than others.

Web address   http://gutenberg.net/index.html

Rating - ☺ ☺ ☺

Wikipedia

This free online encyclopedia provides information on writing as well as a broad range of topics for research reports. Second language learners can access information in their native languages as well.

Web address   www.wikipedia.org

Rating - ✎ ✎ ✎ ✎

236

BOOKS AND SOFTWARE FOR WRITING AND GRAMMAR

This section contains a listing of books which provide students with grammar and writing instruction in various formats.

Basics Made Easy: Grammar and Usage Review

This book provides clear explanations and plentiful practice exercises on grammar, punctuation, and usage. Chapter reviews reinforce concepts taught in each lesson. The book is a thorough and excellent support for aspiring writers.

Pintozzi, Frank, and Devin Pintozzi. Basics Made Easy: Grammar and Usage Review. Woodstock, GA: American Book Co., 1998.
Web address   www.americanbookcompany.com

Basics Made Easy: Grammar and Usage Software

This interactive software program offers a comprehensive review for grammar, punctuation, and usage. Exercises require students to choose the best answers. The software tracks students' scores and correlates with lessons in the companion text, Basics Made Easy: Grammar and Usage Review (American Book Company).

Pintozzi, Frank, and Devin Pintozzi. Basics Made Easy: Grammar and Usage Software. Woodstock, GA: American Book Co., 2000.
Web address   www.americanbookcompany.com

Focus: From Paragraph to Essay

The author, Martha E. Campbell, presents a practical and easy-to-read text that integrates composition and grammar concepts. She includes plentiful exercises, assorted writing topics, and extensive examples of student writing.

Campbell, Martha E. Focus: From Paragraph to Essay. Upper Saddle River, NJ: Prentice Hall, 1996.

Writer's Choice: Grammar and Composition

This hard-back text contains lessons in composition, grammar, resources, and literature. The composition activities are particularly helpful for improving writing skills.

Royster, Jacqueline Jones, et al. Writer's Choice: Grammar and Composition. New York: McGraw-Hill, 1996.

A Writer's Guide to Transitional Words and Expressions

(Classic) This book is a helpful companion reference to A Writer's Guide to Using Eight Methods of Transition (see below). It contains over 1000 transitional words and expressions that will make your writing effective, logical, and easier to read.

Pellegrino, Victor C. A Writer's Guide to Transitional Words and Expressions. Wailuku, HW: Maui Arthoughts, 1987.

A Writer's Guide to Using Eight Methods of Transition

(Classic) A brief but excellent guide, this book is an invaluable reference tool that helps writers choose the best transitional words and expressions for a context. The author, Victor C. Pellegrino, provides many examples of how to create effective transitions and connections in sentences and paragraphs.

Pellegrino, Victor C. A Writer's Guide to Using Eight Methods of Transition. Wailuku, HI: Maui Arthoughts, 1987.

Writing From A to Z: The Easy-to-Use Reference Handbook

This book is organized alphabetically like a dictionary. Consequently, students can easily find, for example, an explanation of a "paragraph" by looking in the letter "P"section. The book covers a wide range of grammar and usage information.

Ebest, Sally Barr. Writing From A to Z: The Easy-to-Use Reference Handbook. Mountain View, CA: Mayfield, 1997.

The Young Person's Guide to Becoming a Writer

Reading this book will be a different experience than reading the others. This particular guide is gently encouraging to those students who want to pursue a career in writing but are not sure how to take the first steps. There are sections on writing skills, literary genres, and how to keep a writer's notebook. This is a first look into the world of professional writing, and it is good for everyone to know the ways to enter that world.

Grant, Janet E. The Young Person's Guide to Becoming a Writer. Minneapolis: Free Spirit, 1995.

Use the writing prompts in **Appendix A** of *Targeting the AIMS in Writing* for writing practice. Keep all of your essays in one folder. As you practice writing essays, you can use the **Writing Progress Chart** below to help you assess your progress.

For each essay, work with your teacher or tutor to assign a grade in each category listed. If you have an excellent grasp of the skill, write **E** for **Excellent**. If you use the skill well enough to pass, write **P** for **Passing**. If you need to practice a skill more in order to master it, write **NP** for **Needs Practice**. The number listed next to each skill indicates the chapter which discusses that skill. Your teacher may also use the six point scale from Chapter 10, **Scoring the AIMS Essay**. Review the chapters you need to improve each concept and skill.

There is a copy of this progress chart in the back of the answer key, also. Teachers/tutors may copy the chart from the **Answer Key** as needed.

Writing Progress Chart

Writing Skills	Chapter Number	Student Name:					
		Essay 1	Essay 2	Essay 3	Essay 4	Essay 5	Essay 6
Writing Paragraphs	1						
Voice	2						
Creating Ideas and Content	3						
Organizing and Drafting the Essay	4						
Revising the Essay for Sentence Fluency	5						
Proofreading the Essay for Conventions	6						
Persuasive Writing	7						
Expository Writing	8						
Narrative Writing	9						
Scoring the Essay	10						